D1860007

COMBATING VIOLENCE AGAINST WOMEN

COMBATING VIOLENCE AGAINST WOMEN

A Reality in the Making

Smita Nayak

KALPAZ

© **Author**

All rights reserved. No part of this book may be reproduced, stored, adapted, or transmitted in any form or by any means, electronic, mechanical, photocopying, micro-filming, recording or otherwise, or translated in any language, without the prior written permission of the copyright owner and the publisher. The book is sold subject to the condition that it shall not, by way of trade or otherwise, be lent, resold, hired out, or otherwise circulated without the prior publisher's written consent in any form of binding or cover other than that in which it is published.

The views and opinions expressed in this book are author(s) own and the facts reported by them have been verified to the extent possible, and the publishers are not in any way liable for the same.

ISBN : 978-93-5128-192-4
Price : ₹ 900

First Published, 2016

Published by

Kalpaz Publications
C-30, Satyawati Nagar,
Delhi-110052
Ph. : 9212142040
E-mail: kalpaz@hotmail.com

Laser Typesetting : Abhishek Mandal, Delhi
Printed at : G. Print Process, Delhi

Cataloging in Publication Data—DK

Courtesy: D.K. Agencies (P) Ltd. <docinfo@dkagencies.com>

Combating violence against women : a reality in the making / Smita Nayak.
pages cm
Includes bibliographical references.
ISBN 9789351281924

1. Family violence—India—Manipur. 2. Family violence—India—Odisha. 3. Women—Violence against—India—Manipur. 4. Women—Violence against—India—Odisha. 5. Women—Legal status, laws, etc.—India—Manipur. 6. Women—Legal status, laws, etc.—India—Odisha. 7. Women—Political activity—India—Manipur. 8. Women—Political activity—India—Odisha. I. Nayak, Smita, editor.

HV6626.23.I4N39 2016 DDC 362.82920954 23

Dedicated

To

All the Brave Women who have faced violence and have overcome it with great courage

Contents

List of Contributors

1. **Dr Beulah Shekhar**, Professor, Department of Criminology & Criminal Justice, Manonmaniam Sundaranar University, Tirunelveli, Tamil Nadu
2. **Dr Ms. S. D. Sasi Kiran**, Associate Professor of English, S & H Department, Vignan's University, Vadlamudi, Andhra Pradesh.
3. **Dr Padmalaya Mohapatra**, Associate Professor, Department of Public Administration,Utkal University, Vani Vihar, Bhubaneswar, E-mail:padma2seema@gmail.com
4. **Dr Smita Nayak**, Associate Professor, P.G. Department of Political Science, Utkal University, Bhubaneswar, Odisha.
5. **Pramod Kumar Ray**, Lecturer in Political Science, L.B. College, Angalo, Jajpur, Odisha.
6. **Dr Ramakrushna Pradhan** and **Smt. Sukanya Kakoty**, *Lecturer in Political Science at the P.G. Department of Social Science, Fakir Mohan University, Balasore, Odisha.**Senior Research Fellow in Centre for Russian and Central Asian Studies, School of International Studies, Jawaharlal Nehru University, New Delhi.
7 **Dr Mamata Dash**, Lecturer, School of Women's Studies, Utkal University, Vani Vihar.
8. **Dr Swapna S. Prabhu*** and **Dr Niranjan Mohapatra**, Lecturer in Political Science, P.G. Department of Social Science, Fakir Mohan University, Balasore, Odisha ** Asst. Professor, Dept. of Political Science, Assam University, Diphu Campus, Assam.
9. **Ms Sagarika Dash*** and **Dr Sanchita Choudhury****, Lecturer Padmanava College of Engineering, Rourkela.**Assistant Professor Padmanava College of Engineering, Rourkela.

10. **Rajkumari Lilapati Devi**, Asst. Professor, Dept. of Journalism and Mass Communication, Tripura University.
11. **Genevive Syangbo** and ****Karma Samten Bhutia**, Assistant Professor Department of Political Science Contact No. 9775961825, Email Id-syangbog@yahoo.com. Assistant Professor Department of History Namchi Government College Kamrang, Namchi South Sikkim-737126 Email Id- dorzapa @ gmail.com Contact No. 9775961825.
12. **Kamalakanta Roul**, Assistant Professor (Ad hoc) Miranda House, University of Delhi.
13. **Sanghamitra Parida, Research Scholar**, CRCAS JNU, New Delhi.
14. **Dr Dilshad Shaik**, Principal, Sri R.K.M. Law College, Chittor-517127, Cell: 09849000331, Email: dshaik786@ gmail.com
15. **Ishaq Ahmad Shah**, Assistant Professor, Monisha Qudri, Assistant Professor, Department of Journalism and Mass.

Foreword

Violence against women, which is a cause and consequence of unequal gender relations in society, men dominating and discriminating women in every sphere of life, has not only affected the mobility and progress of women but arrested the mobility and progress of the society and nations as well. Irrespective of military strength or economic prosperity, no nation has made any remarkable progress that has neglected or overlooked the well-being of its subaltern, underprivileged groups including women. To-day, there is no country in the world where men and women enjoy complete equality. All forms of violence and inhuman treatment to women, even today in twenty-first century are the outcome of dominant patriarchy. Despite plethora of laws and law enforcing mechanisms, violence against women continue to remain unabated and the scourge of crime against women continues to wreck havoc on the nation's thousands of innocent women. Violence against women in any form, i.e., physical, sexual or psychological directly infringes upon the fundamental freedom and liberty and survival of women and at the same time, it adversely the impacts the society in general. Various forms of violence, which include; sexual exploitation occurring in public and private life, sexual harassment at work places, rape including marital rape, female foeticide, domestic violence, dowry torture, bride burning and wife beating etc. has significantly affected the right to life and personal liberty of every women and have lowered their dignity to the nadir. Women across the world irrespective of caste, class, status and culture are subjected to this gender bias and heinous crime. Notwithstanding the progress made in this direction since the first world conference on women, women as a whole are not allowed to live a decent life, which is free of coercion, exploitation and violence. At international level, although spectacular progress has been witnessed, still much more remains to be done to put down the violence against women.

Back home, in India, the brutal Delhi gang rape not only exposes the weakness of India as a civilised nation insofar as the security and safety of women is concerned but also exposes the ineffectiveness of its instrument of governance in combating the crime and violence unleashed against the women. India's commitment to wipe out violence against women is although amply visible in the form of different laws passed by its legislature; its proper application in fulfilling the objective has still remains a distant reality. India's report card in combating violence against women is typically that of a student who has made significant achievement, but still it has a lot more ground to cover. While our women, today are definitely on a steady path to empowerment, a lot many of our innocent women and girls are still deprived of their right to life being victims of gender based crime. Our mechanism and institutions to effectively take on the violence against women is still very sketchy. Reformed laws with accountable and effective enforcement agencies and changed psycho-social approach may ensure safety and justice to the victims rather than laying down a blanket of protection to the perpetrators of the heinous crime. The real battle is to change the way in which men relate to women and create a culture that does not involve subjugation of women by combating crime against them. So, the need of the hour is, coupled with the government to act promptly and decisively, a composite psycho-social and civil societal approach is very much essential to deal with violence against women with firm hand.

A series of baffling and pertinent questions relating to the problem that hunts the minds of policy makers, enforcement agencies, researchers and members of civil society is how to prevent such a terrible tragedy, what could be the operative measures and tools of governance to ward off violence against women effectively?

All these questions require not only a reflection but a close analysis of the issue. Unfortunately, the massive research literature on violence against women built by social scientist over the years has not touched upon many important aspects of the problem. This edited volume "Combating Violence against Women: A Reality in Making" edited by Dr Smita Nayak, a senior faculty in the Post Graduate Department of Political Science, Utkal University, Bhubaneswar and Shri. P.K. Ray, Lecturer in Political Science is no doubt an earnest and a laudable academic endeavour by a group of committed researchers and academia, who through their valuable contributions have focused on various issues, aspects, dimensions and bringing out the much needed solution to this great human tragedy of violence against women.

I am sanguine that this volume for its penetrating research on the crises faced by the women in present day society would no doubt help the policy makers, law enforcement agencies, academia, social activists and the general public to know about the conflicting currents of the dynamics of gender based crime and the legal and institutional measures to combat such an evil confronting to human society.

(Justice B.K. Mishra)

Acknowledgements

I feel that this Book would be incomplete without expressing my gratitude to those who have provided me their valuable cooperation and Guidance.

This book is truly a joint effort of all contributing authors, thus I am deeply indebted and grateful to them. I acknowledge the sincere cooperation of all the authors for their precious contributions to make this book a reality

I am also grateful to Prof. Brahmananda Satapathy and Prof. J.K Baral for their constant inspiration and motivation in bringing out this book.

I am deeply conscious of the fact that this work would neither have been pursued nor completed if not for the tremendous support and encouragement from my husband **Mr.Janardan Samantaray**, who is working in Reserve Bank of India, Bhubaneswar. He was there in each step of this book project. I must also acknowledge the constant encouragement and support of my two loving daughters Disha and **Isha.**

I would be failing in my duty if I will not acknowledge especially the kind of support and help rendered by **Dr. Pramod Kumar Ray**, Lecturer in Political Science in L.B. College Angalo, in bringing out this book. I would also like to acknowledge the support and help provided by Research Associate **Mr. Abakash Sahoo.**

My special acknowledgement is dedicated to my parents **Mr. Surendra Nayak** and **Mrs. Pramila Nayak**. My mother is the true inspiration behind all my success.

Last but not the least, this book project became possible because of the blessings showered upon me by **Lord Graha Maha Raj** and **Lord Jagannath.**

Dr Smita Nayak
Associate Professor,
P.G.Department of Political Science,
Utkal University, Vani Vihar,
Bhubaneswar, ORISSA.

Preface

Violence against women is a phenomenon, the repercussion of which cannot be localized. Gender based crime not matter how local may be, its ramification is rather global and universal. Violence against women is the manifestation of the historically unequal power relations between men and women, which have led to the domination over and discrimination against women by men and prevented women from exercising their basic human rights. Violence and atrocities against women is an age old phenomenon and exists in all forms of societies. In all societies, to a greater or lesser degree, women and girls are subjected to physical, sexual and psychological abuse that cuts across lines of income, class and culture. The low social and economic status of woman can be both a cause and a consequence of violence against women.

Violence against women implies to physical, sexual or psychological harm or suffering to women, including threats of such acts, coercion or arbitrary deprivation of liberty, whether occurring in public or private life. Various forms of violence against women include rape, sexual harassment at work place, dowry torture and bride burning, female foeticide, domestic violence like marital rape and wife beating etc. The neglect, physical and sexual abuse and rape of girl-children and women by family members and other members of the household, as well as incidences of spousal and non-spousal abuse, often go unreported and are thus difficult to detect, which helps the perpetrator of crime go unpunished.

All forms of violence, whether committed or in form of threats, which may occur within home or community or perpetrated by the state, instill a sense of fear and insecurity in women's life. The fear psychosis permanently creates constraints on the mobility of women limiting their access to resources and basic activities. Thus, violence of any form against women with high social, health and economic cost forces women into a subordinate position compared to men. The growing dimension of violence against women has created serious problems for the society. However, to combat violence against women, intervention both at government and non-governmental level appears to be quite inadequate and lack any conviction. Besides, combating crime against women has been greatly affected due to women's lack of access to legal information aid or protection, redundant laws, failure to reform existing laws, inadequate efforts on the part of public authorities to promote awareness of and enforce existing laws and the absence of educational and other means to address the causes and consequences. Thus, inspite of all that is being said and done in combating violence against women, the plight of women in our society remains deplorable. This untold miseries of women due to gender based crimes, has always pained me, which in turn made me obsessed to organize a National Seminar on "Gender and Development". The idea to edit a book on "Combating Violence Against Women: A Reality in Making" originated from the academic debate and discourse that continued for two days of the National Seminar. Some of the papers read and presented with both theoretical and empirical content had attracted my attention to edit this volume.

I, strongly believe, the contributors through their concern, commitment, research and academic insight have tried out focusing various issues, aspects and dimensions of violence against women. All the papers, chosen for this composite volume are of high academic and research standard which may meet the requirement of teachers, researchers, social activist, policy makers, law and other enforcement agencies engaged in combating crime against women.

Beulah Shekhar draws our attention towards India's failure to honour international instrument oriented towards curtailing violence against women. He argues that the plight of the victims of gender based crime has been intensified due to absence of victim friendly legislations and the alternate state initiatives. To combat violence against women, he has emphasized the role of Public Interest Litigations, alternate dispute resolution and the proactive role of NGOs and activists compositely can take the venture ahead.

Smita Nayak has described domestic violence as a heinous and escalating crime against women, which has added new dimension to violence against women. Pointing out the geometrical progression rate of increase in incidences of domestic violence, she has cautioned about its psycho-social consequences and ramifications. She argues that the existing instruments of governance both legal and institutional have failed miserably to protect the victims of domestic violence. To address the unfinished agenda the author calls for a psycho-social and service dynamic approach.

Padmalaya Mohapatra has made a comparative study of human rights violation of women of Manipur and Odisha. She argues that in spite of proactive feminist movement, the issue of violence against women in India still 'remains one of the most pervasive forms of human rights violations worldwide. Economic dependency, discriminatory practices, lack of proper policing and delayed justice delivery system are the main reasons for increase in gender based crimes. The scenario is precarious both in Manipur and Odisha. As a solution she calls for both civil society and state agencies to work hand in hand to ensure human rights of women to the women of Manipur and Odisha.

S.D. Sasi Kiran has talked about role of literature both English and Vernacular (Telugu) creating awareness among women on violence against women. She also has pointed out that how such literacy works have helped in removing gender based barriers and provided information and education to the victim women to find the opportunity for their advancement.

Pramod Kumar Ray has put introspection on the instrument of governance dealing with gender based crime in Odisha. While arguing 21st century witnessing more incidences of gender based crime making the position and condition of women quite pitiable, Odisha is no way lagging behind in committing this act of insensitivity against its women. To fight crime against women and deliver justice to the victim, he has argued for change of legal framework and existing protection mechanism. Besides making suitable modification in the existing legal procedure (IPC, CrPc, Indian Evidence Act pertaining gender based crime), there is urgent need of introspection and social audit of institutions (both public and private) extending support services to the victims of gender based crime. However, for an effective solution, he urged for a composite psycho-social, legal, political and civil societal approach to deal with the terrible insensitivity against women in our society.

Mamata dash in her paper has investigated the forms, causes and impact of domestic violence against women in its plurality in the state of Odisha. The solution to combat domestic violence, she says, cannot be dealt with mere safety nets such as through existing laws, micro credit schemes, capacity building initiative etc but through creating an environment of harmony and justice by renouncing primacy given to materialism.

Ramakrushna Pradhan and Sukanya Kakoty have brought conceptual difference between 'sex' and 'gender'. While highlighting various reasons for violence and atrocities against women, they have pointed out very specific reasons such as lack of social and economic empowerment, lack of political will, ineffectiveness of law, poor enforceability; which have rather given rise to gender based crime. As a solution to combat gender crime, the women of the world should get united and fight back against the insensitivity.

Sanghamitra Parida has discussed about the adverse effect of manual scavenging on the status of dalit women of India. She argues that the practice of manual scavenging even after 67 years of Independence is a clear negation to our Constitutional guarantee of equality, liberty, justice and fraternity. She further argues that manual scavenging is not only a serious kind of social exclusion, rather is a complete violation of human rights and dignity. She has suggested for abolition of manual scavenging through provision of suitable livelihood alternative, abolishment of dry latrines and imparting education to these secluded communities. She calls for government intervention through suitable policies and programmes to abolish the shameful practice of manual scavenging.

Genevive Syangbo and Karma Samten Bhutia in "Violence against women" described the act of insensitivity has a phenomenal rise in the new millennium and continues to thrive unabated in India. They have highlighted various aspects of gender violence and exploitation. They argue that despite of women's development and empowerment, still full advancement of women is affected due to increasing crime against them. They opined that besides government initiative, there is need of advocacy of socio-economic, education, health, gender and political, cultural and environmental awareness.

Raj kumari Lilapati Devi in her study of collective activism of Manipuri women in conflict communication asserts that nupilan or the women's war played an important role in pre-independence period, proved to be very effective in present day Manipur society which has been inflicted with all kinds of socio-political conflicts. She says 'Meirapaibis', the collective activism movement of the Manipuri women work towards restoring equity, solidarity, gender balance, power relations between women and authority. She described the resistance movement more of a matriarch in the patriarchal society.

Dilshad Shaik has discussed about current challenges of violence against women at work place. Which, he described as the worst form and most unreported crimes in our society. It greatly hinders women's employability. He argues that sexual harassment at work place is a violation of the right to life and personal liberty as mentioned in Article-21 of our Constitution. He has pointed out the inadequate irrelevance of the existing law to curb sexual violence at work place. He also has highlighted the ineffectiveness of the new law on prevention, prohibition and redressal of sexual harassment of women at work place. The new law by allowing the employer to initiate action against the complainant (victim) in case of false or malicious complaint is designed as a guerrilla way of escape for the accused. He concludes that, the new law, if implemented with letter and spirit can reduce the incidences of sexual harassment at work place to a great extent.

Ishfaq Ahmad Shah and Monisa Qadri in their empirical study have examined the idea of gender justice, social mobilization and media activism in Delhi Rape case, in which they have talked about the beginning of a new order determining the safety of women in India. They have studied the role of a leading National Newspaper in highlighting the heinous crime; and bringing rapists to the book. They believe that media activism and social mobilization not only forced the government to change its rape law but has given a sense of confidence to women in general and rape victims in particular that ultimately our society has responded to the act of insensitivity against women.

Sagarika Dash and Sanchita Choudhury have examined the status of women with reference to Sarojini Sahoo's novel 'Goddess in Exile'. They have pointed out the sorry state of women's position in Indian society-the women being treated as a play in the hands of patriarchy. They have highlighted about the traumatized situation of a section of ill-fated women, who are forced to lead a cursed life from their marriageable age till death. The status of women, as depicted in the novel is to maintain the honour of their family and to provide pleasure in various samples.

Swapna S. Prabhu and Niranjan Mohapatra have drawn our attention towards gender sensitization in law enforcement. They say that the domestic violence cases, which were largely unnoticed earlier, now get highlighted due to the efforts of women groups and media coverage. They argue that due to growing number of women in police, the handling of domestic violence cases has become easier. They argue that still there is a need of sensitization of the police force to women issues. They emphasized the role of police as a crucial need to be an agent of social change.

Kamalakanta Roul speculates violence as preeminent and that it exists in every society and civilization. Talking about consequence of violence, he says it has affected peaceful co-existence, social cohesion and cultural cooperation. For a better conceptual and ethical debate on the issue of violence, he has examined it from both analytical and exploratory methods of political theory. He argues that violence, which is a leading issue in contemporary global politics and society, suffers from definitional and conceptual ambiguity in political theory and theory of violence lack a normative ethical position among academia, activists and citizens. He has tried to explain the anatomy of violence through dichotomy of Gandhian form of positive violence and Marxian form of negative violence.

Above all, any society which does not believe in gender equality is treading on a horrible path. However developed a society or nation may be in terms of physical, material, infrastructural and technological advances, it would not pave the way of power and glory of any sections of its population (Citizens) especially if the women are denied equal rights in all walks of life par with men. So, combating violence against women is an issue to be taken seriously understanding the ground realities in order to pave a more concentrated approach to deal with this human insensitivity towards their own fellow human beings. This academic endeavour would also ring a caution bell to our otherwise careless political representatives, law enforcement agencies and institutions right from family to state to be as sensitive and caring to address this. To attain this greater objective of gender equality requires elimination of all forms of violence against women which needs a complete eradication of patriarchy from the edifice of the society. For this, we have to strive hard, adopting a composite psycho social and political approach to kill the ills of the problem.

I strongly believe that our duty as a researcher and academia is far more essential than anyone else in this sensitive issue. Let us start thinking in this direction how to combat violence against women. Serious research and academic endeavior can show the record map for broader platform of action for elimination of all forms of violence against women in our society.

1

Violence against Women

Genevive Syangbo and
Karma Samten Bhutia

"Violence against women is a manifestation of historically equal power relations between men and women, which have led to domination over and discrimination against women by men and to the prevention of the full advancement of women.........."

(The United Nations Declaration on the Elimination of Violence against Women, General Assembly Resolution, December 1993).

Abstract

With the rise of new millennium violence against women continues unabated in our country. Violence against women manifests itself as rape, molestation, stripping, eve-teasing, kidnapping and abduction, domestic violence including wife battering, dowry harassment, and dowry death, cruelty to women, foeticide, and female infanticide. Gender-based violence threatens the well being, rights and dignity of women. Women's right as human rights has been a major concern of women's movement in India since 1980's.

The paper attempts to highlight various aspects of gender violence and exploitation of women in areas of socio-economic, cultural, workplace and politics. Recent statistics show that women is molested every 26 minutes, raped every 34 minutes, sexually harassed every 42 minutes, kidnapped every 43 minutes and killed every 93 minutes. Inspite of women's development and empowerment in all fields, women still have to go a long way for its share as the better half of man. So the mission of bringing out women from the disparity should go on with the advocacy of socio-economic, education, health, gender, political, cultural and environmental awareness.

Key words: gender violence, exploitation of rights of women, dignity and status of women, India.

Introduction

Rights of women are knowingly and unknowingly encroached upon. Women constitute half of the population of the world and often referred to as the "Better Half of Man", women have the worst deal at the hands of society. She is wife, mother and unpaid worker in the household. When old she is discarded and disregarded and widow she is considered fair game for all. For so long women have been assigned a low and undignified status in comparison to that of men.

Violation against women has been a raising international concern. It has been a global phenomenon. The issue of violence against women, both physically and non-physical has played a determinant role on the status of women. Status of women underwent many changes in the course of time. Some scholars claim that in society, particularly in India, women had better status in ancient times than in the medieval and the modern times. Violence against women is viewed as one of the most crucial societal mechanism by which women are forced into a subordinate position.

The idea that female oppression stemmed from male control over female sexuality or the institution of monogamous marriage was the first expounded by English in 1940. Mc Kinnon (1988) and Rich (1980) further argued that compulsory heterosexuality and male appropriation of female sexuality are central to male dominance and female oppression. Gender-based discrimination and poverty and violence against women remains important sources of insecurity in today's world. Article 1 of the Declaration on Elimination of Discrimination Against Women (CEDAW) adopted by the UN General Assembly denotes that "discrimination against women, denying or limiting their equality or rights with men, is fundamentally unjust and constitutes an offence against human dignity".

Violence against women did not become a topic for international social movement until the early 1980's. These issues moved rapidly by the mid 1990's and became the most important international women's issue and new international human rights concern. Violence against women is a serious problem in India. Overall, one-third of women age 15-49 have experienced physical violence and about one in ten has experienced sexual violence. Generally violence includes exploitation economic, social, and political of individual by individual. According to the report of the National Crime Records Bureau, there are three specific situations where women are distinctly vulnerable: within home, while in transit and at workplace. According to World Health Organisation, violence against women causes more deaths among women than any other illness. The manifestation of gender violence may differ in different socio-economic and cultural settings but its impact, intensity and consequences on women remain the same. Constitutionally, social justice and human rights are equal to all people without any differentiation in sex, race, class, religion and caste. Practically women in India are deprived from exercising these rights on the account of rampant gender violence in the male-dominated society. The violence against women in India is continuously rising. In spite of the efforts made by the government and voluntary sector, women are not free from various forms of violence. In 2013, National Crime Branch Bureau records 33707 numbers of rape cases, 8083 cases of dowry deaths, 96.3 per cent of cases of insult to the modesty of women and 92.3 per cent of cruelty by husband and his relatives. This considerable rise in violence against women within matrimonial homes shows the declining status of women.

In India, most of the violence against women pertains to rape, dowry death, dowry related harassment, grabbing/ misappropriation of streedhan and widow's property, molestation, kidnapping and abduction, eve-teasing, sexual harassment, desertion by husband, cruelty by husband and his relatives and sexual harassment at work place.

Rape

Women's sexuality is one important area of violence against women and oppression. Women are obliged to provide sexual services to men. Each year the cases of forcible rapes are reported.

Rape is committed by strangers, family members, friends and relations. Rape cases also go unreported due to some social pressure. It is reported that no age group, social status or blood relations can guarantee a women that she is safe from sexual assaults. Married women are also not safe from rapes. Marital rape is also one of the extreme forms of violence against married women. In this new millennium the worst form of violence against women is the offence of rape. There has been an alarming rise of rape cases in India. The states of Madhya Pradesh, Maharashtra, Uttar Pradesh, Rajasthan, Punjab, Haryana, Odisha, Kerala, Karnataka Chandigarh, Delhi, West Bengal and Assam have shown phenomenal rise in the incidence of rape in last one year. Delhi records the highest rape cases (700 rape cases) in the country over the last 10 years. The number of rape cases was 572 in 2011, the number rose to 706 in 2012 and 1636 in 2013. Rapes by minors are on the rise. Reports on juvenile crimes by the National Crime Records Bureau (NCRB) reveal that from 2002 to 2012, there has been a 143 per cent increase in the number of rapes by juveniles.

Dowry death

In India, one woman dies every hour due to dowry-related problems which has seen a steady rise in such cases between 2007 and 2011 (NCRB, 2012). Dowry as defined in the Act means any property or valuable security given by women's family to the other party in a marriage; at or before or any time after the marriage (Devi, 2005). Dowry death means death of a woman when it is caused by any burns or physical injury in connection with any demand of dowry. Dowry deaths occur within the four walls of a house.

Trends in dowry death have shown a phenomenal growth. National Crime Report Bureau has recorded total 8083 dowry death cases in 2013. The states needing special measures to prevent dowry death are Odisha, Assam, Bihar, Haryana, Jharkhand, Karnataka, Madhya Pradesh, Maharashtra, Rajasthan and Uttar Pradesh and West Bengal as evident from the decadal trends that show greater rise in the incidence of this offence in these states during 2001–2011. Dowry murders have witnessed a sustained campaign by several women's organisations and civil rights groups. The Dowry Prohibition Act (Amendment) was passed in 1984. The Act sets a limit to the amount given in dowry but does not ban dowry. Various measures were adopted by various organisations to combat dowry related incidence in the country since 1980's. While cruelty by husband and his relatives leading to suicide or death has become an offence, punishable with imprisonment, still dowry deaths continue.

Domestic violence

Domestic violence is a serious problem in India. It is the most silent form of violence. It is violence within the four walls of a house. It includes mental, verbal, physical, sexual, economic, emotional etc. It is prevalent among both rural and privileged people. Many people do not accept it as a criminal act. Domestic violence in many cases is disguised as love. Domestic violence can be categorised into physical, sexual, verbal, emotional and economic violence. Physical injury is the most visible form of domestic violence. Acts of physical violence include: pushing, shaking, throwing objects, slapping, arm twisting, hair pulling, punching, kicking, dragging, beating, trying to choke or burn and threatening and attacking with any kind of weapon. Cruelty by husband and his relatives seems to be the offence that has shown phenomenal rise in the incidence among most of the Indian states and Union Territories. The rise in the incidence of the offence of cruelty by husband and his relatives has been observed more in the states like Andhra Pradesh, Assam, Bihar, Gujarat, Haryana, Rajasthan, Tamil Nadu, Uttar Pradesh, Andaman and Nicobar Islands and Chandigarh. The state of Assam records the highest incidence of 8636 cases of cruelty by husband towards women in 2013.

Emotional abuse has been the common form of domestic violence within the private home. Psychological abuse has an adverse affect on woman's sense of self-worth and can be incredibly harmful to overall mental and physical wellbeing of women. Emotional abuse can include harassment; threats; verbal abuse such as name-calling, degradation and blaming; stalking; and isolation. Women experiencing domestic violence tend to have more emotional distress and may also lead to suicidal thoughts and attempts. According to a study by the National Centre for Biotechnology Information, suicide attempts in India are correlated with physical and psychological intimate partner violence.

Female infanticide and foetal killing

Killing of the infant soon after the birth or at the foetus stage is called Female infanticide and foetal killing. Foetal killing has been a crucial problem in Indian society where higher value is placed on sons. The birth of a daughter is burden for the family for not only there's insufficient occupation for her but dowry has to be given for her wedding and other gifts to be given to her husband's family on various occasions after the marriage.

Based on demographic information large numbers of women are missing every year from the population statistics in India. Misuse of the sex determination test has resulted in a new type of femicide, i.e, abortion of female foetuses in India. Sex-selective abortion, female infanticide has led to the phenomenon of missing women and girls. The culture of foeticide has given birth to a new culture of bride buying and trafficking. As per the 2011 population census the present sex ratio is 940 females per 1000 males which clearly indicates decline in the female population in India.

Sexual harassment at work place

Women are no less free from sexual harassment at workplace. Supreme Court of India recognised sexual harassment at work place as violation of guaranteed fundamental rights in its landmark judgment in Vishaka Judgement, August, 1997. As per the Supreme Court verdict sexual harassment at the workplace is violation of Article 14 (Right to Equality), Article 19(1) (g) (Right to Practice any Profession, trade or business), and Article 21 (Right to Life). The act of Sexual harassment include any kind of unwelcome sexual advance, request for sexual favours and verbal or physical conduct such as loaded comments, remarks or jokes, letters, phone calls or e-mails, gestures, exhibition of pornography, lurid stares, physical contact, stalking and sounds or display of sexual nature. The impact of sexual harassment has an adverse effect on the individual as well on the workplace affecting the entire work culture.

There are several factors that perpetuate violence against women which includes: cultural, economic, legal and political factors. **Culturally**, women are prone to domestic violence on various lines like; gender-specific socialisation, cultural definitions of appropriate sex roles, expectations of roles with relationships, belief in the inherent superiority of males, values that give men proprietary over women, notion of family as private sphere and under male control, customs of marriage (bride price/dowry) and acceptability of violence as a means to resolve conflict. **Economically**, women gets violated as women are economically depended on men, limited access to cash and credit, discriminatory laws regarding inheritance and property rights, limited access to employment in formal and informal sectors and limited access to education and training for women. In **legal** sense too women enjoy leaser status. Inappropriate legal laws regarding divorce, child custody, maintenance and inheritance have relegated the prestige and self esteem of women to a low position in the society. More importantly insensitive attitude of police and judiciary towards women have undermined the status of women. And **politically**, women are under-represented in the political arena. There is a limited organisation of women as a political force and limited participation of women in organised political system (Heise, 1994).

Studies has been carried on the socio-economic costs of violence against women reveals that all sectors of society are deeply affected by and bear the consequences of violence against women. The study carried by Inter-American Development Bank (IDB) in six Latin American countries–Brazil, Colombia, El-Salvador, Mexico, Peru and Venezuela calculated four categories of costs of violence against women (Coomaraswamy, 1999)–

(i) Direct costs take into account expenditure on medical treatment, cost imposed on the criminal justice system–court case, police services -time spent on arrests and responding, housing and shelters for women and their children; and social services (prevention and advocacy programmes for police, doctors, the judiciary and the media).

(ii) Non-monetary costs include pain and suffering–increased mortality via homicide and suicide, abuse of drugs and depressive disorders.

(iii) Economic effects–includes macro-economic, decreased labour market participation, reduced productivity on the job, lower earnings, lower education attainment of children and decreased investment and saving.

Violence against Women Throughout the Life Cycle

Phase	*Type of Violence*
Pre-birth	Sex –selective abortion; effects of battering during pregnancy on birth outcomes.
Infancy	Female infanticide; physical, sexual and psychological abuse.
Girlhood	Child marriage; female genital mutilation; physical, sexual and psychological abuse; child prostitution and pornography.
Adolescence and Adulthood	Dating and courtship violence (acid throwing and date rape) molestation to schoolgirls, sexual abuse at school, college and workplace; rape; sexual harassment; forced prostitution and pornography, trafficking in women; partner violence; marital rape; dowry abuse and murders; partner homicide; abuse of women with disabilities and forced pregnancy.
Elderly	Forced suicide or homicide of widows for economic reasons; sexual, physical and psychological abuse.

Source: "Violence against Women", WHO, FRH/WHD/97.8.

Table 1: Crime against women–Rape, Dowry Death, Assaults on women, Insult to the modesty of women and Cruelty by husband and his relatives, 2013

State/Union territories	*Rape cases (Sec-376-IPC)*	*Dowry Deaths (Sec-304 B-IPC)*	*Assaults on women in intent to outrage her modesty (Sec-354-IPC)*	*Insult to the modesty of women (Sec- 509-IPC)*	*Cruelty by husband and his relatives (Sec-366-IPC)*	*Kidnapping and abduction of women and girls (Sec-363-369 and 371-373 IPC)*
Andhra Pradesh	1635	492	6930	4702	15084	2119
Arunachal Pradesh	75	0	93	3	29	82
Assam	1937	170	2409	14	8636	3812
Bihar	1128	1182	331	52	4533	4807
Chhattisgarh	1380	109	2261	180	1181	450
Goa	86	0	162	54	40	24
Gujarat	732	29	1243	77	7812	1720
Haryana	971	263	1560	643	3617	1349
Himachal Pradesh	250	0	493	111	328	172
Jammu & Kashmir	378	7	1389	354	428	1093

(Contd.)

(Contd. Table 1)

State/Union territories	*Rape cases (Sec-376-IPC)*	*Dowry Deaths (Sec-304 B-IPC)*	*Assaults on women in intent to outrage her modesty (Sec-354-IPC)*	*Insult to the modesty of women (Sec- 509-IPC)*	*Cruelty by husband and his relatives (Sec-366-IPC)*	*Kidnapping and abduction of women and girls (Sec-363-369 and 371-373 IPC)*
Jharkhand	1204	307	524	18	2084	1056
Karnataka	1030	272	3913	137	3276	1451
Kerala	1221	21	4362	404	4820	281
Madhya Pradesh	4335	776	8252	736	4988	1302
Maharashtra	3063	230	8132	2630	8542	1583
Manipur	72	0	59	0	29	223
Meghalaya	183	2	98	0	23	92
Mizoram	89	0	81	1	5	8
Nagaland	31	1	18	426	4	27
Odisha	1832	395	4829	67	2792	1542
Punjab	888	126	1045	67	1741	919
Rajasthan	3285	453	4829	25	15094	3243
Sikkim	43	0	29	0	5	10

(Contd.)

(Contd. Table 1)

State/Union territories	*Rape cases (Sec-376-IPC)*	*Dowry Deaths (Sec-304 B-IPC)*	*Assaults on women in intent to outrage her modesty (Sec-354-IPC)*	*Insult to the modesty of women (Sec-509-IPC)*	*Cruelty by husband and his relatives (Sec-366-IPC)*	*Kidnapping and abduction of women and girls (Sec-363-369 and 371-373 IPC)*
Tamil Nadu	923	118	1271	313	2471	1945
Tripura	233	29	407	7	827	139
Uttar Pradesh	3050	2335	7303	25	8781	8878
Uttarakhand	228	43	295	72	435	297
West Bengal	1685	481	4913	577	18116	5117
Andaman Nicobar	27	1	45	8	9	8
Chandigarh	45	1	143	26	92	87
Dadra & Nagar Haveli	5	0	1	1	1	13
Daman & Diu	8	0	2	0	2	3
Delhi	1636	144	3515	916	3033	3970
Lakshadweep	2	0	1	0	0	0
Puducherry	17	1	12	8	8	19
TOTAL	**33707**	**8083**	**70739**	**12589**	**118866**	**47592**

Source: India, Ministry of Home Affairs, National Crime Records Bureau, 2013.

(iv) Social effects: impact on interpersonal relations and quality of life. It also includes intergenerational transmission of violence, reduced quality of life, erosion of social capital and above all reduced participation in democratic process.

Despite the fact that women in India are legally protected from various forms of abuse, crime against a woman is committed every three minutes, a woman is raped every 29 minutes, a dowry death occurs every 77 minutes, and one case of cruelty committed by either the husband or relative of the husband occurs every nine minutes. A brief glance at the recorded data pertaining to crimes against women indicates the growing rate of violence in India.

Conclusion

The paper enables to understand the typology of violence pertaining to women, particularly in India. As a response to women's movement that began in late 1970's, the government set up women's cell within few ministries. Women's movement in India involves not only urban areas but also middle class educated women. There are several active grassroots organisations of the poor rural and urban working class women, tribal, self-employed women who are fighting against all forms of oppression, injustice and exploitation. Various national and regional political parties and trade unions have also set up women's wings. The Vishaka Guidelines (1997) on sexual harassment seek to ensure safe working spaces for women. Women's studies or gender studies has been given priority to understand the suppression and oppression of women in various sectors of life.

Efforts have been made through various legislations and movements to combat women's condition, still women have no better place in the society. Hence, it can be understood that the most crucial consequence of violence against women is the denial of fundamental human rights to women (Desai, 2001). Much emphasis has been endowed by governments on women's rights as human rights; violence against women is increasing at an alarming rate. A woman is not only deprived of her dignity and pride but is also a victim of cruelty both within and outside home which relegates women to a subordinate position. In this paper we have referred to various issues of violence against women, now what is required is to support the movements and policies striving towards gender equality. It has been felt that more integrated studies should be carried out to estimate the costs of violence against women in order to advocate national policies and eradicate this largely preventable crime.

References

Aggarwal, Nomita. 2002. *Women and Law in India.* New Century Publications, New Delhi.

Desai, Neera and Thakkar, Usha. 2001. *Women in Indian Society.* National Book Trust, New Delhi.

Devi, Uma K. 2005. *Violence Against Women-Human Rights Perspective.* Serials Publication, New Delhi.

Forbes, Geraldine. 2009. *The Cambridge History of India–Women in Modern India,* Cambridge University Press.

Innocent Digest. 2000, *Domestic Violence Against Women and Girls,* Unicef, Vol. No. 6, June 2000, Florence, Italy.

Crime Statistics, 2013. Ministry of Home Affairs, National Crime Records Bureau. Crime in India, New Delhi.

Parvin, M. Razia. 2005. *Empowerment of Women, Strategies and Systems for Gender Justice.* Dominant Publishers Distributors, New Delhi.

Rhodes, Edward and Mansbach, W. Richard, 2000. Global *Politics in a Changing World,* Houghton Mifflin Company, Boston, New York.

Singh, K.V. 2007. *Women Issues–Empowerment and Gender Discrimination,* Vista International Publishing House, Delhi.

Statistics on Women in India. 2010. National Institute of Public Cooperation and Child Development, Hauz Khas, New Delhi.

2

Resistance and Collective Activism of Manipuri Women in Conflict Communication : an Overview on Manipuri Society

Rajkumari Lilapati Devi

Abstract
Manipuri women have been involving in socio-economic-political matters of the state for many decades. Nupilan or the Women's war which occurred in pre-independence period is a vivid example of their collective activism against any conflict situation in society. The present-day Manipur society which is inflicted with all kinds of socio-political conflicts bestows a picture where womenfolk come forward and move the wave, be it the case of AFSPA, ILP, safeguarding of the territorial integrity of state, extra judicial killing or any social ecological havoc created by armed groups or any kind of community injustice committed by local people. The overall picture of their conflict communication is being carried out through fiery protest rallies, sit-in protests and other demonstrations and negotiations. Their bravery, solidarity, promptness, concern for the community communicates a majestic feminine stronghold in the patriarchal Manipur society.

Key words : Community cohesion, social ecology, geo-political conflict, genealogic social geography, MeiraPaibi, naked protest.

Introduction :

Manipur society bears the characteristic of "community cohesion" (people in the community share common values, respect each other, and have a common identity; and people in the community share goals and responsibilities and are willing to work with others (S Chamard, 2013). Its residents : Meeties, Pangals and Tribals have been residing in harmony for many centuries. Its "social geographical structure" manifests more of homogeneity rather than compartmentalised array of different races doting on it. Looking from the view of geopolitics, the state has come a long way from being an independent kingdom to being a part of Indian union in 1949, then a full flagged Indian state in 1972; its unstable social turmoil, insurgent groups, naïve economy, the politics between the state government and the centre, its people and the state government, the international border mayhem have made this small state of 22,327 sq km area and population of 2,570,390 people a unique mosaic of various kinds of violence and conflicts. The state has seen social movements fighting against destructive power relations for human rights, ethics, identity, market stabilisation, social ecology, cultural preservation and indigenous social wellbeing.

Women have contributed and proved their might in times of instability and conflict. The feminine power at the core and their ability and strength have moved the state in many cases of conflicts. As per Stevenson's article on Women activists and their communities, he categorised women activists into three types : elite women, Perfectionists (who sought to eradicate rather than ameliorate social ills), Ultraists or radicals. Perfectionists concerned less with moral reform of individual men and women but to ameliorate perceived social ills. Women activists in Manipur can be considered to be a homogeneous group of women deeply rooted in community spirit, no matter what their educational qualification and social standing are. They are a collective community oriented informal groups taking part in day-to-day's social, political, economic conflicts. There are elites who pioneered to take up social conflict issues to the international platforms. Their activism reflects the other collective activism of the homogenised platoon. Irom Sharmila protesting against the repeal of Armed Forces Special Power Act, 1958: Binalakshmi Nepram, founder of Manipur Women Gun Survivor network can be put in the last category of activists.

Conflicts can happen at many levels and circles of interpersonal, organisational, community, social, religious, intercultural and international. We will be discussing only the social conflicts of Manipur state. Manipur society is replete with many types of conflicts at various levels: local, district and the state. The origin of its conflicts lies in the deep-rooted indigenous community oriented culture, patriarchy, corrupt practices of authority, insurgency and the colonial nature of centre. From time to time, civil societies, other organisations, local people and student parties have actively put up their voices and sought resolution and answers through protest rallies and sit-in protests. In all of these conflict situations, Manipuri women have taken part either lion's share or solely by themselves only. Women's activism in Manipuri society runs strong, and it takes up the whole picture of any socio-political, geo-political conundrum.

Manipuri women's activism in conflict communication may be analysed through macroprocesses (eg., social, economic, and political structure). Multilevel approaches include terms such as the social ecological framework/model, multiple levels of analysis, and multilevel theorising.(JG Oetzel, ST-Toomey, and WJ Anderson, 2013). Multilevel approaches focus on understanding concepts at multiple levels as well as between different levels. Multilevel approaches have a good fit for "naturalistic environments" (Upton and Egan, 2010).

There are many approaches to examine the specific levels in multilevel frameworks including meso-organisational research (Rousseau and House, 1994) and social ecological frameworks (Stokols, 1996). Conflicts in Manipuri society and women' activism in it are largely shaped by family value system, social ecology, cultural values and inherent community spirit of these people. These are the various levels and strata to be looked at when analysing the conflict situation and the way to communicate for resolution of the conflict.

Any conflict can be analysed at various system levels. The system levels are : (1) micro (face-to-face interactions in specific settings—interpersonal conflict), (2) meso (interrelationships among various microsystems—organisational conflict), (3) exo (forces within the larger social system—community to institutional/ structural conflict), and (4) macro (cultural beliefs, values, and ideologies—intercultural/international

(Bronfenbrenner, 1979, 1989). This article will delve into the exo and macro levels of conflict communication in the Manipuri society.

The State's socio-political conflict and women's resistance

The earliest women's movement and collective activism can be traced back to the historical event NupiLan (Women's war) which occurred in 1904 and again in 1939 AD. It was the collective resistance against monopolist Marwari rice traders of the state. When the government lifted the ban on the export of rice in 1939, there followed excessive uncontrolled export of rice by the monopolist Marwaris creating an adverse effect on the petty women rice dealers of the state. Huge price rise of rice and then artificial famine followed. The fear and apprehension of the common people were aggravated by the heavy rain and floods occurred at that time. Women who were holding the reins of the total household activity came forward against this unruly prevalence of the society and surged a great uproar against the lawmakers of the state.

On 12 December 1939, hundreds of women who were demanding an end to the free trade on rice besieged the President of the Manipur Durbar and the officials who came to the rescue of the President. In the scuffle that broke out between the women and the Assam Rifles, twenty one women and one Indian officer and seven other ranks of the Assam Rifles were injured. In the following months, women targeted the rice-mills owned by the non-Manipuris, which, 'with a daily outturn of 11,200 mounds of rice, absorb the entire paddy available in the state (and)', threw out of employment the bulk of the people who lived by husking'. Women boycotted the main bazaar, i.e., the hub of hoarding and profiteering that was under colonial protection and protest meetings were held in the Paona Bazar. They formed vanguards, intercepted rice carters carrying paddy for sale to the Mayang (outsider) and at times threw cartloads of rice into gutter. In January 1940 alone they held up about 150 rice loaded carts.

In the course of the months long struggle women besieged State Thana and fought several pitch battles with the security personnel. In one of the pitch battles fought on 14 January, forty women agitators and some men were injured. Women organised anti-tax gathering and the leaders advised the agitators to arm themselves with *tem* (a long wooden appliance used for weaving cloth) and wear two phaneks (sarong type of cloth worn by the women of Manipur) while confronting tax-collectors. In short, there was a qualitative shift of the movement towards popular struggle for a responsible Government. The movement, however, subsided as a result of the approach of the Second World War in Manipur in early 1940s.

The primary targets of NupiLan were the agents of exploitation and the visual manifestations that have symbolised the colonial sovereignty, e.g., the Mayangs and the Mayang owned mills.

The NupiLan, which started as an agitation by Manipuri women against the economic policies of the Maharaja and the Marwari monopolists, later on changed its character to become a movement for constitutional and administrative reform in Manipur. The original demands of the women were confined to the banning of rice exports, but later their demands also included changes in, the Darbar and the administrative set-up.

The importance of the NupiLan lies in the fact that it prepared the ground for the leading role played by the women of Manipur in the emergence of a new Manipur after the end of the Second World War (S Yambem, 1976).

Next to the NupiLan, the Nisha-Bandh movement which started in 1970s is regarded as the foundation of the present day Meira Paibi group in Manipur society. Nishabandh movement was a movement against the rise of usage of drugs, narcotics and alcohol among the menfolk of Manipur. The menace of drinks and its consequences in family and the society as a whole were intolerable amongst the homemakers. Social disorder, domestic violence and other crimes started occurring rampantly. Women in the family bore all the brunt of this menace. Groups of women in every locality came forward in order to stop this untoward behaviour of menfolk. The seizure and destruction of drugs and alcohol in mass scale, beating of drunkards and humiliation in public were executed by these Nishaband women. This movement is termed as Nishabandh movement (stopping of drugs, narcotics and alcohol). This Nishabandh movement gave rise to the birth of 'Meirapaibi' groups in Manipur. The literal meaning of MeiraPaibi is 'women holding the torch'. This torch

Picture 1: First NupiLan, 1904.

Courtesy : RK C S Gallery.

Picture 2 : Second NupiLan, 1939.

Courtesy : RK C S Gallery.

is made of bamboo stick filled with kerosene and stuffed with a piece of cloth acting like a torch when ignited the piece of cloth.

Any form of present day women's resistance in Manipuri society, the activism engrained in any case can be seen as woven around the activities of MeiraPaibis of Manipur. Meira Paibis are the interest groups of Manipur society. Interest groups may consist of tightly knit and well-recognised entities or loose coalitions or even emergent (or incipient) networks. Such groups are situated not only within a matrix of political, economic, and social forces but also within the flow of their own experiential histories (G Cheney, G Beck and RJ Cline, 2013).

Currently there are four State level Meira Paibi organisations. the All Manipur Women's Reformation and Development Samaj (also known as Nupi Samaj), the Poirei Leimaro, Kanglamei, the Meekhol. Ideologically, the NupiSamaj is supported by UCM (United Committee of Manipur) and the PoireiLeimaro by the AMUCO (All Manipur United Clubs Organisation). The President of each State level group is selected by an understanding and consensus. There are numerous MeiraPaibi groups in every *leikai* (small locality). The structure of the MeiraPaibis is loose and strong at the same time. They don't have any fixed office in every leikai nor do they meet to discuss issues every day. Only when there is a crises situation do these women gather as MeiraPaibis.

Manipur women Gun Survivors network, an NGO under the organisation, Control Arms Foundation of India describes the MeiraPaibi as a women's association, one of the largest grassroots human rights movements in Manipur, comprising virtually the entire adult Meitei female population in every Meitei town and village. It is the watchdog of civil rights violations at the community level, initiating and engaging in campaigns against rights violations, such as arbitrary detention, cordon and search operations, and torture, committed by the security personnel of the federal government of India.

Every women's collective resistance is associated with MeiraPaibi. Every women in a *leikai* (locality) is virtually a member of Meirapaibi. A formal body exists comprising of president, secretary, treasurer, advisor. MeiraPaibis may work at the leikai level, district level and state level. These MeiraPaibi groups may or may not register under society's registration act.

The advent of MeiraPaibi movement in the valley of Manipur came along with the imposition of AFSPA (Armed Forces Special Power Act, 1958 which legitimised full scale military operations, permitting even a non-commissioned officer to kill anyone on mere suspicion with guaranteed immunity) in Sept 1980. After the imposition of this Act, Indian Army assumed extra power to violate basic civil right of the common people. Young men were randomly picked up, women were raped, and many were killed on suspicion of being insurgents.The NishaBandh women shot up their agenda to safeguard innocent youths from the atrocities of security forces under the aegis of AFSPA. Thus came the birth of MeiraPaibis to counter the inhuman acts under AFSPA. During the time of combing operations, MeiraPaibis stay alert. They communicate with one another, once a signal of danger looms. Hiting the electric post hard with a stone is the way to give the information of urgent summoning of other women. They would form a human shield not letting the army to intrude the area or house.

For years, or even decades, security forces in Manipur have faced allegations of human rights violations and extrajudicial murders committed under cover of the draconian Armed Forces

Courtesy: www.Indianexpress.com

Picture 3 : Irom Sharmila along with Meirapaibis.

Picture 4: Protest on AFSPA.

Courtesy : www. e-pao.net

Special Powers Act (AFSPA). In 2000, Irom Sharmila, shocked by the massacre of 10 civilians, including an 18-year-old National Child Bravery Award winner, by the Assam Rifles, started her hunger fast — that lasts to this day — in protest against the AFSPA.

Meirapaibis' geopolitical landmarks

The geopolitical affair of Manipur has been running rough for many decades even before India's independence. The kingdom of Manipur which extended beyond the present territory upto some parts in Myanmar and Assam before independence is in turmoil now with conflicts running high with its various ethnic groups. The Kuki State Demand Committee demanding separate Kuki land, and the Isak-Muivah faction of the NSCN along with the United Naga Council on the other side demanding Nagalim or Greater Nagaland (a unified country merging all Naga inhabited areas of North East), repeal of AFSPA, demand of ILP (inner line permit system), and other insurgent problems make the state a soup of conflicts. Each and every movement has seen a critical geographical ethnocentrism. Ó Tuathail G, in his book, *Critical Geopolitics: The Politics of Writing Global Space*, says 'Geography is about power. Although often assumed to be innocent, the geography of the world is not a product of nature but a product of histories of struggle between competing authorities over the power to organise, occupy, and administer space'. This is evident in case of the above geo-socio-political conflicts of the state. Each competing party has moved their geopolitical idea and deconstructed the genealogic social geography of the state. Irrespective of the gender, people have fought for their ideology, womenfolk in particular have raised their voices and taken the weight on their shoulder. The MeiraPaibis' socio-political involvement in any conflict situation creates a deeper meaning, a culture which moves on its dictum governed by the ideology of human security. They are the female revolutionary groups, the protective guard of the society who are on move all the time trying to reduce the socio-spatial gap of power management between the ruler and the people or any other destructive power in the geo-political conflict orbit.

The great June Uprising, 2001

On June 18, 2001, Manipur witnessed the biggest mass uprising when about 10,000 people came out to the streets protesting the centre's decision to extend the ceasefire with the militant NSCN(IM) [National Socialist Council of Nagaland (Isak-Muivah)] beyond Nagaland. This militant group has been demanding the formation of greater Nagaland or Nagalim covering Naga inhabited areas of Manipur, Assam, Mizoram, Arunachal Pradesh and Myanmar. The move signalled the fragmentation of Manipuris' territory, giving advantage to the NSCN-IM. (The NSCN-IM is led by IsakChisiSwu and Thuingaleng Muivah)

The protestors burnt down the Manipur assembly building, the chief minister's office, the speaker's residence and other government establishments. A total of 18 protestors – a woman, three minors and 14 young men – were killed and many others were injured that day when the security forces opened fire to subdue the frenzied mob on the 18th June, 2010.

A massive civil disobedience movement followed and state capital Imphal was kept under curfew for nearly a month until July 24 till Govt. of India reversed the announcement that the ceasefire with the NSCN (IM) would once again be restricted only to Nagaland, as had been the case ever since it first came into force on Aug 1, 1997.(hillpost.in, 2012).

Courtesy : The Sangai Express.

Picture 5 : MeiraPaibis protest to save territorial integrity

Courtesy : www.hillpost.in

Picture 6 :The protestors burning government establishments.

The United Committee Manipur (UCM), one of the largest civil society in Manipur has been observing the historic day as the "Great June Uprising." Those eighteen people who lost their lives in the turmoil to save the territorial integrity of Manipur are paid rich tribute every year on this day.

The Naked protest, Thangjam Manorama's case

The infamous Naked protest was born when a group of fiery Meirapaibis marched to an Assam Rifles base in Imphal, stripped naked and raised a searing banner: 'Indian Army Rape Us'. They were protesting the rape, torture and murder, a fortnight earlier, of Thangjam Manorama, 32, who was picked up from her home by the 17 Assam Rifles in the early morning of July 11, 2004 and found in the evening dead with no clothes on in a hill side.

The Asian Human Rights Commission (AHRC) had been in tussle with the Centre for Organisation Research & Education (CORE) on the extra-judicial killing and torture of this woman. Manorama's family believes that she had been raped and then killed by the army personnel.

According to the report from CORE, curfew was imposed in Greater Imphal, Bishenpur and Thoubal Districts of Manipur, India since 15 July 2004 in wake of widespread public protests

Courtesy : www. Tehelka.com

Picture 7: MeiraPaibis protesting naked in front of the Assam Rifle Gate

against the torture and extra-judicial execution of Manorama. Large number of people came out on the streets defying the curfew that caused street battles between the people and Manipur police. It was reported that over 100 people were injured in the police firing on July 16, while the police tried to disperse the people at various places of Imphal and also at outskirts using tear gas and rubber bullets (AHRC, 2004).

Resistance against Muivah's entry

There was a great uproar and resistance against the news that Ţhuinglaeng Muivah, general secretary of the National Socialist Council of Nagalim-Isak –Muivah was visiting his ancestral village, Somdal in Ukhrul district after more than four decades. Denied entry to Manipur due to the strong negative reactions from the Meiteis and especially the Manipur state government, Muivah was camping in Viswema village near the Nagaland-Manipur border since May 5, 2010. The Manipur state government has turned down the Union Government's request to provide security to Muivah during his visit to Ukhrul on the ground that the absence of a ceasefire with the NSCN (IM) in Manipur absolves them of such responsibility. Manipur government took the news as a potential conflagration to the imbroglio of the greater Nagaland (Nagalim) issue.

Courtesy: surahmar.wordpress.

Picture 8 : Manipur women march with a banner during a protest against NSCN (I-M) general secretary Thuingaleng Muivah's entry in Manipur

The picture turned to a whole new game next morning when a heavy deployment of hundreds of Manipur armed forces including police commandos, Manipur Rifles and Indian Reserve Battalion (IRB) personnel moved into the border areas and villages at Mao Gate (on NH 39) to prevent Muivah's visit, scheduled on the 3rd May. They pulled down the traditional welcome arch and banners put up by the Naga community to welcome Muivah at Mao Gate (Mamipur). Soon after, Section 144 CrPc was imposed in Senapati and Ukhrul districts and curfew clamped. There were reports of harassment of travellers by the Manipur police personnel, who had severely restricted vehicular entry from Nagaland. There was a clash between police personnels and those who tried to welcome Muivah. MeiraPaibis staged wide spread protest.

People in the hill districts started protesting against the imposition of Section 144 and the ban on Muivah's entry. In Ukhrul town, there was a public meeting of over ten thousand persons followed by a candle light vigil. Women of nine villages around Mao started an indefinite protest in Mao village, as did women of thirteen surrounding villages in Tadubi. Even as news came of peaceful protests from all Naga inhabited areas of Manipur one also began to hear of more direct action like the attack by a group of women on a police station in Ukhrul and the burning of five stranded trucks with Manipur number plates by unidentified persons late at night on 3 May. (IDSA COMMENT, 2010)

Protest for demand of ILP in Manipur

Manipur has witnessed an alarming increase of the influx of foreigners/non-locals/outsiders since independence. This has led to increase in competition in jobs, and other economic activity between locals and outsiders. Eventually, a threat to the indigenous culture, and social issues like drug trafficking, robbery, and other crimes are seen to increase day by day. In order to check this impending danger, all the people of Manipur have come forward under the aeigis of the organisation Federation of Regional Indigenous Societies (FREINDS) and are demanding now Government of India to implement Inner Line Permit system (ILP) in Manipur. Neighbouring states, Mizoram, Arunachal Pradesh have already implemented ILP. Any Indian

Courtesy : The Sangai Express.

Picture 9 : MeiraPaibis demanding implementation of ILP in Manipur.

citizens who wish to travel to these places, they will need an ILP. This provision was made by Britishers under an Act called as Bengal Frontier Provision Act,1873. An outsider cannot take away any rubber, wax, ivory or other forest product (or any book, diary, manuscript, map, picture, photograph, film, curio or article of religious or scientific interest outside these inner line permit areas. This ILP provision was made to give special protection to the indigenous people.

In 2012, Manipur State Assembly also passed a resolution urging Government of India, to implement the ILP system to Manipur.The year 2014 has seen a rigorous move on the demand of ILP in every places of Manipur. Protest Rallies, sit-in-protest are rampant urging the state government to work on it.

As usual, womenfolk have come forward and shouldered the state's responsibility to effect the demand. Here is an excerpt from www.e-pao.net, Aug 8th, 2014.

'All the arrested 27 members of Joint Committee on Inner Line Permit System (JCILPS), Women Wing, were released from Central Jail, Imphal at around 5:30 pm on 08 August 2014. Earlier during the production of the JCILPS activists in the court, a large number of women attempted to storm the court complex shouting slogans against the authority. Later in the evening, the activists were freed by the authority without imposing any conditions on them and they were received by hundreds of jubilant women outside the Central Jail gate who put garlands around their necks.'

MeiraPaibis and community justice

MeiraPaibis have been taking a great role in delivering community justice in any case of conflicts in the society. Community justice is a concept that addresses how criminal justice operations should be carried out in areas where public safety is a major concern. A definition of community justice, provided by David Karp and Todd Clear (2000) is that it encompasses all crime prevention and justice activities that include the community in their processes and have as their primary goal the enhancement of community quality of life. Such initiatives include crime prevention, community policing, community defense and prosecution, community courts, and restorative justice.(JR Hamilton Jr., 2013)

Picture 10 : MeiraPaibis demanding implementation of ILP in Manipur.

Courtesy : The Sangai Express.

Picture 10: Womenfolks staging sit-in-protests in various social conflicts.

Courtesy : The Sangai Express.

Picture 11 : Womenfolks staging sit-in-protests in various social conflicts.

MeiraPaibis are successful in influencing formal system of social control as well as informal system of social control. Formal system of social control such as criminal justice system, law courts may not directly and immediately provide public safety. MeiraPaibis do many a times the informal social controls weaving around families, neighbours, and the society as a whole rendering public safety. Women's organisation, the so called MeiraPaibis have been doing rounds from time to time the various social services for overall moral, political, socio-economic control in many situations. They work as informal social control mechanism in delivering community justice. These controls have a stronger and longer-lasting effect on reducing crime (*ibid*).

Besides taking part in socio-political movement of the state, other issues taken up at leikai level range from neighbourhood fights, theft, threat from UG for extortion, elopement, extra-marital affair, desertion of women to combing operations done by the Army. The leikai level groups also join the State level groups (whoever they are affiliated to) in order to carry out a protest rally or a dharna. MeiraPaibi groups which are not registered and function on their own.

Conclusion

Every socio-political-economic conflict in Manipuri society has a collective movement staged by women, the so called MeiraPaibis. They move in order to bring authorities into action to stop the unwanted consequences and bring justice. This is evident from the local media text. The discourse on local media text throughout the year are full of narratives of women's collective movement against the authority or the other half of the dialogical party in every conflict situation- micro, meso and exo. The conflict communication has been acted through sit-in-protest, dharnas and protest rallies. MeiraPaibis are the emblem of fervent Manipuri women ready to act against any disharmony in law and order situation of a leikai, or district or the state. Equity in solidarity, gender balance, power relations between women and authority runs high in the Manipuri society. It is more of a matriarch in the patriarchal society as evident in the resistance. That is the brilliance of the repertoires of collective activism amongst Manipuri Women across a range of areas in militarism, ecology, identity, ethnicity, ethics, human rights, social welfare, moral guidance and indigenous self determination.

References

Asian human rights commission - urgent appeals program India:,Torture and murder of a woman by armed forces in India, July 29, 2004, http://www.humanrights.asia/news/urgent-appeals/UA-96-2004.

Bronfenbrenner, U. (1979). The ecology of human development, Cambridge, MA: Harvard University Press.

Bronfenbrenner, U. (1989). Ecological systems theory. Annals of Child Development, 6, 187–249.

Manipur Women Gun Survivors network "MEIRA PAIBI", Product ID:MWGSN-P10, http://www.womensurvivorsnetwork.org/product-detail.php?id=16

Namrata Goswami, "Muivah's Visit to Manipur: Steps towards a Meaningful Reconciliation" in IDSA COMMENT, May 11, 2010, http://www.idsa.in/idsacomments/Muivahs Visit to Manipur Steps towards a Meaningful Reconciliation_ngoswami_110510.html

John R. Hamilton Jr., "Community Justice" in *Encyclopaedia of Community Policing and Problem Solving,* Kenneth J. Peak, Sage Publications, *Ltd.*, Thousand Oaks, 2013.

John G. Oetzel and Stella Ting-Toomey and Willow J. Anderson, "Conflict Communication in Contexts: Organising Themes and Future", in *The SAGE Handbook of Conflict Communication,* ed. John G. Oetzel & Stella Ting-Toomey, 815-830, Sage Publications, Inc. Thousand Oaks, 2013.

IANS, "Great Uprising' of Manipur to be cast on screen", June 20, 2012, http://hillpost.in/2012/06/great-uprising-of-manipur-to-be-cast-on-screen/46126/

Karp, D. R., and Clear, T. R. (2000). Community justice: A conceptual framework. In Criminal Justice 2000. Washington, DC: National Criminal Justice Reference Service.

Ó Tuathail , G. (1996). Critical Geopolitics: The Politics of Writing Global Space. Minneapolis University of Minnesota Press.

Rousseau, D. M., and House, R. J. (1994). Meso organisational behavior: Avoiding three fundamental biases. In C. L. Cooper, ed. and D. M. Rousseau (Eds.), Trends in organisational behavior (Vol. 1, pp. 13–30). New York, NY: Wiley.

Sanamani Yambem, "NupiLan: Manipur Women's Agitation, 1939", Economic and Political Weekly, (Feb. 21, 1976), Vol. 11, No. 8 , pp. 325-327, 329-331.

The Sangai Express, "Women give vent to naked fury in front of 17 AR at Kangla", http://www.e-pao.net/GP.asp?src= 1.10.160704. jul04 accessed on the 5th September, 2014.

Sharon Chamard, "Community Cohesion and Empowerment" , in Encyclopaedia of Community Policing and Problem Solving, ed. Kenneth J. Peak, 35-38. Sage Publications Ltd. Thousand Oaks, 2013.

Stokols, D. (1996). Translating social ecological theory into guidelines for community health promotion. American Journal of Health Promotion, 10, 282–298. http:// dx.doi.org/10.4278/0890-1171-10.4.282

Upton, M. G., and Egan, T. M. (2010). Three approaches to multilevel theory building. Human Resource Development Review, 9, 333–356. http://dx.doi.org/10.1177/1534484310380333

3

Addressing Domestic Violence against Women: An Unfinished Agenda

Dr Smita Nayak

Introduction

Violence against women has acquired a new dimension with the frequent occurrence of domestic violence as escalating crime against women. In contemporary time, there is an increased incidence of domestic violence with geometrical progression rate affecting the fundamental and basic rights of survival of women and girl children, whose psycho-social consequences are far more deplorable and alarming. The perpetrators of this heinous crime find the instrument of governance as safe heaven, since the law enforcement agency allows such categories of criminals to go scot-free under the pretext that such cases as just mere family conflicts. Thus, the existing instrument of governance, both legal and institutional have failed miserably to protect the victims and have increasingly became obsolete as deterrent to the bourgeoning crime against women. The need of the hour to address the unfinished agenda, the author calls for a psycho-social and service dynamics approach to deal with the escalated danger.

Statement of the Problem:

Domestic violence is an issue encountered by both the legal and health systems. The health system addresses the negative health outcomes of domestic violence while the legal system focuses on intervention and prevention through criminal and civil laws. Both systems, however, struggle to give full consideration to domestic violence. The healthcare system often fails to take steps to intervene and prevent the violence while the legal system often fails to consider the impact its laws and procedures have on health outcomes. The shortcomings of the health and legal systems in addressing domestic violence can be resolved through increased awareness by healthcare and legal professionals and improved coordination between the systems. The health system can go beyond simply treating the health outcomes of domestic violence and take an active role in preventing the violence through inquiry of patients, identification of victims and referrals to supportive services. The legal system can go beyond the prevention of future acts of violence and help to address the health outcomes of domestic violence by becoming aware of how its procedures influence the health and well-being of the women who utilise the domestic violence law. These processes can then be modified so that they no longer have a negative influence on women's health and well-being.

Background and Context

Domestic Violence – A conceptual Analysis

Domestic violence is violence against women and girls occurs in the family or within the home, where violence is often tolerated. The neglect, physical and sexual abuse and rape of girl children and women by family members and other members of the household, as well as incidences of spousal and non-spousal abuse often go unreported and thus difficult to detect. Even when cases of domestic violence reported there is often failure to protect victims or punish perpetrators.

Domestic violence is any behaviour or action that causes physical, sexual or psychological harm by one person against another who are related by consanguinity or affinity. Physical harm includes hitting, slapping, burning, and beating. Sexual harm refers to forced intercourse and rape. Psychological harm can be the threat of physical or sexual abuse as well as belittling, humiliating and name calling. Other controlling behaviours, such as isolation from family and friends, monitoring of movements and actions, and restriction of access to information, finances or assistance are also forms of domestic violence. The behaviours and actions that constitute domestic violence occur in all countries and can be found within all social, economic, religious and cultural groups. Domestic violence also occurs in all types of relationships: in same sex relationships as well as heterosexual ones, between unmarried couples, or family members. Women can be the perpetrator of domestic violence against men; however, this type of violence is rare. Men perpetrate the overwhelming majority of domestic violence against women. Women experiencing domestic violence face negative social, economic, and health outcomes and are often reluctant to get help due to being stigmatised, or are unaware of how to get help.

The gender imbalance of domestic violence can be attributed to cultural, social and individual variables. For example, physical differences between men and women make women more likely to be victims of domestic violence. Additionally, attitudes about domestic violence are passed down through generations. A study by Martin, *et al*, in northern India interviewed husbands about their witnessing of domestic violence as children. The researchers found that men who witnessed domestic violence as a child were more likely to be physically and sexually abusive toward their wives than men who did not witness abuse. Often, social norms, patriarchal power structures and rigid gender roles do not adequately prepare women to protect themselves from violent partners. In many relationships where domestic violence occurs the woman is financially dependent upon the man, thereby making it difficult for her to resist the violence or leave the relationship. Many times the violence stems from the man's belief that he is exercising his right to maintain order or punish a wayward woman.

World wide, 10-50 per cent of women have experienced domestic violence. Many incidents of domestic violence are unreported so the actual incidence of domestic violence in any given country or location will likely be higher than estimated. Domestic violence is endemic in many countries. It is a behaviour that is often deeply ingrained and accepted. Women of all ages are affected by domestic violence and it is the most common form of violence against them. Domestic violence has serious impacts on women's health and well-being as well as negative social impacts on families and communities. These factors make domestic violence a recognised public health issue. Instead of a public health issue, prevention of domestic violence is primarily seen as a legal issue with laws prohibiting it and providing legal processes for victims to seek relief. There have been many calls for a multi-sectorial response to domestic violence, including the Vienna Declaration's assertion that elimination of violence "can be achieved by legal measures and through co-operation in fields such as economic and social development, education, safe maternity and healthcare, and social support."

Domestic Violence in India and Odisha

Domestic violence in India is often considered a private family issue which is to be handled within the home. Any external intervention is typically unwanted and seen as unnecessary. These beliefs are based on deep-rooted cultural norms and patriarchal values. Domestic violenceis viewed as "a burden that women are expected to bear in silence rather than, shame the family," examined the association between domestic violence and several socio-economic variables. These variables included high stress factors (e.g., family poverty, education level, age at marriage, and number of children) and privacy factors (e.g., household size, inclusion of family members in household, and urban settings). The study found general support for the relationship between high stress variables and domestic violence; however, there was not strong support for a link between family privacy and domestic violence. According to the NFHS-III survey (India's National Family Health Survey-III, twenty-two per cent (22 per cent) of women who reported experiencing domestic violence from a current husband sought help. Of those seeking help, less than one-half per cent (0.4 per cent) sought help from a doctor or other medical personnel and fewerthan one per cent (0.6 per cent) sought help from a lawyer. Because family violence is such a taboo subject in India and rarely discussed it is likely that the incidence and prevalence of domestic violence is under-reported. The reported data alone, however, indicates a high rate of prevalence within the country.

The state of Odisha and domestic violence. The state of Odisha is located in eastern India on the Bay of Bengal. Odisha's estimated population in 2012 was *40,025,00019* with 14.99 per cent of the population living in urban areas. According to the

NFHS-III 2005-2006, 41.2 per cent of ever married women in Odisha experienced spousal violence, slightly higher than the national rate. Thirty-three and a half per cent (33.5 per cent) experienced physical violence, 15 per cent experienced sexual violence, and 20 per cent experienced emotional violence during the twelve months preceding the survey. Details regarding the types of physical abuse experienced by married women in Odisha are provided here to know the magnitude and proportion of such act of insensitivity against women.

According to the NFHS-III 18.6 per cent of women in Odisha aged 15 to 49 who experienced physical or sexual violence have sought help. Sixty eight and a half per cent (68.5 per cent) of ever-married women never sought any help or told anyone while almost eight per cent (7.7 per cent) of the victims have told someone about the violence perpetuated on them but did not seek their help. Of those who sought help, 1.5 per cent sought help from a lawyer, 2.3 per cent from the police, and 1.0 per cent from a social organization. The vast majority of those seeking help sought the help from their own family (75 per cent). Unfortunately, the data for Odisha does not reveal the percentage of women who sought help from doctors or other health personnel. Overall, it is clear from the data that domestic violence is widespread while seeking help for it is rare.

Domestic Violence and Health Outcomes

Domestic violence has many negative health effects on its victims. These health outcomes are routinely encountered, assessed and treated by the health services system and include physical injuries ranging from assault (e.g., lacerations, fractures, internal organ injury), burns; chronic health problems such as irritable bowel syndrome, backache, headache, chronic pelvic pain, pelvic inflammatory disease; increased unintended or unwanted pregnancies, miscarriages, terminations, and low birthweight babies; gynecological problems; higher rates of sexually transmitted diseases, including HIV/AIDS; and, self-harm and suicide. Mental health issues can also occur as a result of domestic violence and include depression, fear, anxiety, low self-esteem, sexual dysfunction, eating problems, obsessive-compulsive disorder, and post-traumatic stress disorder. With the link between domestic violence and health outcomes firmly established, it is imperative for healthcare providers to take an active role in preventing the abuse. Beyond simply treating the physical and mental injuries caused by domestic violence, healthcare professionals can help prevent the violence and resulting health outcomes by identifying those patients who experience domestic violence and referring them to supportive services.

Role of the Healthcare System in Preventing Domestic Violence

Healthcare professionals can not only provide treatment for the resulting health outcomes of domestic violence but can also help prevent the violence by identifying domestic violence victims and referring them to support services. Healthcare professionals have a unique opportunity to intervene in domestic violence situations since they have access – often private, confidential access – to victims when they seek either related or unrelated healthcare treatment. By taking a proactive role in identifying victims and preventing domestic violence, healthcare professionals can reduce the negative health effects of the violence, thereby reducing the number of women treated for physical and mental injuries and the burden on the health system.

Health Professionals and Preliminary Inquiry about Domestic Violence.

Inquiry about domestic violence by health professionals can uncover hidden cases of domestic violence, change the perceived acceptability of violence in relationships, make it easier for women to access support services earlier, change health professionals' knowledge and attitudes towards domestic violence, help reduce the social stigma of domestic violence, and help maintain the safety of women experiencing domestic violence.

It is important for healthcare professionals to inquire about domestic violence since the disclosure of abuse is unlikely to occur without direct questioning. It is not information women are likely to simply volunteer to their doctor or nurse. With such a high prevalence of abuse, the evidenced health effects of the abuse, and the unlikelihood of voluntary disclosure, it is important for health professionals to inquire directly about domestic violence. The inquiry can lead to disclosure by the victim and successful intervention by the healthcare provider. Health care professionals have the opportunity to inquire about domestic violence because of their frequent contact with individual patients. Women routinely access health services for primary care, maternity care and care for their children. Also, those women who experience domestic violence may access services to address the physical injuries resulting from the abuse. These factors place healthcare professionals in the position to identify domestic violence victims. Additionally, inquiring about abuse and identification of victims by healthcare professionals can lead victims to access support services which have been shown to benefit women and children. The development and implementation of a system of inquiry is dependent upon the organisation and capacity of the health services system as well as the local agencies to which victims will be referred. Inquiring about domestic violence should be made in a non-judgmental manner and healthcare professionals should be able to give clear information on local agencies offering advocacy and support services.

Barriers to inquiry

Factors that prevent healthcare professionals from inquiring about domestic violence include the fear of offending female patients, the potential of putting the patient at risk by asking about abuse, and a belief in possessing a lack of expertise to help patients experiencing domestic violence. Other barriers to inquiring about domestic violence include a lack of time, doubts of the efficacy of inquiry, a lack of privacy in the health services setting and lack of proper training in how to frame the question.

Barriers to disclosure

Inquiring about domestic violence doesn't mean the patient will disclose the abuse and receive assistance. Women may refuse to disclose the abuse due to feelings of shame and denial. She may be fearful of the abuser's or others' reaction to the disclosure. Also, fear of negative consequences regarding children can prevent a woman from disclosing abuse. A health professional with an unpleasant attitude toward abuse can also discourage a victim from disclosing domestic violence, while a perception that the health professional is uncaring, too busy, lacks interest, uncomfortable with the topic, or not listening may also prevent a victim from disclosing abuse. Finally, female patients' concerns about breaches in confidentiality can be a barrier to disclosure.

Training of Health Professionals for inquiry and disclosure

It is recommended that no inquiry be made until healthcare professionals are trained and protocols are established that prioritise the safety of patients. Establishing these protocols and providing training to health professionals on the inquiry about and disclosure of abuse will allow healthcare professionals to overcome ambivalent attitudes about domestic violence, alleviate any difficulties in the framing of questions about abuse or seeing the patient privately, and learn proper recording techniques. Healthcare professionals can also learn more about the legal implications of domestic violence and the need for confidentiality after disclosure. Training can also provide healthcare professionals with awareness of the individual, social and cultural factors surrounding domestic violence, thereby helping them understand the frustration that often comes along with a victim's responses and the safety needs of patients. After a victim makes a disclosure of abuse the healthcare professional must be able to address the problem by identifying available resources and making proper referrals.Therefore, it is important to increase the healthcare professionals' knowledge of local advocacy and support services. It has been shown that training healthcare professionals to properly respond to disclosures of abuse and increasing their knowledge of available services encourages them to inquire about abuse and alleviates concerns about creating controversy. Also, if a healthcare professional feels there is limited time to inquire, he can be trained to recognise the indicators of abuse, thereby allowing him only inquire in suspected cases.

Domestic Violence and the Law

The effective implementation of the domestic violence law and the legal process can bring about substantial relief to the health and well-being of the victims. Understanding how to maximise the law's positive impact on health allows the law to share medicine's principle of "above all do no harm." "Too often, however, we see how the legal system can negatively impact the people who become involved in it. The process of civil litigation, for example, can negatively impact people both emotionally and financially through its time-consuming and often psychologically draining processes." The most obvious influence domestic violence law has on health and well-being is the prevention of future physical injury. Therefore, proper implementation of the laws protecting victims, adequate utilisation of the law by victims, high levels of awareness among victims, and an understanding of the health impacts by legal professionals should result in improved health outcomes for women. Court systems are adversarial by nature and set out procedures that victims have little control over. Victims are asked to recount the abuse and can face questioning about her credibility, memory, and veracity. These factors can prevent victims from utilising the law that is meant to protect her or may cause her to stop the proceedings before they are completed. Lack of social support and severity of abuse have been found to impact a victims effective utilisation of the law. Other barriers to the utilisation of the law include confusion and frustration over delays in the court proceedings, fear, and conflict over whether the abuser should be punished. The ability to effectively utilise the domestic violence law influences a victim's health and wellbeing. If the domestic violence law is not effectively implemented or utilised – for example, when women are not aware of the law or face barriers to utilising the law fully – the legal process will have a negative effect on women's health and well-being. Therefore, it is important for those who take part in the legal process, such as lawyers, judges, and victim advocates, to understand the influence the legal process has on the health and well-being of the women who seek to use it.

Domestic Violence Law in India

Before 2005 there was no law in India specifically addressing domestic violence. Women who experienced domestic violence had to rely upon a variety of criminal and civil laws to gain legal relief and protection from the abuser. These various legal remedies were time consuming and confusing since several different courts had to be accessed and various claims filed. Also, there was no law granting victims of domestic violence immediate relief, which is an important need for women seeking to escape violent relationships. To overcome these shortcomings the Indian legislature enacted the Protection of Women from Domestic Violence Act, 2005 (PWDVA). The PWDVA attempts to solve the problems victims faced with the earlier legal provisions by creating a single law to address domestic violence, provide women easier access to court, and grant immediate relief. Quicker access to court is facilitated through the Protection Officer, who is the governmental implementer of the law charged with guiding victims of domestic violence through the legal process and assisting them in meeting their immediate needs. The PWDVA also directs state-governments to identify Medical Facilities which are instructed to provide free medical assistance to domestic violence victims upon their request or that of the Protection Officer. The Protection Officer is to assist the victim in filling out the form requesting relief and the law mandates a resolution of the case with sixty days of filing.

There are several legal remedies a victim can request under the PWDVA. These requests can be granted as part of an *ex parte* order (i.e., an order issued before a hearing is held) and also in final orders after a hearing. The court can grant a protection order enjoining the abuser from contacting the victim, thereby preventing any further acts or threats of domestic violence. A residence order can be issued granting the victim possession of the marital home. Custody orders regarding the couple's children can also be issued. A maintenance order can be granted immediate relief.

Conclusion and Reflections

To conclude, the psycho-social dynamics of domestic violence often creates barrier for the victims to have access over legal recourse. Besides, failure of the existing laws, inadequate efforts on the part of the implementing authority to enforce existing laws, failure of the government to promote awareness and education to address the causes and consequences of domestic violence instead of containing incidences of domestic violence rather have become the key drivers of its colossal failure.

This paper will help to bring awareness that domestic violence is a public health issue. For some healthcare providers it was a novel reframing of domestic violence from an individual and family issue to a public health issue. Many of issues brought up in the paper are already known components of the domestic violence issue; however, having a study that confirms those suspicions will be helpful. This project also shows local organisations who are already doing domestic violence training where additional training and collaboration is needed. Hopefully this project will help those organisations also influence the way in which the PWDVA is being implemented by advocating for more resources for Protection Officers and resolutions to the reasons for court delays. The project compares nicely with the previous Abstract. It was apparent that the more support a victim had the more likely she was going to effectively utilize the PWDVA. Also, it is obvious from my observations that more than providing training to doctors about domestic violence screening is needed. The training is a valuable step but not the only one needed in order for the health system to address the issue of domestic violence. Above all, domestic violence as escalated problem grossly affecting the victim's basic human rights, family happiness and social solidarity has blown out of proportion which needs more of psychosocial therapy. It needs a greater understanding, a stronger advocacy; knowledge of the biology of gender and a mutual accommodative approach, which together can promote a harmonious survival.

References

Beijing Declaration and platform for Action, Fourth world conference on women, 15 Sept 1999, A/con F. 177/20 (1995) and A/conF. 177/20/Add. (1995), para 136.

Benninger-Budel and Bourke-Martigroni; (2003), "Violence against women": For protection and promotion of the human rights of women, Geneva: World organisation against torture.

Chakraborty, Diponsa (1999), "Atrocities on Indian Women", New Delhi: APH Publishing House.

Roy, Ashine (2003), "Violence against women", New Delhi: Rajat Publication.

Baruah, Arunima, (2004), "The soft Target, Crime against women", New Delhi: Kilaso Books.

4

'Woman' - A *Dalit* in Virtual Sense—With Special Reference to "Goddess in Exile"

Dr. Sarojni Sahoo and Mrs. Sagarika Dash
Dr Sanchita Choudhury

Abstract

Women subjugation or under representation of women is an issue that exists in society since time immemorial. Portrayal of the sorry state of women or the "second sex" has been portrayed by the poets or literatures over the ages. Indian society in every era, has witnessed the exploitation of women, being a ploy in the hands of patriarchy. This paper aims at focusing the plight of Indian women, especially the women of Odisha in the garb of Harsha, the protagonist of ***Goddess in Exile***, who sacrifices her wish to compromise with the situation. Dr Sarojini Sahoo, the author of the novel **Goddess in Exile**, vividly depicts the traumatised situation of a section of those ill-fated women who are forced to lead a cursed life from their marriageable age till death. Taking many illustrations from the novel, this paper portrays the dejected life of the "second sex" population who are treated as devices to maintain the honour of their family or at some other instances to provide pleasure in various forms.

***Keywords*:** Women, second sex, patriarchy, atrocity and plight.

Woman – one of the beautiful creations of the Almighty and a creator in herself, is underestimated and selectively neglected since the time immemorial in spite of her ubiquitous presence in every significant aspect of life. A woman has been considered at par with an object of amusement to be played with or a multipurpose household commodity to be used, reused and recycled. Now, the inevitable question that pops up in one's mind is, 'who is this authority that denies a woman her worth and value?' The answer would unanimously be the opposite gender—the males. It has been a customary instinct of the powerful group to remain in the privileged section, and this might be one of the strong reasons why women, who are supposedly physically less aggressive, are deprived of their due attention, respect and care.

From her inception, a woman undergoes perennial tormentation and sacrifices, which at times results in female foeticide. Every mother as such desires not to witness her reflection, which is nothing but a trauma, in her daughter. From her babyhood days a woman is deprived of many significant things that she craves for, where as her male siblings enjoy this privilege liberally. Even worse, after marriage a daughter is supposedly sent to a lifelong exile. The exile of the Indian epic hero Shree Ramachandra was preordained for the annihilation of demonic forces. But in the present social milieu, women are getting brutally devoured by demons instead of being protected by Rama.

Life becomes dejected if a woman belongs to an orthodox family. Neither can she stay contented in her parental home nor in her in-laws' abode. No one else but a woman with humanitarian values can feel and let the world feel a woman's incessant sufferings and struggle for existence. One such most celebrated woman, a South Asian novelist Dr Sarojini Sahoo, deals with various issues related to the atrocities of women. Harsha, the protagonist of her novel *Goddess in Exile* represents a section of such ill-fated women, raped and brutally tortured by their husbands, who are supposed to be proved as security blankets for their wives. May it be social, educational or economic right–a woman is deprived of everything. She does not have any right even on her own body and life.

Women are conditioned to be caring and sacrificial from their childhood days. In an Indian context, their condition is miserable when it comes to domestic affairs. Once married, they are not supposed to demand anything from their parents. In pre-marriage period too at times they are forced to forget their aspirations whatever it may be, if situation demands. While on the other hand, the male children are encouraged to dream more and achieve that dream at any cost irrespective of a family's financial condition. Harsha, although a bright student who aspires to be an IAS officer or at least an allied officer, is forced to bury her dreams forever under the dark blanket called society. In the words of Harsha, "I had a strong desire to become an IAS or an Allied Officer by taking the competitive examination. But my dreams had no meaning for anyone" (Sahoo, *Goddess in Exile*, 2013: 79). She was also victimised by the orthodox thoughts of her family and forced to marry an unknown person chosen by her family while her brother was allowed to continue his study and work in California.

Although, women are sacrificial in nature, most of the times they are forced to sacrifice even their lives. For some, the fulfillment of a dying man's wish becomes so prominent that they do not think about the wish of the person who is yet to see and know what life is. If the grand parents or parents want to see their children married before their death, it becomes almost an obligation for the family to fulfil their wish and see them happy on their death bed. They don't consider the acceptance or denial of children who are to tie their knot with someone forever. Although, the case is same for both male and female child in a family, the female child suffers the most. The family becomes so enthusiastic and active to give her in marriage that as if in doing so, the ailing and dying man will recover and live long. It is something like offering sacrifice before deities. Harsha being a member of an orthodox family falls a victim to her ailing grandfather's wish. As no one in the family has the courage to stand against this orthodox head of the family, it is quite natural for Harsha that her opinion would not be regarded and taken into consideration. While expressing about her cursed life to Alberto (Harsha's friend), she says, "I was given in marriage against my wishes. My grand father had become very old. He lay on the bed for days together. He insisted that he would see his grand daughter's marriage before his death. ... ... No, at that time he did not at all consider my acceptance or willingness" (Sahoo, 2013: 78 - 79).

When it comes to marriage or choosing a partner for marriage, the male members of the family are the decision-makers. A man as if has solely got the license to go to different places and choose a bride while the woman is deprived of this privilege. If a man rejects her, she has to wait for someone else to come and select. If she is lucky enough to get selected by a man she is compelled to marry, irrespective of her desire. She plays a negligible role in the game of selection and rejection. It is true that parents are the well-wishers of children. They always look for the best or the most suitable for their children. While taking one of the most significant decisions of their daughter's life (regarding her marriage), they look for a well-educated, well-settled and well-blooded groom. Although, they look for a well-behaved man too, all requirements of them are not fulfilled. Later, everything is left in the hands of an unseen force called 'destiny'. If the girl is fortunate, she gets a good friend in the form of her consort but if destiny does not befriend her, a life gets silently spoiled. After marriage, a daughter becomes an outsider or a guest to her parental home and is prohibited to take part in some of the significant decisions. In Indian context, it is believed that a girl leaves her maternal home in a palanquin for her in-law's abode, supposedly her real destination, after getting married and from her in-law's home she heads only towards the final destination called graveyard or crematory. However, she is sent to exile for her entire life. If she comes to her parental home to get some relief for a longer period, she becomes a burden for the then family, and is forced to return to her in-laws' place. So, neither does she have an option to go to her parental home nor to stay contented in her connubial life. When she gives up, she opts for killing herself or the person who makes her life a hell. Harsha's husband although apparently an established gentleman with a sound family background, is actually a rude spoilt brat. During the formalities of pre-marriage period, Harsha's father and uncle go to the doctor's (the groom is a doctor) clinic to enquire about him. There, "...they found him lying on the floor dead drunk. He had urinated in his pant, the impression of urine was left on the floor, a procession of ants in and around the place. Had they not heard the snoring sound, they would have misconstrued that the man was dead" (Sahoo, 2013: 84). Even if the truth about their would be son-in-law was known to them, still they proceeded for Harsha's marriage to that beast. Although Harsha's father was in a dilemma regarding the marriage, later he agreed with his brother-in-law (Harsha's uncle) that the man had taken alcohol as a result of his loneliness and would be changed after marriage. Here, some obvious questions strike in mind and have still remained unanswered: Are the ladies some magic wands that their touch would change the habit of men which has been adopted for a long period of time? Do the parents always take the right decision regarding their children, especially the daughter? Don't they regret if their decision is proved wrong? Or, they just leave everything in the name of destiny?

No one can feel the plight of a woman without being placed in that situation. A father can only understand a daughter's agony where as a mother feels them. As the feelings of a mother and daughter are reciprocal, they empathies with each other and hence are best friends together. Although Harsha's mother is the only person who can sense and feel each pulse of her daughter, she cannot come out with any solution as she is a social entity and is dominated by others. Harsha's friend Sarita, a girl of her age but unmarried, scorns Harsha when she expresses her agony that her husband keeps physical relation with her. Harsha becomes a laughing stock for Sarita because for any layperson keeping such relation is quite natural in between spouses.

"Karyeshu Daasi, Karanyeshu Mantri, Bhojeshu Maata, Shayaneshu Rambha, Roopeshu Lakshmi, Kshyamayeshu Dharitri, Shat Dharmayukta kuladharma patni" – the *shloka* is derived from the *'Manusmriti'* of sage Manu. *Manusmriti* is abundantly crammed with the description of a woman, womanly qualities, her duties and responsibilities. But no-where does it mention the qualities of a virtuous man or husband. Whatever may be the aim of Sage Manu in prescribing the qualities and duties of a virtuous wife, nowadays this *shloka* is being misconstrued and pointed towards women to disgrace them. Every man wants his wife to be a servant in household chores and a heavenly beauty on his bed but he never realises about his own duties and responsibilities towards his wife as no such duties in the form of *shlokas* have been prescribed in *Manusmriti.* Dr Shukla (CMO of the hospital where Harsha's husband works) makes Harsha understand about the characteristics of an ideal wife by citing the *shloka* from *Manusmriti.* "A maid in household chore, a minister to advise, a mother in feeding, a fairy like

Rambha on the bed, an earth in forgiving" (Sahoo, 2013: 83). Although many such *shastras* or religious textual inscriptions have propounded duties of a virtuous wife, is not there any such quality required for of a husband? Is he only to derive carnal pleasure out of the wife? Is a woman only to run a family? Many such unanswered questions crop up in mind. Male hegemony is prevailed in the society since time immemorial whose outcome is such *shlokas* about women. Since no *shlokas* have been formulated for men, does it mean that all men are virtuous and can be regarded as ideal for every purpose?

There is a saying in Hindi – *"Shaadi ka laddoo jo khaaye pachtaye aur jo na khaaye wo bhi pachtaaye"*. This is aptly proved in the novel by Harsha and Sarita. Harsha has a detestable experience about marriage while Sarita regrets for not getting married. So she asks Harsha to get back to her husband if he does not have any unnatural relationship with her. It is strange that Sarita, a maiden girl who does not know what conjugal life is, talks about unnatural relationship! While explaining Sarita about her relation with the doctor Harsha says, "Do you know, Sarita, each time while ascending the chariot of this body he presented me something or the other as a kind of fee. Sometimes a pair of earrings, sometimes a saree. Sometimes he poured a lot of coins into my lap" (Sahoo, 2013: 91).

It's true that a woman desires for new *saree*s and ornaments but her husband's love, affection and adoration are her real ornaments. If she does not receive love from her husband, everything else appears insignificant. Before making love (rather can be said "making sex" as there is no love in between them) Harsha is presented with *sarees*, ornaments, coins, etc. by her husband just like a customer pays fee to a prostitute. Sage Manu's word *"shayaneshu Rambha"* is made alive. Harsha is unerringly presented as the heavenly beauty Rambha to satisfy the lust of her husband. At the refusal, she is maltreated and brutally beaten. The beast extracts her life till the last drop. In spite of being aware of the brutality of the man, Dr Shukla urges Harsha to control and prevent her husband from taking alcohol. Actually, a human being can control everyone except a beast incarnated as a man. One has to come down to the level of a beast or go to the level of the omnipotent God to control such a beast.

A man demands his wife to be an angel in his life but often fails to design a heaven for her. A lady naturally desires for physical satisfaction but it is not her ultimate desire. Apart from getting physical satisfaction, she feels contented with a suitable companion in the form of a husband who wipes her tear and at the same time whose absence brings tear in her eyes. It's quite obvious that, if she does not get such a legal companion (husband), she looks towards another one. Harsha too like any other woman expresses that she does not crave for any material presentations rather love and co-operation from her husband. That's why, absence of love from her husband becomes an oblique reason for Harsha's fondness towards Alberto whose loving words and touch allures her.

People say much about unconditional love. But, does anyone really love someone unconditionally? Can he/she continue her love if no reciprocation is received from the opposite side? A number of such questions remain unanswered. Although, Alberto often declares his love for Harsha, is actually not unconditional. He seeks love and wants her, as she is a great help for him in quenching his intellectual thirst for Indian culture. Alberto, who shows another aspect of a man, enjoys Harsha's company and feels comfortable with her. While the doctor needs Harsha to gratify his carnal desire, this "white skinned Pundit" exploits her in an intellectual manner. A man as if has been certified to interact with a lady in any way he likes. During such an interaction if a lady comes closer to that man, she is either physically exploited or left alone and consequently blamed for everything that happens to her. On the other hand, a man pretends to be clean-handed and gets ready to welcome a new day with a new lady.

A lady needs someone who could understand her. She does not hesitate to sacrifice anything for that man. However, it is unfortunate for her if the man, whose presence and tender touch should have made her feel solaced, treats her as an object to be experimented with. Harsha represents a section of those ill-fated women who find themselves shackled in their conjugal life. After marriage too they do not get a chance to know what love or romance is. In Indian context, to love a man before marriage is a taboo for a woman. For her, the husband must be her first and last love. She cannot defy the contract of institution called marriage. Harsha, too although young and married does not know what love or romance is? When she thinks of the word, her eyes are closed and a picturesque scene flashes before her. But with eyes open, everything vanishes as a fantasy making her realise of the actual state.

A man (if he is not her first love) enters into the life of a lady during her weakest moment of life. Usually, when she is cheated by a man and makes up her mind not to trust anyone whosoever he may be, a man succeeds to touch the tender chord of her heart with his consoling words and she feels as if she has got the right person. Ultimately, her vow is broken and she again falls into the trap of Cupid. But unfortunately, she is completely shattered if that most reliable man simply intends to have a bath in the flowing stream of her youth. However, Harsha's union with Alberto is not her first union with a man. Although, she has united with her so-called husband many a times, she has not felt blissful as she experiences with Alberto. She considers it as the first touch of a man. She blossoms with love and love-making whereas she regards the union with her husband as rape. She feels crushed under the weight of her husband's body. Being a doctor, he just succeeds to touch Harsha's body but not her heart. For him, she is just a body laid on the operation table for surgery or a dead body to be torn open for experiment. On the other hand, Harsha feels consoled with Alberto and considers him as her first love who she has been waiting for. Harsha shows her desperation and concern for Alberto as if he is very dear to her. She asks worriedly, "What happened to you Alberto? Why did you not inform me before? Where are you now? I have been trying the whole day to contact you but failed. Don't you think me as your own? Then why did you not inform me about your illness?" (Sahoo, 2013: 54). But the same loving Alberto whose days used to spoil without meeting and discussing with Harsha intends to take a halt on the flowery bed of her body but feels reluctant to make her a part of his sweet home.

A lady is to be blamed for everything whatever happens in a family or in the society. If a daughter gets married at her own wish, she brings shame for her family even though she leads a happy conjugal life. If she marries at her family's wish and unfortunately cannot live in peace, then too she is blamed for not being able to win the heart of her husband and in-laws. If due to some unendurable circumstances at her in-laws' she comes back to her maternal home to get some relief she becomes a burden for them. The society too does not allow her to feel relieved as if it has the responsibility to take care of her. A storm is raised in the family when Harsha remains still at her word of not going back to her in-laws'. Her father says, "How can I show my face to the world outside? What explanation should I offer? What will people say?" (Sahoo, 2013: 89). The daughter, who once used to be the pride of her family, becomes a shame for them if she wants to stay at her maternal home after marriage. People are so obsessed with their prestige that they can go to any extent to safeguard it. They also don't hesitate to kill their children if situation demands. The in-laws, who say they cannot show their face as their daughter-in-law has left their home, do never realise of the reason that has forced the lady to bring such a disgraceful situation. They also do not ever think of the lady who is driven out of the home by their son or gets a divorce. It is as if a lady is born to endure everything and also to be blamed.

Women are at times taken for granted especially by their male counterparts. They consider that their wives would do everything to them and understand them properly. When the wife shows her love and sense of insecurity to the man, she becomes possessive and is blamed for not giving any space to him. The condition is miserable in case of unmarried couples. The lady is mocked at by the man as well as by the society if she tries to execute her right on that man. She also becomes a laughing stock when she demands for an identity to their unidentified relationship. A woman is regarded as the symbol of sacrifice. That's why, to carry on this tag and to prove how sacrificial is she, she is often put to test by the society. Like the mother earth, she is to satisfy everyone; even the physical hunger of men but cannot demand anything in return. Men agree to continue their so-called love relationship till they are alive and even if they are married to other women. But they retreat at the moment, their beloved's demand for an identity for their clandestine affair. Men demand for virgin women to make their wives, irrespective of how many girls he has slept or sleeping with. Alberto is an archetype of such men who wants to bring ecstasy in the life of their beloveds by uniting with them physically. But they do not dare to stand by their side in the broad daylight. Alberto although married and is leading a healthy conjugal life, does not hesitate to make an extra marital relationship with Harsha and says, "You promise me, Hana, you will always give me company as long as I am there in your country, you won't desert me. Why in your country, I want you for the whole life. Oh, my sweet babe!" (Sahoo, 2013: 74). For some men like Alberto, to have intercourse with women is just like television soap. Just like viewers of television soaps forget their pent up feelings after watching an emotional scene, men too become suitably oblivious of what has happened after a successful intercourse. For them, there is no difference between a success from any other job and their own successful intercourse.

Dr Sahoo has aptly portrayed the sorry state of women and also the patriarchal domination in Indian society. Harsha is the voice of women from the orthodox Indian family. Harsha's condition is so miserable that neither can she tolerate the brutality of her husband nor can she complain against it. Rather, she is made responsible for the drunken state of her husband. Not only Harsha but another girl Kishku (the doctor's ex-girlfriend) too is kept responsible in making the doctor alcoholic.

At times, it is seen a man going to an extent of begging for the body of a woman, whatever her mental state may be. He wants to show his possession on the body of the woman but her soul does not carry any value for him. Alberto too begs Harsha as, "My Hana, I can't stop thinking of you. I dream of you. Please take me to your flowery bed, I want to be there forever. ... When can we meet, Hana? ... I can't wait, I need you today. I am waiting for you" (Sahoo, 2013: 132-133). If, the lady due to some difficulty gets late in responding to the man, she brings storm in their relationship. She commits a crime when she does something without informing the man. But in case of the man informing the wife about everything is discouraged. Alberto who once used to share everything with Harsha and never wants to desert her blurts out, "Was it a mistake that I went without telling you?" (Sahoo, 2013: 156).

Consciously or unconsciously, a woman is used and reused under male domination. In most of the cases she is exploited physically and at some other cases emotionally or intellectually. But it gets too late when the lady realises and repents for it. "Harsha was a plate of rice for that man which he would devour like a cow, and for Alberto, she was a book in which he would underline every page of it. ... The truth remained that she was used" (Sahoo, 2013: 160).

Dr Sahoo has not only penned down but voiced the atrocities of a woman through her protagonist Harsha. According to an American journalist Linda Lowen, "Sarojini Sahoo has written extensively as an Indian feminist about the interior lives of women and how their burgeoning sexuality is seen as a threat to traditional patriarchal societies" (Wikipedia). Harsha is presented as a social entity. Her identity and existence is well rooted to an orthodox Indian society and culture. The society allows her to live but if something goes against the interest of the society, it does not hesitate to kill her or force her to kill herself. She is repeatedly reminded of the societal norms and taboos especially formulated for her. As Harsha is one of the social beings, she cannot defy its canon and stay away of her husband and in-laws.

Under representation and social subjugation of woman is there from her inception. Indian society being patriarchal, often suppress the women as well as daughters; as if this 'second sex' of the society is going to pose a threat to them. A daughter is considered as *Lakshmi* in Indian context. But unfortunately, they are not worshipped rather are taken care of as sources of wealth to be exploited and reused in multiple ways. The birth of a daughter is welcome and celebrated for her multifaceted usage in the family. From her babyhood days she is exploited invariably. She is an unparalleled companion to her male sibling and a helping hand to her mother. Being the property of her in-laws, she is properly taken care of in her parental home. In post-marriage period, that so called invaluable property of the in-laws is asked to bring some more property from her (maternal) home. While on the other hand, her parents insist her to solve everything in her (in-laws) home if any disturbance occurs. In short, she belongs to none but used and enjoyed by all.

References

Sahoo, Sarojini. 2013, *'Goddess in Exile'*, New Delhi, India, Tr. Suman Mahapatra. Authorspress. Print.

Wikipedia. *'Sarojini Sahoo'*. Web. 24 Jan.2014. <http://en.wikipedia.org/wiki/Sarojini_Sahoo>

5

Gender Sensatisation in Law Enforcement: Major Issues and Challenges

Dr Swapna S. Prabhu and Dr Niranjan Mohapatra

Abstract

A society is judged by the status its women enjoy. The growing violence against women in the country has been a matter of great concern for both the government and civil society. Earlier while cases of violence against women went largely unnoticed (most of these cases being confined to the domestic arena and went unreported) for the past few decades due to the efforts of women's groups and media coverage, a large number of such cases have been highlighted. This has helped in creating a climate to build up public opinion about the urgent need for adequate state intervention not only for action against such offenders but also to sensitise the police forces in the country to prioritise such cases.

The growing number of women in police and their increasing visibility has led to a positive statement about the country's prioritisation of cases of violence against women and to handle the victims compassionately. But did this also lead to the sensitisation of the police force to women's issues?

The present article intends to look at the above-mentioned issue in order to assess the ground realities of the situation. An attempt has been made, in this article, to establish the probable link between increasing number of women in police and sensitisation of the police force towards women's issues.

Key Words: Gender Sensitisation, Women Police, Pro-active Policing, Administration, Law Enforcement.

Women police have now become an integral part of the police forces in almost all countries of the world, including India. However, the possibility of women functioning as full members of a police force and playing a role for achieving its objectives was not well perceived in the early years of the evolution of police system. This was so, perhaps, because traditionally law enforcement has tended to remain primarily a masculine job involving substantial use of physical prowess. Changes in social attitudes, however, has led to an increased association of women in field duties such as *bandobust duties* at places where women assemble in large numbers and field investigations in several branches of administration during the last few decades. The myriad problems arising from increased juvenile delinquency, rising social tensions, and involvement of women in crimes, either as victims or accused, progressively necessitated the employment of women police officers as such in a variety of police tasks. Gradually, women have now become an integral part of the police organisation.

However, the fact remains that India has about 97,518 women police of all ranks in the 1,660,666 strong police force as on 1st January 2014. They are at a stage when they are confronting the negative attitudes and values of society and struggling to find their feet. Ironically, many a times they themselves get bogged down by their own patriarchal upbringing, and bring in the societal biases, prejudices, predilections, dogmas, myths, stereotypes, etc., when dealing with women victims. A lot of gender related work is being done. Still, a lot remains to be done (Singh, 2002:27).

Gender sensatisation in law enforcement—a rationale

Gender sensitisation, involves a higher responsiveness to the inequality and unequal power equation of gender relations, heightened receptivity to gender fair value framework that challenges the patriarchal stereotypes in order to ensure gender justice. It denotes a process of resocialisation—a process of unlearning the gender bias, both societal and organisational (Panigrahi, 1998: 124).

The rationale for gender sensitisation in law enforcement can be summed up as follows:

1. Police are the initial decision-makers in the Criminal Justice System and enjoy wide discretion. Differential law enforcement, indifferent police response and fear of police deny women the access to justice.

2. It is in dealing with women that police are often accused of inadequate and aggressive policing.

3. There is a perceived reluctance among women to turn to police for help due to various factors. Such reluctance is "potentially damaging to the role of the police as protectors in society" (Panigrahi, 1998: 124).

4. A total of 3,09,546 cases of crime against women (both under various sections of IPC and SLL) were reported in the country during the year 2013 as compared to 2,44,270 in the year 2012, thus showing an increase of 26.7 per cent during the year 2013. These crimes have continuously increased in reporting during 2009 - 2013 with 2,03,804 cases in 2009 and 2,13,585 cases in 2010 and 2,28,649 cases in 2011, 2,44,270 cases in 2012 and 3,09,546 cases in the year 2013.

5. In addition many sensational incidents of police involvement in gang rape, custodial rape, molestation, running protection rackets in prostitution, conniving with offenders in dowry death cases and other atrocities against women have also been highlighted. All these make it imperative for the police to recognise the need to re-affirm its moral authority and to rebuild the confidence, which it has lost among people, especially women and other weaker sections of society.

6. Women victims are differently placed than their male counterparts. The victims of sexual violence suffer from a sense of shame, self-guilt, fear and are often humiliated, abandoned and traumatised. In case of domestic violence, offence is committed in the privacy of the home, by a

person on whom the victim is emotionally and economically dependent. In such cases police role is not one of interrogator but of facilitator and empathiser (Panigrahi, 1998 :124).

Where the gender of the officer involved should be a paramount consideration is in cases where this is a factor of significance to the victim. The onus is on the police as professionals, and as the gatekeepers to the justice system, to determine this fact through sensitive procedures oriented towards empowerment of the victim as a necessary prerequisite for obtaining quality information to assist in law enforcement.

Increasing Violence against Women

As more and more women in the country started asserting their rights, got educated and took up jobs, they increasingly became targets of attack. Crime against women in the country is on the increase. The following statistics published in ***'Crime in India-2010'*** speak loudly about the alarming picture of crime against women in the country.

- One case of violence against women took place every four minutes in 2010.
- One woman/girl was raped every 35 minutes in the same year. In 1998 there was one rape every 38 minutes.
- Some unfortunate woman got molested every 17 minutes.
- One dowry death took place every 75 minutes. In 1997, there was one dowry death every 87 minutes.
- There was one instance of torture every 13 minutes.

If we take into consideration the instances of violence that do not get reported because of illiteracy and ignorance of women and other social factors and also the amount of crime that does not get registered in the police stations due to various reasons, the true picture of violence against women would be more shocking.

Response of police personnel to increasing violence against women

In spite of the frightening and alarming picture, the police response to violence against women continues to be highly inadequate and inappropriate. Besides the reasons for the generally poor response to instances of crime such as increasing workload, lack of resources, political pressure to maintain crime figures at a low level, mal practices in the organisation, there are certain specific reasons for the lack of appropriate response to offences against women. The cult of masculinity prevalent in the department makes the police officers hold some stereotypes about violence against women. The stereotypes lead to certain standard patterns of police response. For instance, below mentioned are some stereotypes held by the police about sexual violence/ harassment:

- Rape is victim-precipitated. Women ask for rape/sexual violence by provocative mode of dress and behaviour or by going out after dark or going to shady and lonely places.
- Women sub-consciously desire rape and 'cry rape' only when they are caught.
- Rape cannot occur if a woman resists.
- Women's place is at home. If they go out, they must take what comes their way.
- Sexual harassment at work place and eve-teasing are fun and women enjoy it.
- Male sexuality is an uncontrollable force. Women should not arouse it.

Rationale for Gender Sensitisation training in police: In order to make police officers behave and act in a gender sensitive manner, there is an urgent need to conduct gender sensitisation training courses for police.

The following findings of a research study conducted about the opinion of the male police personnel regarding the role of women colleagues also reflect the attitude of a majority of the police officers towards women and the lack of awareness about the concept of gender :

1. There is no need to integrate women into the mainstream of police.
2. Women police should be given only specific tasks related to women and children.
3. Women are not enthusiastic about their jobs.
4. Women may work as cooks in the police mess.
5. Women should escort only female prisoners and not male prisoners.

6. Women should not be engaged in operations against militants, extremists and insurgents.
7. Women officers are very gentle and are not capable of handling hardened criminals (Saxena, 1995 : 49).

Women's job in the police should not become an extension of their jobs at home. They should not just be employed for working as cooks, office clerks, but they should be encouraged to enthusiastically investigate crimes, participate in law and order duties and even operations against militants, extremists, and insurgents. In this regard the mind set of men needs to be changed and this can be achieved by making men and women work together, rather than separating them.

Police Contact Situations and Gender Sensitisation

Police contact situations and categories of women who come into such contact can be broadly summarised under the following heads:

Women as victims: Police response to women victims is generally categorised by sexism, bias, victim- culpability and social stereotypes regarding violence against women. A gender sensitive police response would be patient and empathetic listening, identification with the women's view point, communication skills to make the women feel at ease and not feel intimidated, initial counselling and referring to other support services, prompt registration and investigation of the case and follow up at the trial stage.

Women as offenders: Female criminality offends the social conscience more severely because it challenges the ideological constructs regarding gender roles. Police response to female offenders/ suspects is known to be improper and insensitive as also indecent and obscene. A gender- sensitive police response to women offenders shall include observance of due regard to their dignity and modesty and procedural norms in all aspects of investigation, search, seizure, arrest, confinement in police lock-up, interrogation and forwarding in custody.

Women considered to be on the margins of "respectable society" : Police response to women who are on the margins of the society, whom they perceive as unrespectable and thus undeserving of protection—prostitutes, women in the slums, women labour, widows, divorcees–ranges from indifference to intimidation, hostility and violence. These women considered to be less "respectable" as they are subject to not just gender bias but multiple biases of caste, class and race, are not less but more deserving of the protective arm of law and gender sensitive policing should ensure their fullest access to legal help.

Women's groups: Pressure for gender sensitisation in police comes not so much from the new laws which are again differently enforced as from below. The feminist groups who have launched an organised campaign to seek justice on women's issues like sati, dowry death, and custodial rape come in regular contact with the police. Their relationship with police is one of mutual distrust and confrontation because they complain of police inaction, harassment and victimisation. Gender sensitive policing would accept these women's groups as equal partners in their fight for gender justice (Panigrahi, 1998 : 125).

Modes of Gender Sensitisation in Law Enforcement: An Agenda

In India, the State response to increasing violence against women has been threefold : legal reforms, gender sensitisation programmes for all levels of bureaucracy and giving the police some new powers with regard to dealing with cases related to women. The present article deals with the second and third aspects of response to increasing violence against women.

Gender sensitisation effort in police organisation may be conceived at three levels : in the process of recruitment, in training and the administrative measures for greater gender equality and gender sensitive policing.

Recruitment: At the level of induction into police force, some psychological tools should be employed to test the character, social sensitivity, responsibility and commitment of the candidates. As crimes against women are mostly personal and intimate in nature, there should be larger representation of women in the force who can inspire confidence of the victims and better appreciate and investigate cases of sexual and domestic violence. Induction of women can also prevent complaints of indignity and misbehaviour to female victims/offenders, help tackle the women demonstrators and ensure better coordination with women's groups (Kriplani, 2005: 40).

Mahatma Gandhi had once said, "*the right method for securing justice for women from men, is to make women strong. A man like me may guide you and awaken other men to a consciousness of their duty. But my capacity for serving women is limited. Women alone can serve women perfectly*" (Kriplani, 2005: 40).

However, the induction of women should not confine only to basic grades but also in managerial positions and appointed not simply as police women, but as police surgeons, psychologists and forensic scientists in the police organisation.

For better integration and involvement of women police in the mainstream and providing them with equal opportunities, the fifth report of the National Police Commission (NPC) in November 1980, has recommended recruitment of women in vacancies in general duty posts and not against only women specific vacancies.

Training : Training is a continuous process involving induction, pre-promotion, refresher, reorientation and is a vital tool for unlearning the male bias and learning to deal with the needs, concerns and priorities of women more sensitively. Thereby, proper perceptions of gender and behaviour, critical understanding of laws for women, social investigation and role of police need to be built into the learning content.

Administrative Measures : This mode, may consist of the following measures :

- Special, officer-intensive units to deal with crimes against women with an appropriate mix of men and women police in investigation cadre and not a parallel force of women investigators which will lead to sexual division of labour.
- Screening of personnel to be posted in these special units and non-posting of officers who have come to adverse notice for involvement in offensive activities against women.

- Relatively fixed periods of tenure of these personnel and a scheme of incentives and disincentives.
- Posting of women duty officers even during night especially at railway stations and market places to record women's complaints and to look into cases of harassment of women.
- Women under-trials/suspects not to be kept at police station but at women crisis/support centres in voluntary sector under police guard.
- Periodical meetings with voluntary agencies at the police station and higher levels to brief about the action taken against the offenders against women, discuss provision of support and sort out complaints and grievances.
- Constitution of an apex body at the state level consisting of representatives of police, judiciary, administration, prison, prosecution, women activists, lawyers, civil liberty activists, legislators, academicians and media to spell out a formal policy and code of conduct on gender sensitive policy, monitor the implementation of such policy at regular intervals and effect modifications in the light of new experiences.
- Lateral entry of professional psychologists and community workers into police to supplement the amateurish effort of police in these fields (Panigrahi, 1998 : 129).

The Indian Penal Code (IPC) and Crime Against Women : The Indian Penal Code (IPC) covers wide range of issues with regard to crimes against women. It is the basic criminal law, prescribing deterrent punishment in cases of crime/violence against women. Cases under the IPC are investigated by the police more seriously and tried in higher courts of law more effectively.

The programme of gender sensitisation in police should ensure that the participants i.e. the police personnel are aware of all the legal provisions with regard to prevention of crime against women. For instance, Section 46(1) of Cr PC holds that a police officer making arrest is required to be actually tough or confine the body of the person to be arrested but in case of a woman, their submission to the custody should be prevented unless proved otherwise and there should be no instance for a police officer making arrest of a woman to touch her person. In bailable cases, bail should be granted to women without any delay. Further, Section 51 (2) and 100 (3) of Cr PC make it obligatory that a woman should be searched by another woman and with strict regard to decency.

However, in such a male-dominated milieu, there is every reason why the police officers are adequately sensitised so that they could handle women and children with care. According to P.M. Nair, the purpose envisaged in this sensitisation are to ensure that:

1. There is no secondary victimisation or secondary traumatisation of the victims of the crime.
2. Basic human rights are not violated by anybody.
3. No atrocities are committed on them and no modesty is outraged by taking advantage of the situation.
4. Basic decency and courtesy is extended to women/ children.
5. Minimum comforts and prerequisites required for a human-being, especially a woman, is extended.
6. A congenial atmosphere is created by which the victim/ suspect/ accused is free to speak out without a fear or favour or any reservation.
7. An atmosphere of camaraderie is built up so that the person (especially the victim) is helped to get out of the trauma, both physical and mental.
8. Adequate assistance is extended to prepare the victim to face the legal processes involved (Nair 2004 : 155).

The fourth report of the NPC in February 1980, recommended more active and direct involvement of women police in the investigation of crimes relating to women and children and to be employed on intelligence work connected with such crimes.

In this regard, a mention can be made of some of the best attempts that have been made both by law enforcers individually as well as with the help of other well-meaning and committed individuals and institutions to do their bit in this area. Some such examples have been listed below:

Some Major Individual Initiatives towards Gender Sensitisation in Police

1. Community Policing as a tool to fight crime against women by Shri. Nikhil J. Gupta, IPS in 2000 in Sindhudarg district in Maharashtra.

2. E-learning initiative for women police by Shri. K. Radhakrishnan, IPS in 2001 in Chennai.
3. Empowering women by making them work with Anti-liquor Movement in Balasore, Odisha by Shri. Sudhanshu Sarangi, IPS in October 2002.
4. Special panel to safeguard women staff in police stations by V. Naveen Chand, S.P., East Godavari district, Andhra Pradesh in Nov., 2005.

State Police Initiatives towards Gender Sensitisation in Police

The Delhi Police, has been making efforts to impart gender sensitisation training to Inspectors/Sub- Inspectors with the help of Gender Training Institute, New Delhi. The credit for organising these training courses in New Delhi goes to Dr Kiran Bedi, former Director of Bureau of Police Research and Development (BPRD), New Delhi.

Training courses are also being organised for the Inspectors and Sub-Inspectors in Maharashtra on the basis of gender sensitisation training module developed by a team comprising of top police officials in the state and the faculty members of Chavan Academy of Development Administration, New Delhi; National Police Academy, Hyderabad; Tata Institute of Social Sciences (TISS), Mumbai and SNDT Women's University, Pune. The module developed by the above team is also being used for conducting gender sensitisation training courses by Madhya Pradesh Police (Mishra. 2004:98).

Further, in Tamil Nadu, since 1992 All Women Police Stations (AWPS) have been established to combat crime against women in the state. The Mobile Counseling Centers established in the state in the recent past is a measure intended to instill a sense of confidence in women seeking justice and redressal of their grievances. The establishment of a Women Commando Force and an All Women Police Battalion, in 2003-2004, are first of its kind for any state police force at the national level (Mishra, 2004 : 92).

Similarly, in Andhra Pradesh, a community policing initiative called "Maithri" was introduced in 2001. It was a police-public partnership programme and provided an organisational strategy that motivates police officers to solve community problems, especially those related to women's issues, in new and innovative ways, by allowing average citizens a say in the police process.[8]

However, it is to be noted that the reach of all the above mentioned programmes and training courses in terms of the area covered and the number of police officers covered has been very limited so far (less than one per cent of the total strength of the police organisations). Further the training courses are limited only to officers of the rank of sub-inspectors/inspector or senior officers in the police organisations. Systematic efforts have not been made so far in the State and Central Police Organisations to impart gender sensitisation training to the constabulary, which constitutes nearly 80 per cent of the police force (Mishra, 2004:98).

Institutional Initiatives towards Gender Sensitisation in Police

Several institutional initiatives are being adopted by various social organisations including non-police institutions to induce gender sensitisation in law enforcement. Some of these institutional initiatives have been discussed as below:–

(1) On the initiative of the National Commission for Women (NCW), the S.V.P. National Police Academy, a premier IPS training institution in the country, set out preparing a structure for gender sensitisation training in police in 2002-2003. Further, in order to ensure that gender sensitisation forms a part of the training curriculum of police officers at every level, the NCW decided to hold regional conferences, inviting the Heads of Training Institutions, to participate and formulate action plans for themselves for introducing gender sensitisation into the police sub-culture. The Regional Conference for the Southern States held on 11th and 12th of July, 2003 at S.V.P. National Police Academy, Hyderabad, is the first of this series (Mishra, 2004 : 102).

(2) The Delhi Commission for Women (DCW) after a careful study of the cases handled by its counseling units felt the need to sensitise the police personnel handling the cases of women in the Central Crime against Women Cell and District Crime against Women Cells in Delhi. DCW with assistance from

lawyers collective, held a two-day workshop for police personnel at India International Centre, Lodhi Estate, New Delhi on 24-25 July, 2001.

The subjects covered in the discussion at the workshop included:-

- Constitutional Law and Women.
- Section 498A, IPC - Quantitative and Qualitative Analysis.
- A critique of the working of the Crime against Women Cells.
- Effective prosecution of offences against women etc.

The workshop proved to be a success in inducing gender sensitisation in the police personnel working in the Crime against Women Cells in Delhi (Mishra, 2004: 57).

(3) The Tata Institute of Social Sciences, Mumbai, has been holding a field action project called 'PRAYAS', since February 1990, to demonstrate the need for social work intervention in the Criminal Justice System. It is based in Mumbai and the workers are based in the various sub-systems of the Criminal Justice System, such as police stations, courts, prisons and rescue homes, with the aim of carrying out social work intervention within the system (Raghavan, 2004 : 129).

(4) 'Springboard' is a programme organised to empower women in the police. Launched in February 2000 in India, it was implemented under a joint collaboration of the Bureau of Police Research & Development (BPR&D), India, and the Springboard Consultancy, United Kingdom. This initiative is an attempt at forging a new future for women in police and seeks to awaken the police to issues which must be tackled if it is to develop women's potentials as a deliverer of quality services to the public in the twenty first century (Singh 2002 : 27).

Conclusion

The above discussed initiatives to induce gender sensitisation in law enforcement indicates that serious attempts have been made both by law enforcers individually as well as with the help of other well-meaning and committed individuals and institutions to do their best in this area. Still, a lot remains to be done.

The only institution that is perceived as the state by the masses in rural areas are the police stations. But its functioning leaves a lot to be desired. In principle, priority is supposed to be given to crimes against women, which are to be supervised by senior officers. This norm, however, is not implemented in practice since there is acute shortage of women in the police force.

The growth, status and development of the women police personnel besides their training and role representation can no longer be dealt with in an ad hoc manner. There is an urgent need to integrate women to mainstream policing and their working conditions also need to be improved.

The First National Conference for Women in Police, held in 2002 at New Delhi grew from the realisation that an increasing number of women are joining all levels of the police force and large scale attitudinal and workplace changes were needed if the talents and services of these women were to be optimised. The participants suggested several organisational and attitudinal changes towards women in police.

The Second National Conference for Women in Police was held on 27th-29th July, 2005 at Mussoorie in collaboration with Uttaranchal (present Uttarakhand) Police and under the aegis of Bureau of Police Research and Development (BPRD). The former President of India, Dr A. P. J. Abdul Kalam, inaugurated the conference. Several recommendations were made in the conference such as mainstreaming of women in police in order to increase their representation, training needs and attitudinal changes towards women police, lifestyle management for women in police, the issue of sexual harassment at work place and other such issues.

The third National Conference for Women in Police which was organised by Haryana Police under the aegis of BPR&D/ MHA from 7-9 March 2009 at Panchkula, Haryana introduced a theme on "Optimising the Contribution of Women in Police to the Organisation and Society". The Conference was attended by 193 delegates from 24 states and UTs. 28 IPS officers, 34 Gazetted Officers, 19 Inspectors, 51 Sub-Inspectors/Assistant Sub-Inspectors, and 59 Head Constables/Constables participated in this Conference besides the eminent domain experts acting as Moderators/ Resource persons (www.bprd.gov.in).

The fourth and fifth Conferences held in Bhubaneswar, Odisha and Thrissur, Kerala in 2010 and 2012 respectively called for equal opportunities for women police for career progression. Similarly, the sixth national conference also stood for recruitment of more women in the police force.

The above mentioned National Conferences for Women in Police are a clear indication of the realisation of the role of gender sensitisation in law enforcement. A gender sensitive police is ultimately, the product of a gender sensitive society. Segmented police reform in this direction may be token (without undermining the sub cultural resistance), divisive (selective application to upper-class, educated, urban women defined as "respectable"), counter-productive (the other side of police protection is increasing social control on the movement and opportunities for women) and isolationist (the other wings of criminal justice system maintain gender bias). However, the crucial issue is the perspective on role of police in society— as a defender of *status quo* or an agent of social change.

Notes

Fifth Report of the National Police Commission, Government of India, November 1980, 56.

Data on Police Organisations in India, BPRD, Ministry of Home Affairs, New Delhi, January 1st, 2014, 36-38.

Crime in India – 2013, National Crime Records Bureau, Ministry of Home Affairs, Government of India, p. 79.

Interview dated 12th December 2005, with Shri. K. Laxmi Reddy, Superintendent of Police, Women Protection Cell, C.I.D., Hyderabad.

Poornima Advani, member, National Commission for Women, Workshop on Gender Sensitisation of Police Officers (July 21-22, 2000), held at S.V.P. National Police Academy, Andhra Pradesh.

Interview dated 21st December 2005, with Smt. Aruna Bahuguna, Addl. D.G., Coordination, DGP Office, Hyderabad.

Reported in 'The Hindu', 6th November 2005.

Interview dated 21st December 2005, with C. V. Narasaiah, I.G.P., Director, S.C.R.B., C.I.D., A.P., Hyderabad.

References

Panda, Rekha and Subhash Joshi, Gender Issues in the Police, SVP National Police Academy Publications, Hyderabad, 2000.

Panigrahi, Debasis, Gender Sensitisation in Law Enforcement, Prize Winning Essays, Golden Jubilee Publication, SVP National Police Academy Publications, Hyderabad, 1998.

Kriplani, Shyama, Women – Conflict for Basic Rights, Vol. I, RBSA Publishers, Jaipur, 2005.

Saxena, Shabha, Crimes Against Women and Protective Laws, Deep and Deep Publications, New Delhi, 1995.

Mishra, Renuka, Compendium on Good Practices in Police – Gender Issues, Vol. IV, SVP National Police Academy Publications, Hyderabad, 2004.

Singh, Jija Madhavan, Women Leaders in Police – International Law Enforcement Issues, Vol. 47, No. 2, SVP National Police Academy Journal, July – December, 2002.

Nair, P.M., Gender Sensitisation of Police Officers in Dealing with Women and Children During Investigation of Cases, Compendium on Good Practices in Police – Gender Issues, Vol. IV, SVP National Police Academy Publications, Hyderabad, 2004.

Raghavan, Vijay, 'PRAYAS', TISS: Social Work at the Police Stations, Compendium on Good Practices in Police – Gender Issues, Vol. IV, SVP National Police Academy Publications, Hyderabad, 2004.

Pande, Rekha, Women in Police – Looking for Lessons Learnt and Best Practices, Compendium on Good Practices in Police – Gender Issues, Vol. IV, SVP National Police Academy Publications, Hyderabad, 2004.

Sen, Sankar, Human Rights and Practice of Policing, S.V.P. National Police Academy Journal, Vol. 48, No. 2, Jul – Dec 1996.

Khanna, Tejendra, Creation of People Friendly Governance Systems, S.V.P. National Police Academy Journal, Vol. 52, No. 2 Jul –Dec 2000.

Dikshit, R.C., Police: The Human Face, Gyan Publishing House, New Delhi, 2000.

Menon, Nivedita, Gender and Politics in India, Oxford University Press, New Delhi, 1999.

Aleem, Shamim, Women in Indian Police, Sterling Publishers Ltd., New Delhi, 1991.

Shah, Giriraj, Encyclopaedia of Crime, Police and Judicial System, Vol. 14, Anmol Publications, New Delhi, 2000.

Crime in India – 2005, National Crime Records Bureau, Ministry of Home Affairs, Government of India, New Delhi.

The Andhra Pradesh Police Manual, A.P. Police – Crime, Detection, Investigation and Prosecution, Part – I, Vol. 2, Director General of Police, Hyderabad, 2002.

6

Violence and Political Theory

Kamalakanta Roul

Abstract

Violence is continuous, eternal and inevitable thus getting accentuated according to the passage of time. Every society and civilisation at every stage of life is experienced with some kind of violence. The eternality of violence has afflicted the human society more in comparison to other species of nature. Peaceful co-existence of human life has collapsed; social cohesion and cultural co-operation has been politically contaminated. Consequently, the growing contours of violence encourage scholars about the raucous and venomous violence that has raised a new debate in the academic world.

The issue of violence could have been examined in more analytical and exploratory methods of political theory through more systematic and serious conceptual and ethical debates. It must lead the study on violence and should also challenge the popular perception about the entirety of negative performance of violence. All the time violence is not evil. It is very often also appears with a reformist performance for mass interest and common good. In the same vein, the entire article has been divided into five major strands of analytical underpinnings. The concerned article argues that violence is a leading issue in contemporary global politics and society but political theory is little concerned about it because of that definitional and conceptual ambiguity persists in the theory of violence with lack of normative ethical positions among academia, activists and citizens.

Key Words: definition, positive violence, negative violence, state violence and political theory.

Introduction: Political Theory and the Question of 'Violence'

Political theory fosters general awareness for a humanistic study of political processes and events in an organising way of contexts and circumstances. It is an 'interdisciplinary endeavour whose centre of gravity lies at the humanities end...' (Dryzek *et al.*, 2006: 4). It understands political reality of society so as to supply ideas and theories for the purpose of interpretations and criticisms. It explains the 'attitudes and actions arising from ordinary political life and to generalise them in a particular context...' (Crick, 1973: 5). It not only understands but also solves the problem of group life and organisation (Sabine, 1973:3). Group life has regular persistence of violence which is also a leading issue in contemporary global politics. It has become a very common phenomenon in our social and political life. Probably, human beings are the sole creature who craves life on the edge of random violence. They are obsessed by violence in all forms i.e. from individual to group violence: Black-White tensions; causes of Hamas and Al-Qaeda, or the invasion of Iraq and Afghanistan; Civil war in Arabian continent; economic violence in African countries; conflict in Tibet, ethnic violence in South Asia; and communal and anti-displacement violence in Odisha and India are exemplified the fact of sporadic violence.

The issue of violence could have been examined in more analytical and exploratory methods of political theory through more systematic and serious conceptual and ethical debates. Meanwhile, political theorists claim to be more prone into 'conceptual sensitivity' and perfect with 'rational structure' for a humanly achievable truth and objectivity (Bhargava, 2010: 17). It also advocates for a 'rigorous theoretical investigation' (Parekh, 2010) of any social issue and political reality. However, the role of political theory is quite little and passive in the matter of violence. Political theorists who share commitment for 'a humanistic study of politics' (Dryzek *et. al.*, 2006: 4) have said little about the normative ethical position of violence. They urge for individualism, welfare state, human security, justice for least advantaged group and multiculturalism. But they would probably fail to address some specific questions relating to violence. Consequently, political theory must lead the study on violence and should also challenge the popular perception about the entirety of negative performance of violence. Of course, violence is full of negative concomitants but it is also a fact that all the time violence is not evil. It is very often also appears with a reformist performance for mass interest and common good. However, the concerned article has been divided into five major strands of analytical underpinnings. It argues that violence is a leading issue in contemporary global politics and society but political theory is little concerned about it because of that definitional and conceptual ambiguity persists in the theory of violence with lack of normative ethical positions among academia, activists and citizens.

The Violence Issue

Every society is experienced with some kind of violence in its vicinity and of its veracity. The vacuity of study over the votary of violence veils its versatile parts in each sphere of human civilisation. Violence is continuous, eternal and inevitable thus getting accentuated according to the passage of time (Roul, 2013:1). It has stayed put as a constant universal phenomenon in the socio-cultural processes of both primitive and modern societies. No doubt, 'there is an element of violence in life itself' (Gandhi, 1934). Throughout the human history 'violence has played an enormous role in every society created by man' (Arendt, 1960: 8). The eternality of violence has afflicted the human society more in comparison to other species of nature.

The concept of violence can even be traced back prior to human community. The primitive men/women could have acquired the quality of violent and aggressive manners through the perpetual struggling process with 'nature' and 'wild animals' for their survival, security and food. The contemporary human society is under constant outrage of several types of violence. Individual is inflicted with hatred and raged attitude. Group life has also been pervaded with intolerance, obscurantist and irrational belief including narrow thoughts. Conflict and aggression are guiding individual and group behaviour and social interaction. Violence is the state of mind comes from human behaviour, attitude and activity. It is not only an individual pursuance and group performance but it also crops up as structural violation. Individual violence evolves as a part ofinner disturbances or disorder of socio-political systems but group violence would be possible with the matters of inequality, injustice, and mobilisation. Structural violence comes up in the form of institutional dysfunction, dominant and exploitative mechanisms, and discrimination in deliberation of services to people. In fact, individual, group and structural violence combines most of the concomitants of common violence that usually take place in society.

Consequently, human growth, prosperity and security have been disturbed by the menace of violence in daily life. Peaceful co-existence of human life has collapsed; social cohesion and cultural co-operation has been politically contaminated. Moreover, the variety of violence invades to end human existence and social subsistence. Thus, the growing contours of violence raises a question in the mind as to what would happen to human civilisation and society if violence would occur very frequently? It has ignited scholars about the raucous and venomous violence that has raised a new debate in the academic world.

The Task of Political Theory

Political theory tends to emphasise over the study of 'cosmologies' and 'common sense' which urge that cosmologies frequently inform and become part of a society's common sense (Bhargava, 2010: 19). The theoretical reflections of cosmologies would be an incomplete lesson without leaning on the violence issue. Human anatomy reveals that violence pervaded with every stage of its civilisation, growth and development. Moreover, violence becomes an embedded fact of human existence appeared in the forms of conflict, confrontation, crime, threat, attack, war, terrorism and injuries. In this context, political theory would play very larger role to carry forward a theoretical investigation and ethical normative position of violence for the holistic understanding of cosmologies and human survival. In fact, exploratory and normative analysis of violence would be the appropriate method to understand the problem of violence in political theory. The issue of decline and fall of political theory might be an attempt to put it into the intellectual captivity but it has probed its impact and influence in capturing the human emotion and expression for a better understanding of human and its cosmos. In this regard, political theory has three major tasks of analysing violence: observation, exploration and generalisation of violence issue.

The twentieth century world has correctly been identified as the long century of violence (Keane, 1996:3). The number of victims, the magnitude of devastation and the new technologies of destruction are without historical parallel (Wolin, 1963: 20). It has been calculated that war-related killings in the twentieth century exceeded 105 million, including 62 million civilian victims (Steger, 2003, p. xiii). The magnitude of violence cannot be confined to the dead only. Rather those who survive it may even be worst hit. "For every person killed by an act of violence there are many more who have survived torture, brutality, persecution, the loss of loved ones, or (if they are lucky) the loss of all their belongings and livelihood. One can safely speculate that every person living today will experience, directly or indirectly, some type of violence" (Bufacchi, 2005: 193).

The persistent proliferation of political violence should not come as a surprise because violence has always been the essence of politics. Writing in the seventeenth century at a time when the modern state, and modern philosophy, acquired its present identity, "Thomas Hobbes famously depicted the pre-political 'state of nature' as a place of violence, where everyone endeavours to destroy or subdue one another, making life solitary, nasty and short" (*ibid*). Therefore, Hobbes affirmed that society is "a conquest of violence" (Johnsons, 1968: 9). Society as a viable enterprise, according to this school of thought, comes into being after its individual members have ascended from the 'state of nature' in which "every man was at war with everyone" (Singh, 1988: 19). Even John Locke, who entertained a much rosier picture of the state of nature, admitted to a problematic level of violence, which made life 'inconvenient'. The other school of thought however "begins its inquiry from a prior assumption of the existence of social order and then, tries to see violence as an endemic social data of all social structures" (*ibid*).

The modern human lives escaped from the pre-political state of promiscuous violence by forming a political society under the rule of a centralised authority. Max Weber justifies state's monopoly over the legitimate use of violence. The force used by state institutions may be legal, even legitimate, but it is still violence (Brady and Garver, 1991) and when the state is incapable of providing protection for its subjects, private agencies will take over the role of dispensing violence and security, as in the case of the Russian mafia (Varese, 2001). "Following in the footsteps of Hobbes and Weber, today the vast majority of political theorists see collective violence as integral to political life" (Bufacchi, 2005: 194). No one is immune from political violence, whether living in a wealthy western democracy or in a country undergoing late economic development (Bates, 2001).

There is an academic agreement over the issue that every society is infected with the problem of violence. In fact, the subject of violence was a taboo area of study among the academia. It was not recognised in academics till 1970s, neither by the Encyclopedias of Philosophy nor Social Sciences. The 'Encyclopedia of Sociology' has only one entry on 'violent crimes' (Singh, 1999: 23; Singh, 1976: 58). There was plenty of literature on war and warfare dealing mainly with the implements of violence, but not violence as such. No social scientists and political scientists in particular, can afford to neglect its role and manifestation in political life. Nevertheless, very few have tried to consider violence in politics systematically and empirically. Georges Sorel rightly said that "the problem of violence remains very obscure" (1941: 61). Violence has never been taken, although Socrates was killed, as a theme in itself by the great thinkers of the western philosophic tradition before the nineteenth century. It had to wait for Georges Sorel, till the dawn of the twentieth century to make violence the centre of his studies (Singh, 1999: 24). Georges Sorel's 'Reflections on Violence' first published in 1908 with the core title of 'Violence'. It is the first systematic literature on violence.

The Concept of Violence

The syntax of violence can be examined by two words: violent and violence. The term 'violent' qualifies a certain act or person which has exceeded some generally recognised limit or norm. But the act of violence is different from the violent act. The term 'violence' is derived from the Latin word 'violentia' that means 'vehemence, a passionate and uncontrolled force (*ibid*: 14). In fact, some scholars' attempts to define violence tend to combine the idea of an act of physical force with a violation. Hence, T. Honderich defines violence as 'a use of physical force that injures, damages, violates or destroys people or things' (2002:91; 2003:15).

Violence is said to be a universal phenomenon. Instinctive theorists say it is a human intuition and biological trait. The Oxford Dictionary defines violence as 'the exercise of physical force so as to inflict injury on, or cause damage to, person or property'. But with the changing of times, violence has obtained much comprehensive and complex range of meaning. Raymond Williams defines violence as 'use of physical force to unruly behaviour' (1976: 278). Violence is a generic term that may include many forms of overt, and often noxious, expressions, ranging from internal physiological changes in the organism to external behaviour that directly impinges upon the safety and security of other organisms. Hostility, psychological and physical aggression, anger, and rage are all terms that have been associated with the meaning of violent responses to stimuli (Wolfgang, 1996: 2).

There are many ways to define the concept of violence that is what social scientists have followed so far. But scientific understanding of human violence is one of the most urgent tasks of our time. However, there is no agreement among the scholars concerning a definition of what exactly 'violence' is (Stanko, 2003: 3). The popular practice of defining violence always considers 'forms of criminal violence and to argue that violence is the use of force that has been prohibited by law' (Riedel and Welsh, 2002: 3). Nevertheless, violence conventionally denotes physical attack. David Riches defines violence as "an act of physical hurt deemed legitimate by the performer and illegitimate by (some) witnesses" (1986:8). Riches claims that this definition is compatible with "basic properties" of violence, which have cross-cultural validity. Willem de Haan says that this cross-cultural validity refers to "the performance of violence." (2008: 30).

Further, Haan (2008: 27) argues that "violence as an essentially contested concept" which has two types of definitions: (a) "restrictive definitions of violence are being offered which tend to limit violence to physical attack" (2008: 30) and 'inclusive definitions of violence' which is "an attempt to introduce a more systematic, comprehensive analysis of violence something missing here several propositions have been made for a more extended notion of violence to be defined in a more inclusive way" (2008: 32). F. Neidhardt favours the restrictive definition of violence because of two reasons: physical violence is a universal media of communication and the monopoly of violence always applied to physical rather than mental violence" (1986: 135). Furthermore, he has considered the feasibility of other definitions. But scholars like Nedelmann (1995: 8) and von Trotha (1997: 20) are convinced that the question of how to define violence has been adequately solved, at least for the time being, by defining it as bodily harm by physical use of force.

Willem de Haan contemplates that "the concept of 'violence' is notoriously difficult to define because as a phenomenon it is multifaceted, socially constructed and highly ambivalent" (2008: 27). Haan also says that "violence is multifaceted because there are many different forms of violence, which are exhibited in a wide range of contexts" (*ibid*). However, a group of scholars (S. Henry (2000), M. Jackman (2002) and G. Barak (2003)) have offered an inclusive version of definition of violence i.e. 'to take into account the full range of harms associated with a variety of interpersonal, institutional, and structural relationships and behaviours and to not exclude any forms and expressions of violence, whether they refer to individual acts, institutional arrangements or structural conditions as well as whether or not they are prohibited by law'. Similarly, Henry (2000) suggests that a more inclusive, integrated definition of violence is necessary, which replaces the term 'force' with 'power' and takes a more comprehensive view of harm. Thus, violence is defined by him as "the use of power to harm another, whatever form it takes" (Henry, 2000: 3). In this case, harm is not only physical pain and suffering. It can also occur along many dimensions beyond the physical to include psychological or emotional, material or economic, social or identity, moral or ethical, and so on. Within each dimension, the harm can be of two kinds: 'harms of reduction' and 'harms of repression' (Henry and Milovanovic, 1996: 103). Some scholars tried to clarify how the term violence ought to be distinguished from other terms of a similar nature such as power, aggression and coercion. Hannah Arendt's "On

Violence", 1969, clarifies the confusion how violence is different from power. However, Max Weber defines "power as the ability to change the incentive structures of another actor or actors to bring about certain outcomes" (*ibid*).

The Theoretical Tradition

Every stage of the civilisation realised the importance of violence and has given primacy to violence. The pre-Enlightenment philosophies of all the major religions of the globe have advocated the use of violence when all other modes of redressing a wrong have failed. The idea of *'just war'* of radical Christianity, *jihad* in Islam and *dharmayuddha* in Hinduism and Sikhism advocates "to take violence only at its extreme to restore order in society and grant justice to the suffering people".

Violence as Biological Trait

The classical theorists believe that primitive men acquired the quality of violent and aggressive manners through the perpetual struggling process with 'nature' and 'wild animals' for their existence, security and food. The Paleolithic period of hunting and food gathering gradually evolved to the Mesolithic phase of use of stone weapons that fostered this inherent process of violence and aggression. The climatic changes and use of stone weapons impelled them to take violence as their mean. Probably, the muscular strength of young men was the only motive force employed to operate the elementary tools and weapons. Later on, conflict persisted among ancient human community relating to the 'distribution of foods' and other similar 'resources' (Roul, 2012). The tribal authority managed this conflict among the individuals. Such societies have been described as the 'pre-state societies'. This primitive form of social organisation later on developed into the state. Consequently, the instinctive theorists say violence is a human intuition and biological trait (Turnbull, 1999: 32). The contemporary research on "genetics have raised the possibility of a greater biological basis for much of human behaviour" (*ibid*: 32) relating to social problems such as violence. Sometimes the physiological changes can account for some episodes of violent behaviour. These biological or physiological explanations of violence are neurological, hormonal, genetic and other physiological changes.

Violence as Force, Power and Authority

There is a broad consensus among the classical scholars that violence and other kinds of force are perennially associated with the exercise of power. They also consider authority as the authentic form of power, based on consent, voluntary obedience, and persuasion, and consider violence as a symptom attending the breakdown of authority. These ideas may be found in the Socratic opposition to Thrasymachus, and in Plato's conviction that persuasion is morally superior to force. This idea was also later on carried out by Rousseau. Most of the classical theorists believed that all politics is a struggle for power; the ultimate kind of power is violence. Many scholars such as Machiavelli, Hobbes, Manu and Kautilya are representing this tradition that power is the bitter reality.

Violence as Revolution

The modern philosophers did not give more importance on the thematic study of violence but suggested that violence could be the last and only remaining alternative with the oppressed majority to seek justice for their oppression by the minority. In the mid-nineteenth century, Karl Marx assigned proletariats to liberate not only itself but the whole human community and he also prescribed if necessary violence or bloodshed could be used as means for it. The last paragraph of the *Manifesto of the Communist Party* states: "The Communists disdain to conceal their views and aims. They openly declare that their ends can be attained only by the forcible overthrow of all existing social conditions. Let the ruling classes tremble at a Communist revolution" (quoted in Adam Schaff, 1973: 263). Similarly, talking on the nature of revolution, Engels says: "A revolution is...the act whereby one part of the population imposes its will upon the other part by means of rifles, bayonets and canon..." (Singh, 1989: PE-15).

Vladimir I. Lenin suggested the relevance of guerrilla warfare in the proletarian struggle for socialism. He argues that "guerrilla warfare is an inevitable form of struggle at a time when the mass movement has actually reached the point of an uprising and when fairly large intervals occur between the "big engagements" in the civil war" (Lenin, 1968: 163). Leon Trotsky (1961:48) defends against Karl Kautsky's "charge of terrorism both in the Russian Revolution and Bolshevism". Mao Tse-tung's philosophy occupies the significance place after the above mentioned first generation of revolutionaries and the theoreticians of violence. The most popular slogan of Mao was 'power comes out of the barrel of the gun' which gained currency among the practitioners of guerrilla warfare. Mao believes that 'war is the continuation of politics' (Tse-Tung, 1977 and 1965 ed.: 150). The anarchists too consider violence is necessary and inevitable. Michael Bakunin (1990: xxxiii) states that this would be possible by 'organising a society 'from below upwards' composed of small, voluntary communities federating into larger associations for larger purposes'. Bakunin gathered hopes for revolution on the most alienated sections of the society- the most destitute and desperate toilers- including the lumpen proletariat. Bakunin says they are the real social rebels and the real spirit of revolution to establish a new free society.

Violence as General Strike

Generally, Georges Sorel's theory of violence has both creative and destructive dimensions. Sorel argues that the strike violence not only keep the revolutionary spirit alive, but also encourage the middle class. He says, "it is here that the role of the violence in history appears to us as singularly great for it can, in an indirect manner, so operate on the middle class as to awaken them to a sense of their own class sentiment" (1941: 90). Further, Sorel tries to clarify two concepts i.e. force and violence which are used more often interchangeably. For Frantz Fanon, violence is only a means to an end, which is the formation of a just society. Fanon states: "the violence which has ceaselessly drummed the rhythm for the destruction of native social forms and broken up without reserve the systems of reference of the economy, the customs of dress and external life, that same violence will be claimed and taken over by the native at moment when, deciding to embody history in his own person, he surges into the forbidden quarter" (Fanon, 1980: 31).

Violence as Healing Character

Jean Paul Sartre said that "a man feels himself more of a man when he is imposing himself and making others the instrument of his will", which gives him "incomparable pleasure" (Arendt, 1999: 3). Sartre vehemently criticised 'imperialists for unleashing violence in the colonies not only to keep them at an arm's length, but dehumanise them'. He says, 'the violence of the colonialists itself emerges as an indefinite necessity or, to put it another way, the colonialist reveals the violence of the native, even in his passivity, as the obvious consequence of his own violence and as its sole justification' (Sartre, 1982: 720). Sartre subscribed Fanon's contention concerning the 'healing character of the native's violence'. He supports Fanon's view that violence can heal the wounds that it has inflicted.

Violence as Power

Hannah Arendt states that a consensus exists among the political theorists to the effect that "violence is nothing more than that the most flagrant manifestation of power" (1999:3). She says power corresponds to the human ability not just to act but to act in concert. Power is never the property of an individual; it belongs to a group and remains in existence only so long as the group keeps together (1999: 6). Power is an instrument of rule, which rule owes its existence to "the instinct of domination". Ardent supposes power relations are essentially cooperative. On the other hand, Ardent says "violence...is distinguished by its instrumental character. Phenomenologically, it is close to strength, since the implements of violence, like all other tools, are designed and used for the purpose of multiplying natural strength until, in the last stage of their development, they can substitute for it" (1999: 7). Arendt argues that 'power is the quality of the people constituting the public realm; violence is the property of the state which is used against the people'. Violence relies on the instruments of its application; hence it can be held in possession. She asserts, "Where power is absent, violence may emerge to fill the gap" (1999: 9).

Violence as Moral Vacuum

Gandhi observed that many have instrumentalised violence to achieve their self-interest and turned to violence as the only effective method of securing justice (Parekh, 1997: 65). He rejected violence on moral grounds. Morality consisted in doing what was right because one believed it to be right and required unity of belief and conduct. Since the use of violence did not change the opponent's perception of truth, it compelled him to behave in a manner contrary to his sincerely held beliefs and violated his moral integrity (*ibid*: 66). Gandhi urged that the "rational discussion or persuasion was the best way to resolve conflict" (Parekh, 1997:64). But he affirmed that "I do believe that, where there is only a choice between cowardice and violence, I would advice violence" (Gandhi, 1960: 3).

Violence as Social Injustice

Johan Galtung (1969) depicted violence as social injustice through his concept of 'structural violence'. He equates violence with 'social injustice', arguing that "violence is present where human beings are influenced so that their actual somatic and mental realisations are below their potential realisations". "Violence is here defined as the cause of the difference between the potential and the actual, between what could have been and what is". "Violence is that which increases the distance between the potential and the actual, and that which impedes the decrease of this distance".

The State Violence and Political Theory

The notion of violence also grappled with the use and practices of individual as well as state and non-state actors. Little attention has been given by political theorists on violence generating by state actors, although state is a basic concept of political theory. Some scholars even, do not agree that violence by state should be equated with violence by individuals or non-state actors. But the illegitimate violence by state officials has become a wide practice. The idea of 'coercive network' to understand the interconnected institutions, laws, and practices that made up the state's coercive repertoire. "Far from being limited to a single institution, coercive practices ranged from firing on crowds and bombing from the air, to dismissal from one's place of work or study, to collective fines, imprisonment and corporal punishment" (Sherman, 2010:1).

Taylor C. Sherman (2010: 5) provides two scholarly arguments on state violence: counter insurgency measures, and cultural turn. Sherman says, "state violence in India was often not centrally planned. Instead, it tended to be perpetuated by individual officers operating under their wide discretionary powers. These acts of violence became battlegrounds of representation: Indians represented state violence as they pursued their own political goals; but official rhetoric attempted to assure the public that government servants used forced only as a last resort" (*ibid*: 6). Steffen Jensen and Andrew M. Jefferson (2009: 14) argue that "state officials occupy a position of structural undecidability. On the one hand, they are the active perpetrators of violence against whom communities and individual must be protected. On the other hand, when state officials are targeted for training, they are seen less as agents of state-sanctioned violence and more as potentially rights-promoting legal subjects...State officials are thus made into objects of intervention whose beneficiaries are someone else". Similarly, Steffen Jensen (2009: 60-78) argues that the state officials commit violence on behalf of their superiors. But Sherman (2010:11) argues, "the state was not a static entity; not only was its constitutional structure regularly recorded, the lower levels of the state were constantly adapting to changing circumstances" (2010: 12). "It is surely not surprising that those sectors of the state often responsible for upholding authoritarian states through political repression, suppression of voices or downright oppression are targeted for rights-based reform, be these members of the state security apparatus or local chiefs" (Jensen and Jefferson, 2009: 15).

Ruth Blakeley (2010: 12) discussed about the 'state terrorism in social sciences'. He says state terrorism is a constitutive element must be consistent with non-state terrorism. Some scholars do not accept that terrorism by states should be equated with terrorism by non-state actors. Walter Laqueur has argued: "there are basic differences in motives, function and effect between oppression by the state (or society or religion) and political terrorism. To equate them, to obliterate them is to spread confusion" (1986: 89). He further argued that including state terror in the study of terrorism "would have made the study of terrorism impossible, for it would have included not only US foreign policy, but also Hitler and Stalin" (Laqueur, 2003: 140). Richard Jackson, Eamon Murphy and Scott Poynting (2010: 3) states that "we understand state terrorism to be the intentional use or threat of violence by state agents or their proxies against individuals or groups who are victimised for the purpose of intimidating or frightening a broader audience". In 1980s, a group of scholars attempted to define state terrorism with the incorporation of Eugene Victor Walter's (1969) core characteristics of terrorism. They were Christopher Mitchell, Michael Stohl, David Carleton, and George Lopez. They argued: "terrorism by the state (or non-state actors) involves deliberative coercion and violence (or the threat thereof) directed at some victim, with the intention of inducing extreme fear in some target observers who identify with that victim in such a way that they perceive themselves as potential future victims. In this way they are forced to consider altering their behaviour in some manner desired by the actor" (Mitchell *et al.* 1986: 5).

Conclusion: Ethics of Using Violence and Political Theory

Violence is one of the oldest human practices. It is universal and ubiquitous which has multiple forms. It is also said that human society begins with violence and would end with violence. As Nietzsche says 'violence is everywhere' (Polin, 1974: 66), we can only choose 'good and bad usages of violence' (*ibid*: 69). The importance of violence has been realised in very stage of human civilisation. However, the debates on the definition of violence states that it has been defined very *restrictively*. It denotes violence as physical attack or injury. On the other hand, a group of contemporary political theorists argue that violence is essentially a contested concept which requires *exclusive form of definitions* that refers to non-physical, institutional, or any action harms individual. Gandhian theory of symbolic violence is considered as exclusive definition of violence. In this context, violence has been appeared as a large challenge for political theory in regard to produce a general definition and theories. Although in mid 50s political theory witnessed a phase of crisis and the question of irrelevance that has again reemerged in a slight different way in late 80s and early 90s onwards. Rajni Kothari (1986) depicted a very 'dark picture' of Indian political theory and thought which had been recapitulated and enlarged by Bhiku Parekh in 1992. Parekh argues on the poverty (underdevelopment) of Indian political theory which is falling short of finest mind and a commitment of theoretical understanding (Parekh, 2010: 29). Moreover, Partha Chatterjee (1998 and 2010) exposes the 'poverty of Western political theory' which is considered to be parochial and unsuitable for non-Western countries or background. When both East and West's political theory falls in the problem of thematic insufficiency and conceptual isolation because of their underdevelopment and parochialism of theoretical tradition, violence issue will of course add into it as one of the major themes for a wider interrogation.

Political theory enquires the ethics of use and abuse of violence which would be helpful for the conceptualisation and generalisation of the issue. It explores all these problems towards 'the understanding of the relevance of violence to persons, and the relevance of persons to violence' (Stanage, 1974: 207-208). Some people highly appreciate the success of violence when it achieves immediate results. They give an instrumentalist view on violence. On the other hand, there is a popular perception about the entirety of negative performance of violence in society. But the nature of multiple violence shows that all violence is not evil. It is very often also appears with a reformist performance for mass interest and common good. However, the use of violence can be classified into two major parts: negative and positive violence. The *negative violence* intends to cause harm to other in different forms. Its basic purpose is to destroy the dignity of others through coercion and compulsion and to impose self-honour. Some specific features are embedded to negative violence: physical injuries, killings, pogroms and destructions against the will and desires of others. It includes all types of violence like structural, religious, ethnic, caste, gender etc. The *positive violence* is the epitome of constructive and creative changes in the society. It stands for a socio-political change and collective mass interests. The mass interest is much above the narrow and vested interests. It requires personal sacrifice and commitment. People's democratic revolution- Narmada Bachao Andolan, and Niyamgiri *Suraksha Samiti*- through united front mass movements is also an example of positive violence in India. In addition, Socrates denounces negative violence as loss of 'moral integrity' whereas he has used positive violence against the Spartan government.

Mahatma Gandhi discarded any kind of violence even in thought, words or deeds but his clarion call for "do or die" against imperialist forces is a clear example of positive violence. Gandhi did not reject violence absolutely. However, he advises others on many occasions to use it (Pontara, 1965: 198, 200, 201) as he admitted it openly to choose violence instead of cowardice. He did provoke mass people by asking them for the collective action of "do" at the expense of any odd circumstances. Moreover, Gandhi also injected a strong element of motivation while asking people to "die" for victory of good over evil on moral ground. Although, in this context both provocation and motivation could be considered as the trait of violence but it was a kind of revolutionary violence for the production of a larger political change: Swaraj and Swadeshi. In this form of violence Satyagrahi is asked to sacrifice life before brute force for common interest but has not been asked to kill them. On the other hand, the Marxist forms of violence could also be considered as a part of positive violence as it stands for larger mass interest and common good. But it is different from Gandhism and Gandhi's view on violence. The basic difference between these two ideas is based on their means i.e. Gandhism believes in reconciliation and Marxism emphasises over bloodbath/confrontation. Both kinds of violence are revolutionary in nature. Marxist violence too has a positive end i.e. establishing communism and equality by overthrowing capitalists. But the means of overthrowing capitalists and bourgeoisie intends to do an act of physical hurt. Here Comrades were asked to mitigate inequality by organising revolution and if that is not possible through revolution then they were advised to adopt violent methods. On the other hand, Gandhi's Satyagrahis' were asked to invite 'suffering love' to put a moral and ethical pressure over the evil minded authority. In fact, Gandhian form of positive violence has been widely accepted but Marxist form of violence is still contested. However, violence has very broad perspective to deal with many aspects such as social, cultural, economic and political. Consequently, the positive and negative dichotomy of violence can subscribe all these aspects from a broader perspective of understanding the anatomy of violence in society.

Notes

1. In this article, Political Theory has been used as a general subject of Political Science to represent the broader view of theoretical tradition of study apart from any geographical barriers.
2. I am thankful to the organisers of seminars of National School of Decency, Jajpur, Odisha and RGNIYD, Sriperumbudur, Tamil Nadu where I put forward my idea and debate on conceptualisation

and distinction of positive and negative violence. I too obliged to the Editor of Mainstream Weekly, Sumit Chakravarty who published my article which was carried the idea of negative and positive violence in 2012.

3. I am thankful to Lalit Mohan for his intervention on spiritual perspective of positive violence.
4. The concerned article is an abridged form of a chapter titled "Theorisation on Violence: Quest for a New Perspective" of my Ph.D thesis.

References

Arendt, Hannah, *On Violence*. New York: Harcourt, Bruce and World Inc., 1960.

Arendt, Hannah, 'On Violence', in Steger, B. Manefred and S. Nancy Lind, eds., *Violence and Its Alternatives: An Interdisciplinary Reader*. London: Macmillan, 1999.

Ashcraft, Richard, On the Problem of Methodology and the Nature of Political Theory, *Political Theory*, Vol. 3, No. 1, Feb., 1975, pp. 5-25.

Bakunin, Michael, *Statism and Anarchy*, ed. and trans. by M.S. Shastz. Cambridge: Cambridge University Press, 1990.

Bhargava, Rajeev, *What is Political Theory and Why do We Need It?*. New Delhi: OUP, 2010.

Bates, R. H., *Prosperity and Violence: The Political Economy of Development*. New York: W.W. Norton, 2001.

Blakeley, Ruth, 'State terrorism in the social sciences: Theories, methods and concepts'. In the edited book of Jackson, Richard, Murphy, Eamon and Poynting, Scott, *Contemporary State Terrorism: Theory and Practice*. New York: Routledge, 2010.

Bufacchi, Vittorio, Two Concepts of Violence, *Political Studies Review*, 2005, Vol. 3, 193-204.

Brady, J. and Garver, N., eds., *Justice, Law and Violence*. Philadelphia PA: Temple University Press, 1991.

Bates, R. H., *Prosperity and Violence: The Political Economy of Development*, New York: W.W. Norton, 2001.

Crick, B., *Political Theory and Practice*. New York: Basic Books, 1973.

Chatterjee, Partha, The Poverty of Western Political Theory: Concluding Remarks on Concepts Like "Community" East and West, in Aakash Singh and Sikha Mohapatra, *Indian Political Thought: A Reader*. New York: Routledge, 2010, pp. 287-99.

Dryzek, John S., Bonnie Honig and Anne Phillips, eds. Handbooks of Political Science. Oxford: OUP, 2006.

Ehrlich, Ludwik, The War and Political Theory. *California Law Review*, Vol. 6, No. 6 , Sep., 1918, pp. 418-442.

Fanon, Frantz, *The Wretched of the Earth*, trans. C. Farrington. Harmondsworth: Penguin, 1980.

Gandhi, M.K., *Young India*, September 28, 1934.

Gandhi, M.K., *My Non-Violence*. Ahmedabad: Navajivan, 1960.

Haan, Willem de., 'Violence as an Essentially Contested Concept' in S. Body-Gendrot and P. Spierenburg, eds., Violence in Europe, *Springer* 2008.

Honderich, T., *After the Terror*. Edinburgh: Edinburgh University Press, 2002.

Jensen, Steffen and Jefferson, Andrew M., *State Violence and Human Rights: State officials in the South*. New York: Routledge, 2009.

Jensen, Steffen, 'The vision of the state: Audiences, enchantments and policing in South Africa'. In the edited book of Jensen, Steffen and Jefferson, Andrew M., *State Violence and Human Rights: State officials in the South*. New York: Routledge, 2009.

Jackson, Richard, Eamon Murphy, and Scott Poynting, *Contemporary State Terrorism: Theory and Practice*. New York: Routledge, 2010.

Johnsons, Chalmers, *Revolutionary Changes*. London: University of London Press, 1968.

Keane, J, *Reflections on Violence*. London: Verso, 1996.

Lenin, Vladimir I. (1968): *Marx, Engels, Marxism* (Moscow: Progress Publishers).

Laqueur, Walter (1986): 'Reflections on Terrorism', *Foreign Affairs*, 1986, 65:86-100.

Mitchell, C. Stohl, M., Carleton, D., Lopez, G., 'State Terrorism: Issues of Concept and Measurement', in Michael Stohl and George Lopez, eds., *Government Violence and Repression: An Agenda for Research*. New York: Greenwood Press, 1986, pp. 1-26.

Parekh, Bhiku, The Poverty of Indian Political Theory, in Aakash Singh and Sikha Mohapatra, eds., *Indian Political Thought: A Reader*. New York: Routledge, 2010.

Parekh, Bhiku, *Gandhi: A Very Short Introduction*. New Delhi: OUP, 1997.

Polin, Raymond, 'Nietzschean Violence' in Philip P. Weiner and John Fisher, eds., *Violence and Aggression in History of Ideas*. New Brunswick: Rutgers University Press, 1974.

Pontara, Giuliano, The Rejection of Violence in Gandhian Ethics of

Conflict Resolution. *Journal of Peace Research*, Vol. 2, No. 3, 1965, pp. 197-215.

Riches, David, ed., *The Anthropology of Violence*. Oxford: Basil Blackwell, 1986.

Roul, Kamalakanta, *Kandhamal Violence and the State: A Study of the Politics of Ethnicity, Caste, Class and Religion*. Unpublished Ph.D thesis, Delhi: University of Delhi, 2013.

Roul, Kamalakanta, "Decoding Decency and Violence: Role of Youth in Contemporary Odisha", *Mainstream*, Vol. L, 2012, No. 38, September 8, pp. 28-35.

Sartre, Jean-Paul, *Critique of Dialectical Reason*. London: Verso, 1982.

Sabine, G.H., *History of Political Theory*. New Delhi: Oxford and IBH, 1973.

Sherman, Taylor C., *State Violence and Punishment in India*. New York: Routledge, 2010.

Steger, M., *Judging Non-violence: The Dispute Between Realists and Idealists*. London: Routledge, 2003.

Singh, Rajendra 'Some Reflections on the Study of Collective Violence and Indian Social Structure', in the edited book of K.S. Shukla, *Collective Violence: Genesis and Response*. New Delhi: Indian Institute of Public Administration, 1988.

Singh, B. P. *Problems of Violence: Themes in Literature*. Shimla: Indian Institute of Advanced Study, 1999.

Singh, Gopal, Politics and Violence, *Social Scientist*, 1976, Vol. 4, No. 11, (June), pp. 58-66.

Sorel, Georges, *Reflections on Violence*. New York: Peter Smith, 1941.

Singh, Rustam, 'Status of Violence in Marx Theory of Revolution', *Economic and Political Weekly*, 1989, Vol. XXIV, No. 4, pp. PE-16.

Singh, Gopal (1976): Politics and Violence, *Social Scientist*, Vol. 4, No. 11, (June), pp. 58-66.

Turnbull, John and Brodie Paterson, eds., *Aggression and Violence: Approaches to Effective Management*. London: Macmillan, 1999.

Trotsky, Leon, *Terrorism and Communism: A Reply to Karl Kautsky*. Ann Arbor: University of Michigan Press, 1961.

Tse-Tung, Mao, 'On Protracted War', in *Selected Works of Mao Tse-Tung*, Vol. II. Peking: Foreign Languages Press, 1977.

Wolfgang, Marvin E., eds., *Collective Violence*. New York: Aldine Atheton, 1996.

Wolin, S., 'Violence and the Western Political Tradition', *American Journal of Orthopsychiatry*, 1963, 33, 15-28.

Varese, F., *The Russian Mafia: Private Protection in a New Market Economy*. Oxford: Oxford University Press, 2001.

7

Domestic Violence Against Women in Odisha–A Feminist Discourse

Dr Mamata Dash

Abstract

Violence, and more specifically domestic violence against women in India is an issue deep-rooted in societal norms and economic dependence. Discriminatory socio-cultural practices coupled with inadequate and delayed legal service and ambiguous legal framework and laws favouring men deny female victims proper protection and justice. Although national and state statistics shows progressive change in status of women in terms increased literacy rate, wider scope of employability, ameliorated female workforce as well as public participation in India state like Odisha is still prominent as regards violence against women. While plethora of legal amendments, policy formulation and implementation by state government attests Govt's proactive concern towards violence against women, researches shows that at national level Odisha occupies seventh position in dowry murder, eighth in rape and tenth position in violence against women (NCRB, 2011). However, these figures are just the tip of the iceberg as the number of actual happening particularly in case of domestic violence in its manifold manifestation is even more than these recorded facts and its effects of insecurity and conflict on the victims many times is irreversible and affect their welfare throughout their lives.

This paper investigates the forms, causes and impact of Domestic violence against women in its plurality in the state of Odisha.

Key words: Women, Domestic violence, status of women, Cross cutting issues, Odisha, (Total words-190).

Introduction

Difficult as it is to generalise the complex levels of violence against women both inside and outside the home. Violence threatens life, more often, of women in all its plurality and diversity across the world. As defined by The UN Declaration on the Elimination of Violence Against Women, "violence against women is a manifestation of historically unequal power relations between men and women" and that "violence against women is one of the crucial social mechanisms by which women are forced into a subordinate position compared with men." Thus this can be deduced that domestic violence is also one of the end results of disproportional power game between men and women. In the opinion of Kofi Annan Secretary-General of the United Nations, [2006 report posted on the United Nations Development Fund for Women (UNIFEM) website] "Violence against women and girls is a problem of pandemic proportions. At least one out of every three women around the world has been beaten, coerced into sex, or otherwise abused in her lifetime with the abuser usually someone known to her.

Not every man is a rapist but every woman is a victim of violence in some form or other. She is cursed with a differential, unequal treatment in every step of life till her death. She is made to be silent from inside the mother's womb to tomb beyond time and space. Gender-based inequality is an age old phenomenon. It is as old as mankind and present in all forms and in all walks of life across the globe. Violence against women can fit into several broad categories. These include violence carried out by 'individuals' as well as 'states.' Domestic violence is one of the violence perpetrated by individuals related or known to the victim very closely.

The present study on "Domestic Violence against Women in the states of Odisha was undertaken in the backdrop of the reports appearing in visual and written media depicting inhuman treatment to the women meted to them by their own family members.

The present study was undertaken with the following objectives –

OBJECTIVE

The present study is undertaken with the following principal objectives –

1. To study the nature, extent and incidence of domestic violence against women.
2. To identify the correlates of domestic violence against women.
3. To find out the relationship between the traditional sex-based roles and the Domestic violence.
4. To examine whether dependency, objective or subjective or both is the cause, condition or instigating factor for domestic violence.
5. To find out whether the abused women seek the help of informal or formal agencies and to what extent these agencies are successful in solving the problems of the abused women.
6. To trace the reasons for which abused women continue to stay in abusive relationships.
7. To examine the impact of domestic violence on the abused women, their children and intra-family relations.
8. To suggest measures to control, minimise and, if possible, eliminate domestic violence against women.

Methods used

The present study was conducted both in urban and rural areas of the state. A random sample of 250 families (125 from urban and 125 from rural areas) drawn from urban and rural areas represented the families from upper class, middle class and lower class, middle class and lower class. While drawing sample the geographical area of the state was divided into five zones i.e. East, West, North, South and Central. The selection of districts and places was also done on random sampling basis. A sample of 50 families (25 from urban and 25 from rural areas) was also drawn on purposive random sampling basis to give proper representation to families belonging to different socio-economic groups and religions.

For collecting primary and secondary data from different sources the following tools and techniques were used -

1. Interview Schedule for women respondents.
2. Observation Schedule for Investigators.
3. Informal discussion with family members and neighbours.
4. focus group discussion with the women other than who were interviewed. The collected data was processed and statistical analysis carried with the help of computers. The respondents (women) covered by the study were equally spread over the urban and rural areas of the two states in which the study was conducted. Data relating to their demographic and social background was collected for proper analysis and interpretation of their responses.

Findings

Present Age of Respondents

Out of 250 respondents about 33 per cent are in the age group of 25-30 years, followed by 25 per cent in the age group of 31-35 years and about 18 per cent in the age group of 18-24 years respectively. About 13 per cent of the respondents are above 41 years and about 11 per cent in the age group of 36-40 years. To conclude a very large majority of 33 per cent respondents are in the age range of 25-30 years.

Age at Marriage

Age at marriage is an important variable in the study of domestic violence against women. Younger age at marriage puts a lot of stress for adjustment which may result in use of violence on the part of young husbands.

In Odisha as whole the percentages of respondents who have married at 16 to 20 years of age dropped down to about 63 per cent while percentage of respondents married between 21-24 years and 25-30 years is 24 per cent and about 11 per cent respectably.

Marital Status of Respondents

It is generally assumed that domestic violence is a peculiar phenomenon in which only married women are involved. However, in reality, any woman who is dependent, whether married, unmarried, divorced, separated or widow may fall pray to domestic violence exerted by persons on whom she is dependent. About 93 per cent from Odisha are married followed by 3.5 per cent of separated and two per cent of widow. However, No. of unmarried or divorced respondents is also two per cent.

Educational Level of Respondents

Educational plays a significant role in the life of any individual. Higher the level of education, higher is the potential for resisting any action of injustice, exploitation and torture. As far as women are concerned, education gives them a voice against all types of evils effected on them and empowers them to fight for justice. The percentage of illiterate respondents is only 14 per cent as against that of the respondents in primary level which is about 36, and matric level which is about 24 . However, 2.4 per cent of respondents are in post graduation level and percentage of respondents in middle and senior secondary level is 13 and 3.1 respectively.

Occupational Background of Respondents

Occupational background of the women is an important indicator of their social status. Good occupational background provides higher prestige to the women in their families and in the society. Studies indicate that women engaged in occupations of lower prestige are more likely to be abused.

A large percentage of respondents i.e. about 73 per cent are housewives. As Odisha is economically backward, about 14 per cent of respondents in Odisha are engaged in casual labour as against 4.7 per cent in service, 3 per cent as domestic helper, 2.8 per cent as farm labour. Percentage of respondents engaged in any professional job or business is very low i.e. 1.6 and 1.2 respectively.

Type of Family

The household composition plays an important role for understanding the phenomenon of domestic violence against women. Both joint and nuclear family structure positive and negative impact in promoting and curbing domestic violence. Joint family, the traditional Indian family structure, provides a better scope to share the feelings as well as settle any type of misunderstanding or conflict between the couple or between the daughter-in-law and any of the family members thus curbing the violence on one hand while on the other hand the parents-in-law and other kinsmen continue to have greater affiliation with sons as compared with daughters-in-law. This gives rise to maltreatment of wives by their husbands. Hence, presence of a large number of members in the family not only creates the problem of adjustment but they also act as instigators for domestic violence against women. Nuclear family on the other hand is better for the women to handle the situation with least interference of the in-laws. Secondly, as there is no one else to support, the husband has to find a way out and compromise with the wife. It is observed that almost all the respondents in rural area live in joint family while nuclear family is the trend in urban area.

Religious Backgrounds

Religion is an important institution, which instils a particular philosophy of life in an individual. In the case of women it is observed that their behaviour pattern is influenced by their religious beliefsystem. Ninety three per cent of the respondents interviewed are Hindus while 6.3 per cent are from Christian community and less than one per cent are from Muslims community.

Social Class Background

Maximum respondents i.e. about 39 per cent belong to lower class while 26 per cent belong to middle class, 24 per cent to lower middle class and about six per cent to higher middle class. Only about 5 per cent of respondents belong to upper class which adds testimony to the poor economic condition of the state.

Respondents belonging to families living below poverty line

The respondents belonging to families with and without BPL card does not have much difference i.e. about 49 per cent and 51 per cent respectively.

One of the reason of such anomally may be due to lack of knowledge to of how to procure such card many genuine families living in abject poverty might not be having BPL card with them. However it is observed that domestic violence does not need nor ask for a BPL card to spoil the life of woman living within it.

Condition of Respondents' houses

Percentage of respondents living in Pucca house is only about 19 per cent while that living in semi pucca houses is 24.4 per cent. More percentage of Respondents i.e. 36 per cent live in kutcha houses as against 21 per cent of respondents living in hut / thatched houses.

Nature, Incidence and Extent of Domestic Violence

For the purpose of the present study, domestic violence has been defined as an act carried out by any elder member of the family against any female member with the object of harassing her mentally or causing her a physical injury. Thus, a broader view of violence is taken for the purpose of the study. Further, for the purpose of analysis domestic violence against women has been classified as (i) Physical, (ii) Emotional and (iii) Economic. While describing the nature, incidence and extent of domestic violence, different forms of violence used by perpetrators were considered.

Premarital/Childhood Experience

About 29 per cent of respondents disclosed that their mothers are ill treated by her in-laws where as 71 per cent do not have any such experience.

The reason for more No. of respondents not having experience of their mothers torture may be that they do not want to disclose about their family. And did not answer and the investigator took it as "no" i.e. Not "yes".

Childhood experience of disparity in treatment compared with male siblings-83 per cent have reported not to face such discriminatory treatment as against only 17 per cent have experienced such treatment. The reason for this anomally between the actual practice prevailing in our male dominated society and the response of the victims may be that many of us are not very much conscious about such behaviour, we have internalised such treatment as not a violence or we not know at our childhood days how should we be treated at par with our male siblings.

Experience of Physical Violence in childhood–55 per cent of respondents have experienced physical violence in their childhood.

Types of physical violence faced as a child

It is found that apart from slapping (18 per cent), beating (28 per cent) and mental cruelty (9 per cent) the respondents also categorised pushing (9 per cent), kicking (1 per cent), throwing objects (2 per cent), and worst as holding with rope (2 per cent) as form of violence as they perceived/suffered as a child.

Persons causing Physical violence in childhood

Analysis shows that a majority of the respondents, (about 45 per cent) were indecisive regarding the persons causing physical violence. Percentage of respondents blaming father as causing the violence is about 31 per cent, while respondents blaming mother for this is about 13 per cent, blaming brother is about two per cent, blaming relatives is about eight per cent. However, in 2.4 per cent of respondents blamed some other persons who are not their relatives but caused violence against them.

Frequency of violence in childhood

Percentage of respondents experiencing such violence daily and once/twice in a month is almost same i.e. 13 per cent and 13.4 per cent respectively. There are respondents who suffer from such violence from their own people once/twice in a week (3.9 per cent) while for about 8 per cent of respondents the frequency of violence is uncertain which is still worse for a child.

Pre-marital experience of Sexual Abuse

17 per cent have faced pre-marital sexual abuse as expressed by the respondents.

Persons causing Sexual Abuse

Regarding the persons causing sexual abuse apart from about 83 per cent respondents who kept silent, percentage of respondents blaming relatives and that blaming outsiders for such violence is same i.e. about 9 per cent.

Frequency of Sexual abuse before marriage

Disclosure of pre-marital sexual abuse—In a patriarchal and traditional society like India disclosure of any untoward sexual experience adds more misery to woman and more so to the unmarried girls. Most of the time, without any fault her integrity and morality will be questioned and her character will be assassinated by her own family as well as community members. So she prefers silence and tolerance to disclosure or any discussion with any body. 91.4 per cent of respondents have never discussed as against 8 per cent who have discussed.

Respondents Perceptions of Domestic Violence

The perceptions of domestic violence by respondents who are victims in their childhood and of those who did not experience any violence so far are likely to be different. Such a perception depends upon their life situations, values and availability or non-availability of alternatives. From a study conducted by We Can Campaign, supported by OXFAM, India, it was found that in rural Odisha a woman does not think it any violence up to third slap from his husband. Some of them even think that beating/ slapping to wife is a matter of right of a husband as he takes the charge of maintaining her for the whole life and also as he provides bangles, vermilion and saree which are three basic auspicious symbols of a married Indian lady. Thus, all it depends how one takes it and interprets it.

Further, their reactions are likely to be coloured by presence or absence of other family members. Those who are abused in the presence of others are more likely to feel humiliated as they may develop a feeling of having been let down in the eyes of others.

To understand the perception of domestic violence the respondents were asked as to what in their opinion constituted domestic violence against women. To make it easy violence is divided into three categories like physical, emotional and economic, each is again divided into a No. of types.

Types of Physical Violence faced by women

It is found that beating, pushing and slapping is faced by maximum percentage of respondents i.e. 64,41 and 36 respectively.

The most heinous type of physical violence is torture during pregnancy which is reported by around 39 per cent. Such violence does not hurt physical body only but leaves a grave impression on mind and emotion which has a life risk for the foetus inside the mother's womb.

Other forms of physical violence like kicking, throwing objects and burning is reported by about 27 per cent, 24 per cent and 11 per cent respectively. Beating with cane and holding with rope was also reported. Percentage of sexual coercion reported by about about 11 per cent.

Types of Emotional Violence faced by women

More than half i.e. 51 per cent of the total 250 respondents are the victims of abusive language where as about 49 per cent are insulted in the presence of children/relatives and 45 per cent are treated as servants. Forty three per cent of respondents reported that they are not given freedom to express their views on family matters while 42 per cent are criticised and underestimated for lack of / less intelligence. About 39 per cent of the respondents are blamed for everything that went wrong in the family, 32 per cent are neglected by responsible persons in the in-laws house even their husbands during illness and regarding serious health problems. 30 per cent of respondents are frequently charged for small and negligible matters. Around 29 per cent of the respondents who are compelled to feel guilty for no fault of theirs as against around 28 per cent are blamed for improper house keeping as if it is the duty of the wife only. 26 per cent of respondents are emotionally abused by keeping a constant watch on their movements. About 24 per cent respondents are reported to be victims of this type of emotional violence. Around 21 per cent of them are even prohibited from meeting their parents, relatives and friends and same percentage of respondents are kept under constant stress by giving threats of divorce by their husbands and parents-in-law. About 14 per cent of the respondents were being harassed on the suspicion of their extra-marital relationships, and thereby emotionally abused. From the childhood Indian women are socialised to consider husbands as next to God. Thus, they are emotionally dependent on the husbands objectively and subjectively. This situation is exploited by the husbands for keeping women under constant stress by giving threats of committing suicide by their husbands as reported by 12 per cent of the respondents. However, almost an equal percentage of respondents complain about emotional violence caused by giving them verbal threats of using physical force (7.5 per cent) and by repeatedly harassed by calling names (7.3 per cent).

Types of Economic Violence faced by women

Out of 250 highest percentage of respondents i.e. 64 per cent have no freedom to make purchases of their choice. Thus, their access to the economic resource is denied. Similarly around 56 per cent are being pressurised in some form or other to bring more money from their parents time to time after marriage. By this the women as well as their parental family are under constant mental pressure. The woman knows in spite of poor economic condition of her parents if she does not bring money from them then she will be tortured both physically and mentally by her in-laws. On the other hand, if she brings it will be an added economic burden on their parents who have already spent a lot for her up bringing along with her marriage ceremony itself. May be for this reason it is observed that in both the states initially women prefer to face torture at in-laws place rather to ask any further money after marriage. It is only when the situation goes beyond tolerance they ask money from their parents. Parents too in the hope of a secured and peaceful future give money to their daughter, sometimes even by taking loan from others or even by mortgazing or selling their property.

Another form of economic violence is forcibly making the women dependant by preventing them from taking jobs outside or by forcing them to leave the existing job. Around 14 per cent of respondents are prevented from taking out side job as against nine per cent are forced to leave the existing job. There may be three reasons for such situation. First, that the husband and other seniors in the family intentionally prevent outdoor job so as to exploit the woman for the domestic duties for the whole day and to make her dependent on them for every thing she needs : secondly, some families feel that if women take job outside the home it shows that the husband is not capable enough to maintain the need of his wife and thus the social prestige of the family goes down. This feeling was observed in greater degree in rural Odisha. When the woman is employed she gets a status in the family and as a result she exercises authority. Husbands who are authoritative/dominant in nature may not tolerate this. As a result the husband may force his wife to leave the job.

Apart from all these the worst form of economic abuse is to forcefully collect the full amount of salary or any earning as such from the women and to keep nothing with them for their personal expenditure. In other words though they are earning members in the family they are not free to spend even a single rupee on them. About 15 per cent of the total 254 respondents reported that full amount of their salary or daily income is taken away from them by their husbands or heads of the families.

Causes of Domestic Violence

The causes of domestic violence range from the trivial to bizarre, as just anything can serve as an excuse to severely beat up a woman who is often clueless about how to avoid it. Some of the trivial causes are looking ugly, dressing fashionably, incapable of cooking tasty/palatable food or earning for the family, giving birth to girl child, coming from comparatively well-off family, and difference of opinion etc.

The analysis of data discloses that the phenomenon of domestic violence is not the outcome of any single cause. The violence is caused due to different reasons in different types of families. The personality factors of both the victim and the perpetrators are also responsible for the outbreak of violence. Some of the significant causes as found during the research are: (i) Alcoholic habit of the husband (49 per cent), joblessness of their husbands (40 per cent), husbands stressed constantly under tension due to problems at work place (23 per cent), dowry (31 per cent), doubt of love affairs of the respondents before marriage (25 per cent), lack of education (22 per cent), resistance on their part to sexual abuse (20 per cent), incapability to contribute to the family economy (18 per cent) etc.

However, the overall picture shows that domestic violence against women is caused due to a variety of reasons. A mixed trend of causes of domestic violence is observed in both rural and urban areas.

Instigators of Domestic Violence

It is found that husband is the frequent instigator of domestic violence as reported by about 33 per cent. In 31 per cent of the respondents blame mother-in-law for encouraging violence in the family while 22 per cent of the respondents held other relatives of the husband responsible for instigating violence against them. Only about six per cent of the respondents blame father-in-law followed by around five per cent respondents blaming sister-in-law and around two per cent to brother-in-law as the instigators of violence against them.

However, it is observed that respondents from rural areas blame their mother-in-law and those from urban areas mostly blame their husbands as the main instigators of violence.

Frequency of Violence

To find out the frequency of such violence the respondents were asked to state the frequency of violence they face. The options provided for response were –(i) Daily, (ii) Once/ Twice a week, (iii) Once/Twice a Month, (iv) A number of times in a month, (v) Occasionally and (vi) Uncertain.

It is seen that frequency of violence is influenced by various socio-economic factors like area (rural/urban), economic status and head of the family, Occupation of the women, fulfilment of Dowry demanded by the groom's side etc. Following is the detailed analysis of the frequency of the violence depending upon various such factors.

Frequency of violence in relation to rural/urban area

Violence occurs daily more in urban areas i.e. 16 per cent than in rural areas which is only about six per cent.

Out of total 22 per cent of cases reporting violence occurs once/twice in a month, it is 15 per cent in rural Odisha as against eight per cent in urban Odisha.

Frequency of violence is Once/Twice in a week is more in rural areas (eight per cent) than in urban area (about four per cent)

Cases of violence occurring occasionally is same i.e. about 7.5 per cent for rural and urban area.

Frequency of occurrence of violence is almost same in rural and urban areas of Odisha. But the frequency of violence occurring daily which is 16 per cent and least frequency is 'a number of times in a month' which is 3.5 per cent–both are reported from urban cases.

> However, it is difficult for the victims to calculate the frequency as well as to disclose it to an outsiders as many of them still think it as their personal affairs. Is it really a personal afire!!

Frequency of violence in relation to Economic Status of respondents

It is interesting to note that domestic violence occurs irrespective of one's economic condition, in all families. From the analysis it is found that there is no such structured/ proportional relationship between the economic status of the family and occurrence of the domestic violence.

Frequency of violence in relation to occupation of the respondents

During the study, it is evident that frequency of violence is maximum in case of non-earning wives which is around 73 per cent. Housewives have to face all the tantrum of torture as they have hardly any option to go outside. Maximum housewive's opinion that the frequency of violent activities they face is about 20 per cent. Around 11 per cent of housewives experience violence occasionally. Around 16 per cent housewives are confused about the frequency of violence which is uncertain.

Professional women face least violence

Excepting housewives, women in any other occupation experience violence less frequently. Cases of violence faced by women who are doing formal jobs is around five per cent, . Though such women contribute quite substantial to the family economy, they also face violence as reported by around 14 per cent and three per cent of victims respectively. Around three per cent of women, who work as domestic helper, reported about the violence they face. Professional women face least violence. During the study no such case was found. May be the victims who were interviewed during the study did not hold any professional job.

Frequency of violence in relation with Women Headed Family

The paradox that a woman only better understands the plight of another women is clearly implied in the above table. It is expected that the frequency of violence is less or zero in a woman-headed family. Around 23 per cent of respondents, living in woman-headed family reported violence which is less as compared to those living in man-headed family.

Frequency of violence in relation to Types of Marriage

The frequency of violence is more in arranged marriage i.e. 78 per cent as compared to that in case of love marriage which is only 22 per cent. The frequency of violence is once or twice in a week in case of arranged marriage as reported by only 9.4 per cent of respondents in Odisha. However, the frequency of once/ twice in a month in case of arranged marriage is reported by more percentage 21.3 per cent of respondents.

Duration of Domestic Violence

Duration for which the respondents were facing domestic violence is not identical in different states. Women are keeping silent for years together and tolerating the violence as part of their life. Around 27 per cent of respondents are tolerating domestic violence since one to three years. While maximum of 35 per cent of respondents experience it for less than one year, percentage of women who are facing domestic violence for more than five years is around 17 per cent.

Though the domestic violence act is more than four years old, sizable section of women as evident from the table experiencing domestic violence for more than three years and even the number of victims, suffering since one year is not less.

'The reason why they are living in abusive situation'-(FGD report)–

- There is no other alternative, we have already married them and to tolerate as our bad luck,
- As parents are no more, who will look after our children and feed us! No brother or any other relatives will like to take the burden.
- If we will leave our in-laws' place, we will be criticised by our community for our incapability to manage our own married life.
- Our broken marriage, if disclosed in the public it will defame our parental family which will be a problem for the marriage of our younger siblings.
- We do not want to be humiliated by the wife(ves) of our brother(s) nor to be a burden to our parents.
- Women's life is to tolerate all the miseries of the world, that is why God has created women. Our mothers, their mothers have gone through this stage of life.
- If we will go to any short stay home, what will happen to the future of our children.

It is important to notice how they have internalised the fact that domestic violence against women is part of life. Secondly, it is evident from their statement that even after much intervention of many GOs and NGOs women are not assured for an empathetic attitude of the society towards the survivors of domestic violence. Last but not the least one of the major reason of their staying in abusive situation is their feeling of insecurity for food and shelter as they are not self sufficient.

Abortion due to physical or mental torture

Harassment during pregnancy is the worst form of domestic violence which affects the health of the unborn child. The analysis shows that domestic violence has resulted in abortion of pregnancy as reported by 21 per cent respondents.

However, this percentage is much less than what happens in reality. The reason for such underreported might be; (a) The women themselves do not know the very fact that domestic violence can affect pregnancy and (b) Victims of domestic violence in many cases do not disclose the truth before doctor. So domestic violence is not identified as a proper antenatal care and other common factors are made responsible for abortion.

Impact of Domestic Violence on Children

Change in the behaviour of child / children due to such family disturbance

Women are harassed and tortured even in front of their children. And this experience influence the innocent and immature mind of the children which is reflected in their behaviour. 52 per cent of respondents have observed behavioural change of their children. The frustration and confusion of the child's mind is manifested in their unexpected behaviour. Many a times they are associated with many antisocial activities.

Reactions to Domestic Violence

The reactions by the victims are likely to be different depending upon their level of education, family background, life situation and availability or non-availability of alternatives. Further, their reactions are likely to be different by the presence or absence of other family members in the family or outsiders.

In a patriarchal society like India the plight of a girl/woman is miserable both before and after marriage. Ever since she realises her own existence she is trained to keep silent. Gradually as she grows she loses the confidence to say "NO" to any violence against her, especially when it is caused by her husband or in-laws. Secondly, a good married life is dream as well as pride of every woman. So any apprehension that the disclosure of disturbed married life or about domestic violence may affect their pride. They usually don't discuss or inform it to anybody as long as they can tolerate. But when it goes beyond their tolerance their first reaction is to inform their parental or in-laws family.

When asked about as to if they have informed their parental family it is shocking to notice that more than half, i.e. 51 per cent of the victims have not shared the issue even with their parental family.

It is found that the percentage of respondents sharing about the violence with in-laws is about 32 per cent. It can be said that the first reaction or immediate reaction to unbearable domestic violence is sharing or informing about the torture to their own people. Secondly, as seen the percentage of respondents sharing their feelings/grievances with their close family members.

When they do not get any satisfactory or expected help they would venture to seek the assistance and guidance from outside (informal) sources. It does not mean that all the victims of domestic violence will seek intervention from formal sources after having failed to control the abusive situation. It is, however, expected that few victims of violence will seek intervention from formal agencies. It is in this context that the victims were asked "Did you ever seek the help from outside (formal agencies) to prevent your husband or parents-in-law from abusing you"?

Sharing the information with formal institution -

Around 91 per cent have not gone to any formal institute as against only nine per cent who have gone to a formal institute for help.

Intervention/Guidance by the members of parental family, in-laws' family : (FGD with 20 rural women)–

- Family members of the respondents' families did not intervene when the respondents were being abused (reported by 5-6 out of 20 participants).
- The members of both parental as well as in-laws' family advised the victims to patch up with their family members.
- The family members valued the continuation of the victims in the family and advised them to reconcile to the situation for saving their marriage and the future of their children.
- The victims are even advised by the family members (12 out of 20) to mend their behaviour and try to tolerate the violence as that will restore the social prestige of both the families.
- Initially some of the members of parental family even advised to evaluate their (victim's) own personal situation and then to work out their own strategies to deal with the situation.
- After a long time of tolerance and compromise very few parental families (as reported by three out of 20) advised to break off marital relationship and to report the problem to police authorities.

Suggestions by the victims for Reducing/Curbing Domestic Violence

The victims were asked about their own suggestions regarding the way/strategies to curb and protect oneself from domestic violence. It was found that more percentage of respondents i.e. 20 per cent opine that self employment is the one of the best way to protect women for domestic violence while around 13 per cent suggest to we wise to tackle the situation.

Around 10 per cent of the total respondents think that facing problems with self confidence will protect the women from domestic violence. While six per cent encourage the women to face the problem with enthusiasm. The other remedial suggestion given by the victim are to be silent (5.15 per cent), to be literate (3.57 per cent) and to take help from the law (4.96 per cent), however, few of them (1.38 per cent) suggested that one should not take the domestic abuses seriously so that it will make us mentally weak rather they should neglect such violence and be firm inside. Maximum respondents i.e. around 13 per cent suggested self employment as one of the alternative strategy to protect women from domestic violence as it will reduce the dependency of women on their husband and give them recognition in the family. Education is suggested by 4.3 per cent of respondents.

However, around two per cent of respondents opine that women should help themselves to face the challenge of domestic violence. It shows that maybe they stress on the fact that the women should break the silence to eliminate domestic violence.

Conclusion and Suggestion

Conclusion

Domestic violence in its manifold manifestations is inherent in the current patterns of society irrespective of economic, educational status of victim or even beyond rural-urban setting. It is deeply embedded in the consequent increase of social and economic insecurity for victims and survivors. It cannot be dealt with by safety nets and superficial solutions, or by palliatives such as micro-credit schemes, capacity building workshops, etc. we have to recognise that it is important not only to support the pluralities of living but also to challenge the primacy we have given to materialism over all other forms of human action and expression. The dominant and dominating pursuit of material wealth has negated more comprehensive value systems. The challenge is not to regulate and reform laws and policies against such violence but to transform them to action so that we can all live in harmony and justice with the richness and diversities of all cultural and life forms.

Following are some of the feasible but time taking suggestion to overcome the age old pandemic gender based social problem:

- Domestic violence (D.V.) should be defined and documented separately White Paper (SWETA PATRA) of State Govt.
- The Central and State Governments should conduct regular training programmes of law enforcement officers, judges, other court personnel and prosecutors to identify and respond more effectively to the cases of domestic violence against women in particular and crimes against women in general. The units of law enforcement officers specially targeting domestic violence against women should be created, developed, trained and expanded.
- Similarly, data collection and communication systems, linking police, prosecutors and courts for the purpose of identifying domestic violence against women should be introduced at the earliest.
- A massive awareness campaign involving the civil societies, NGOs, community, religious leaders, women's organisations, National Service Scheme, and opinion makers at all levels is necessary to counter the present trend of violence against women in general and domestic violence in particular.
- Domestic violence against women is an area where rights of women are not fully secured by laws and there are laws which are either discriminatory against women or provide a weak enforcement and punishment mechanism which do not deter the recurrence of crimes against women. It was observed that the victims of domestic violence have not approached to seek relief available to them under different legislations as they were not sure that the law would give them sufficient and durable relief. Hence, it is necessary to see that the laws and orders against perpetrators of domestic violence are strictly enforced and no one is left without punishment.

- Moreover, the entire gamut of laws related to abuse and harassment of women need a comprehensive and thorugh review in the light of the present trends and requirements.
- The Central and State Governments should develop, enlarge and strengthen social support services programmes for the women who are victims of domestic violence.
- Very few victims of domestic violence approach to medical professionals for treatment. Very few, again, disclose that the mental or physical injury is caused due to domestic violence. It is, therefore, necessary to give proper training to our medical personnel in dealing with and treating the cases of domestic violence against women. The training should cover the collection and preservation of evidence, analysis, providing expert testimony and treatment.
- The State Governments should carry out the implementation of comprehensive strategies addressing domestic violence against women that are sensitive to the needs and safety of the victims and hold offenders accountable for their crimes.
- Free legal aid and advice should be made available to Victims of Domestic Violence who are uneducated, backward and economically disadvantaged.
- A carefully planned mass media strategy is of critical importance for women's employment in general and domestic violence against women in particular. Issues relating to domestic violence against women and awareness of family members on the tragic effects of domestic violence should be packaged in interesting, viewer friendly programmes for assimilation and absorption in social psyche.
- The Central and State Governments should encourage to develop and support projects to implement community driven initiatives to address the needs of victims of domestic violence. A large number of NGOs have emerged in different parts of the country, having to their credit significant contribution, expertise, and experience at grass-root level in projecting and addressing women issues. The services of these organisations should be encouraged, supported and availed of, so that the eradication of the evil of domestic violence against women becomes a truly national and peoples' movement.

- Another deep concern of women in the rural areas of the state is the tremendous physical and emotional violence which they experience when the men in their families are drunk. Freedom of families from liquor is their first need. The State Governments should enforce the prohibition in more widespread and effective ways in their efforts to minimise the incidence of domestic violence against women.

References

Kothari Smitu and Wendy Harcourt, The violence of development, Development(2004)47(1), 3–7. doi:10.1057/palgrave. development. 1100024.

Visaria, L. (2000). Violence against Women: A Field Study. Economic and Political Weekly, 35(20), 1742-1751. Retrieved December 2, 2013.

Abbey,A., BeShears,R.,Clinton-Sherrod,A. M.,andMcAuslan, P.(2004). Psychology of Women Quarterly, 28, 323–332. "Similarities and differences in women's sexual assault experiences based on tactics used by the perpetrator".

Fried, S. T.(2003). Violence against Women. Health and Human Rights, 6(2), 88-111.

Uma Narayan, Cross Cultural Connections, Border Crossings, and "Death by Culture": Thinking about Dowry Murders in India and Domestic Violence Murders in the United States. In Dislocating Cultures: Identities, Traditions and Third World Feminism (New York: Routledge, 1997): 83-117.

8

Gender in India Discrimination and Violence towards Women

Dr Ramakrushna Pradhan and Smt Sukanya Kakoty

Introduction

The very fact that the words 'sex' and 'gender' are in common parlance used interchangeably reflects the extremely in-depth nature of a 'gender-blind' society that we have been living in. Gender studies and women issues are being discussed and debated extensively and is widely available in literature, yet the violence and atrocities against women have not been seen diluting in both private and public spheres. As explained by Andrew Heywood, *"Gender refers most basically, to the social construction of sexual difference. As such, 'gender' is clearly distinct from 'sex'....... 'Sex' highlights biological and therefore ineradicable differences between females and males, while 'gender' denotes a set of culturally defined distinctions between women and men."*

In a place like India where women are worshipped in forms of goddesses and Hindu mythology itself provides with varied examples of emancipator roles played by goddesses like Durga and Kali, the paradox lies in that the Indian women are brutally beaten up in their own homes. The scars are not just physical but mental as well. The issue of gender has been already made so complicated in spite of the fact that it is not so. Gender has been a pressing issue world over, however in the context of India it is further more knotty and puzzling due to the presence of so many other factors.

The concept of 'feminism' is mostly misconstrued. It is understood as something to do with the emancipation of women at the cost of their male counterparts. This kind of implication is rather wrong and back-fires the whole idea of a fair understanding.

As Liberal philosophy suggests, *"If human beings are thought of first and foremost as individuals, they must be entitled to the same rights and the same respect, meaning that all forms of disadvantage or discrimination, based on factors such as gender, race, colour, creed, religion or social background, are viewed as morally questionable, if not indefensible."* Therefore, one can gather two things from it; one that in terms of rights and respect, gender difference should not be considered and that it denotes a moral call. As such in fundamentally liberal societies, women rights are seen to be protected in a more conscious way.

Evolution of women's rights

It was in the nineteenth century when for the first time women's rights were recognised in the political platform. Until then only men were allowed to vote hence having a say in the political decisions of a state. This kind of gendered discrimination meted out to almost half of the population reflected a patriarchal state-system. But, with the result of the broad suffrage movements, the 'first-wave feminism' appeared bringing for the women the right to vote and contest for electoral offices. This was a big leap forward as it gave women the power to decide for themselves and make changes they wanted for themselves. The problems related to women however persisted in the private spaces. That called for a more sweeping and revolutionary social change process bringing about the 'second-wave feminism' in and around the 1960-70s. Hence, it was basically the beginning of discovering feminist aspects within the sphere of family and society. The 'third-wave feminism' was an extension of the second and related mostly to the power relationships that gender in society plays. The inherent problems associated with the institution of patriarchy as a norm started to be questioned. This came to be known as 'radical feminism' and dealt in addressing the issue of subordination of women as an outcome of patriarchy.

While on one hand liberal feminists advocate for gender equality in terms of achieving equal rights like men in the public sphere including right to education, suffrage, pursuing a career and so on; socialist feminists press for upholding the social rights of women. Radical feminism argues for 'equal personal power' for women. In a sense, all support that the prevailing order of a 'difference attitude' towards women reflecting both a latent and apparent subordination or 'looking down upon' in legal, social, private, political and other spheres needs to be addressed and checked. However, a distinct division within the broad parameters of feminist theories is 'difference feminism' that advocate on the factor of accepting the 'difference' between the two genders in terms of the biological differences that exist and that in its pursuit of establishing equality should not be at par to wanting to become 'like-man' but celebrate female values and feel emancipated through 'difference'.

The Indian Context

The struggle for women's rights in the public arena was quite rigorous in the West, the outcome of which is the already mentioned women suffrage. It was undeniably the first attempt in recognising the importance of a political decision of a woman, especially in a highly male-centric society, a vote that had the power to affect both the sexes. The movement behind the assurance of political rights for women itself speaks about its significance for an identity that was always there lying dormant and not acknowledged until then. But, in context of India, the circumstances are slightly different. India (independent India) attained its independence in the year 1947 and since then women of India were not discriminated on the basis of gender as far as political rights were considered. They enjoyed equal rights just like the Indian men. This feature of a newly independent India definitely demonstrated a progressive nature of the Indian society and the high regards it had for the 'fairer sex'. Not only that, innumerable examples of women leading the public or political platform or walking at par with men has been there in every page of history. India has been boasting about women leaders since the time of Razia Sultana to Jhansi Ki Rani Lakshmi Bai to Indira Gandhi. Apart from that, the freedom movement of India is affluent with female population, a time when women did not hesitate to come out to the streets and fight for a nation's independence. Some of the names to be mentioned are Rani Channama of Kittur, Rani Begum Hazrat Mahal of Awadh, Rani of Ramgarh, Rani Jindan Kaur, Rani Tace Bai, Baiza Bai, Chauhan Rani, Tapasvini Sarojini Naidu, Vijay Laxmi Pandit among many others. In fact, a large number of women were part of Mahatma Gandhi's campaigns and processions. As Maharani Kamala Devi Chattopadyay said, *"The politics of the nation square measure the supreme need of humanity in its decided to scale the ladder of freedom. No one sex can build up a nation. Woman has her own distinctive contribution to create for the purpose of enriching life so that it should fulfil its own divine mission to perfection, so within the struggle for freedom they're destined to play their legitimate part and bear their share of the responsibility in breaking the chains that weigh heavily on people".*

However, gender problems existed during the pre-independence period also and even in more cruel forms of social practices like *Sati* system, child marriage, polygamy, war, displacement, migration has seen plight of women.

Gender in India: Discrimination and Violence towards Women

Confusing Identity Issue?

The tricky part in India is that if any form of violence is committed against women, it is seen through the prism of multiple identities. The confusion arises because of the presence of varied forms of social and economic stratification and different religious and other identities; an issue of gender violence like rape, molestation etc. is examined under various lenses. Question such as— "Is it because she was a Dalit girl? Was she too 'urban' and 'open-minded'? Was she wearing 'proper clothes'? Was she at a wrong place at a wrong time?" seem to come naturally to peoples' mind.

Although in an instance of a recent rape and murder case of Badaun, a state in Uttar Pradesh is a striking example for confusion in '*multiple identity crises*'. In the unfortunate Badaun gang rape case, the victims (two girls) were not only brutally raped and murdered but also hung openly in a tree which adds the 'caste' layer. Although the 'caste' issue cannot be completely ruled out observing the brutality of the act of hanging for public display, this depicts more about an archetype of power patterns in a male dominated society. As in this particular case, it was judged also on the basis of social stratification as the girls came from a very backward caste, because of the presence of different identities in the Indian society the issue of 'gender concern' gets often little diluted. Gender violence and women subordination exists widely and ignores the parameters of being rich or poor, coming from upper or lower strata of society, educated or literate *et al.*

Women at home

The most fundamental form of gender discrimination starts at home. In the context of Indian society, subordination of women has seen many forms. Signs of both conscious and casual attempts start since the time of birth of a girl child. The undesirability of a girl child seems evident from the presence of social evils like female foeticide and infanticide. And if at all the girl child gets a chance to come into this world, a sense of rejection towards her becomes a daily affair. Subordination of women is seen in rituals and practices as if it is a part of natural order. Indian languages and common dialects are affluent with metaphors and terminologies for women as daughters, wives and mothers such as '*Paraya Dhan*' meaning 'Someone Else's Property', blessings such as '*Sau Putravati Bhava*' meaning 'May you become a mother of hundred sons', etc. Not only that, if the woman of the house transcends the male member in every chore, she is understood to be the '*Man of the house*' and when a man displays cowardice traits he is cursed calling '*Churiya Pehen Lo*' that means 'Go and be a girl (wear bangles like one does)'. This explains the roots of other issues like separation, divorce and maintenance rights, rights of inheritance of property by women that if fundamentally dictated by the patriarchal norms of society or personal norms of a household.

Women at work

"Women do two-thirds of the world's work and receive ten per cent of the world's income and own one per cent of the means of production." Violence against women have been not just sexual exploitation but non-sexual as well. Forms of gendered discrimination are very much evident in the work place where they are paid unequally for the same kind of job as men. They are mostly hired on short-term contracts with low wages and poor working conditions. In a developing country like India with a teeming population serves as a perfect destination for Transnational Corporations (TNCs) to find cheap and vulnerable workers. These corporations mainly target women to work in their sweatshops as they are easily exploited in terms of denial of minimum wages and long hours of work, poor and unsafe working conditions and verbal and physical abuse whenever there are signs of protest. In fact, in sweatshops, there are 90 per cent of women workers. The fact, that these women workers are poor and uneducated makes them carry on with such injustice. But if poverty and lack of education would be the sense behind exploitation of women, then probably it wouldn't count just as a 'gender issue'. Gender problems are such deep-rooted that even educated women in fine work places face a lot of sexual exploitation from either their superior or any other male co-worker.

Woman as a Commodity

Another gender-crooked argument in Indian society lies in its obsession for fair skin that is targeted mostly towards women. Fairness products, media and marketing strategies target women with darker skin colour and as a result promote the 'commoditisation' of female physical attributes. The worst part is how the 'desired complexion' agenda has repercussions not just over one's physical appeal but nudges social acceptance. Matrimonial sections of Indian newspapers are flooded with demands for 'fair-skinned' women as thought to be more appealing and in fact social evils such as dowry system is still sustaining (in spite of its illegal status) and constantly determining the price of a bride in terms of her physical attributes in general and 'fair skin' in particular. All of it poses a question mark on the course of gender justice in Indian society and it has to be realised that in this process both a fair-skinned or a dark-skinned women are being subjugated because for the former, her social inclusion lies merely on her outer appearance rather than the inner qualities that define her.

Women in Social Sphere

As if restrictions on women in every walk to life was not enough that in India another dimension on moral policing on women exist in the form of 'Khap Pachayats'. Khap Panchayats are kind of 'caste councils' prevalent in the villages of Haryana majorly, that have self-established themselves as moral and societal guardians of women and constantly comment and instruct on how a woman should dress or behave. According to a report in *The Hindu*, Khap Panchayats of Haryana not only dictate on the dress code of women but also restrict them from using of mobile phones. Such actions of extra-constitutional bodies depict nothing but an extreme practice of male patriarchal system evident and visible widely in public life. The bodily honour or physicality of a woman is concluded to be a part of wider social or community responsibility.

Positive Developments

Indian society appears to be a land of paradoxes when women issues are concerned. On one hand, it claims to emerge as a powerful state, but on the other hand, a bulk of the population that are women are ignored their basic rights of a secured existence as if it a part of the natural order. Policies and laws encouraging women's rights are many, but successful implementation is sketchy. One boasts about a 'Kiran Bedi' whenever 'courage and woman' is discussed but a simple woman cannot gather courage enough to walk the streets alone. An important query arises whether rights of a woman should be her 'call' alone? Shouldn't the men be a part of women's movements too? Should women's issues and literature be discussed only by largely female scholars alone? In India, the saddest part is not just Indian women being unsafe but even female foreign nationals to come to visit the country feel unsafe about it. Goa, which has been one of India's most desired foreign tourist destination has been in news from time to time for all bad reasons. According to estimates made by the Associated Chambers of Commerce and Industry of India, visits to India by female tourists have dropped by 35 per cent in the first three months in 2013. In this way India is likely to lose foreign currency injected by its tourism industry. For once and for all the image of man as the 'protector' should stop. As evident from the very unfortunate 'Nirbhaya' case in the capital city of Delhi, this girl was brutally gang raped and mutilated in a moving bus in front of a male friend of hers. This explains how the universal image of a man to be the 'protector' is defied. If there is anything that can protect our men and women is education and change in mentality. However, this incident displayed a sea-change in the outrage of both Indian women and men against grave sexual offences. This incident generated widespread public protest both in the country and internationally. Men came out in the streets to protest in great numbers.

A silver lining in the cloud and light at the end of the tunnel is always welcome. The 'Nirbhaya Gang rape' did change the vision of many men and women in India and abroad about a radical change in the concept of recognising a 'Rape victim'. Report of Justice Verma Committee that came out in the aftermath of the 'Nirbhaya case' has been a ground-breaking attempt for the first time in India as it was a serious attempt in laying down protocols for wrecking patriarchy in almost all forms and institutions. Its recommendations included upholding the 'honour' of a rape victim by replacing it with the word 'survivor'. The Report also includes redefining the concept of rape and various forms of sexual crimes like stalking, cyber crimes, molestation, acid attacks etc. Also 'marital rape' and sexual violence in the LGBT community was noticed. The Report also suggested protocols for the police in attending rape cases in terms of both registering it and questioning of 'victims'.

Conclusion

India though an old civilisation is a new state. Notwithstanding the remarkable changes in the position of women in free India, there exists a great divergence between the constitutional position and stark reality of deprivation and degradation. Whatever whiff of emancipation has blown in Indian society, has been inhaled and enjoyed by the urban women, their population belonging to the rural areas are still totally untouched by the wind of changes. They still have been living in miserable conditions, steeped in poverty, ignorance, superstition and slavery. There still exists a wide gulf between the goals enunciated in the Constitution, legislations, policies, plans, programmes and related mechanisms on the one hand and the situational reality on the status and rights of women in India, on the other. The human rights scenario in the country continues to be dismal and depressing. Women are being brutalised, commodified, materialised and subjected to inhuman exploitation and discrimination. In fact, the plight of Indian women is such that, the Thomson Reuters Foundation's global poll attributed India as the fourth most dangerous place for the women in the world. With this background, the paper analyses women right as human right: constitutional and legal provisions in India.

Situational Reality

For women in India, discrimination begins even in the womb and at birth. When it comes to sex ratio, the latest census figures show that the number of girls in the 0-6 age group has fallen to the lowest since independence – a mere 914 girls for every 1000 boys. The governments at the Centre and states have been lax in implementation of the PC and PNDT Act (Pre-conception and Pre-natal Diagnostic Techniques Act, 1994) that bans sex selective abortions. In the health and survival front, the Global Gender Gap Report 2011 shows that India's performance is at rock-bottom (at 134th place among 135 countries). The government's policies on food security and women's health far from urgently correcting this appalling situation are only calculated to make women even more vulnerable. The discrimination against women is even more when it come political representation. In a country where the President of the republic and the Speaker of the Lok Sabha are women, it is quite unfortunate to witness abysmally under representation of women in Indian Parliament and Assemblies in states. With great fan-fare, the UPA-II government passed the Women's Reservation Bill only to derail it in the pretext of lack of consensus in the Lok Sabha. This pure political theatre is organised by the government of the day with golden collaboration with the MPs across party lines illustrating their patriarchal prejudices. Further, in Panchayats, 50 per cent of the seats are reserved for women. However, in the style of 'Panch Pati' syndrome, the husband acts on behalf of the elected woman, relegating her to a mere puppet.

Women continue to have an unequal access to land and other resources. At work place too gender bias is rampant. Even in

MGNREGA for instance women are often denied work on the ground of their gender. In many colleges and Universities, women teachers are asked to observe dress codes while their male counterparts are free at their mercy. In many professions, there is a sexist emphasis on women's appearance and attractiveness rather than on their skills. For instance, norms related to weight and appearances are applied only to female air cabin crew and not to male stewards. A Maharashtra Tribal Development Minister recently said that Tribal women trained as airhostesses could not get jobs since their looks were not physically attractive enough. Women Badminton players few months back were told that they must compulsorily wear short skirts to look attractive rather than to choose clothes that they as sportspersons find comfortable. Very recently, the Indian Air Force Vice Chief described women fighter pilots as a bad investment because they might take maternity leave. Similarly, an Army Vice Chief said that appointing women as army officers was undesirable because male jawans could not be expected to take orders from a woman.

Not the least, women are demeaned and denied dignity throughout their life. Their labour inside the home and family continue to be kept invisible. They have unequal access to work. The Global Gender Gap 2011 ranks India at 131st place among 134 countries on the question of women's economic participation and opportunity. Only 35 per cent of women in the country above 15 years of age participate in economic activities in compare to 85 per cent of male counterparts. Unemployment rates are very high for women. According to NSSO 61st round, the unemployment rate in 2004-05 in 20-24 age groups was 15 per cent for rural women and 27 per cent for urban women while 12 per cent and 16 per cent for their male counterparts in rural and urban areas respectively. The tragic fact also doesn't stop there. It continues to be more staggering as 64 per cent of women in rural are self-employed only means to more exploitation and subjugation. Eighty three per cent of rural women workers are tied down to primary sector activities like agriculture. More than 12 per cent of all urban women workers are domestic workers. Women are paid less than men for the same work - at all levels of employment. The government has not done anything substantial in this regard.

In the front of violence against women particularly sexual terrorism, the data of National Crime Records Bureau are alarming. Among all major crimes including murder, robbery or kidnapping, instances of rape have risen at the steepest rate in the past 40 years. Incidents of rape in the country have increased by 791 per cent since 1971 whereas murder increased by just 240 per cent and robbery by 178 per cent. Kidnappings though increased by 630 per cent – but the rate of rape is far higher than this. The national capital of India – Delhi only constitutes 25 per cent of all the rapes in India. And 97 per cent of rapists are known to their victims (family members, neighbours, friends, acquaintances etc.). After sustained campaign by women groups, the Government of the day has drafted the Criminal Procedure Bill 2011 to expand the scope of sexual assault laws, but nothing has been done substantially to prevent sexual terrorism against women since then.

It seems that in a country like India, the problem of violence against women is a result of a long standing power imbalance between men and women. Men have control over access to property and resources. There is also a sexual division of labour in India that results in female exploitation – physically, mentally, and commercially.

What can be done?

When women protest against their exploitation, many try to silence them. The experience of Bhanwari Devi, the 'Sathin' from Rajasthan, is a case in point. She was gang-raped for working against child marriage practiced by the upper castes in her village.

According to the NCRB (National Crime Records Bureau) 2008, respect for women seem to be the worst in Andhra Pradesh, which accounted for 83.5 per cent of cases under Indecent Representation of Women (Prohibition) Act of total cases across the country. Out of a total 1,200 such cases, Andhra had registered 1,005 incidents in this regard. The NCRB data clearly points to the profile of the average rapist – over 75 per cent were known to the victims. In fact, nearly 10 per cent were relatives. Another disturbing aspect was that about a quarter of the rape victims were minors.

During the Fourth World Conference on Women held in Beijing in September 1995, the United Nations Secretary-General, Boutros Boutros-Ghali, said that violence against women is a universal problem that must be universally condemned. The United Nations has termed violence against women as a gross violation of human rights. What are the reasons for this sorry state of affairs? Issues may be various and varied, however a few basic issues deserve specific mention: lack of awareness, lack of social and economic empowerment, lack of political will, feebleness of accountability mechanisms, lack of enforcement by the police force and lack of gender culture. To overcome this iron chain, the women of the world must unite and to fight for their rights. They have nothing to lose but their chains. Hence, wake up, stand up and fight for your rights.

References

Heywood, A. (2011), "Gender in Global Politics" in *Global Politics*, UK: Palgrave Macmillan.

Heywood, A. (2011), "Society in a global age" in *Global Politics*, UK: Palgrave Macmillan..

Heywood, A. (2011), "Gender in Global Politics" in *Global Politics*, UK: Palgrave Macmillan.

Ibid.

Singh, M. (2014), "Role of Women in India's Struggle for Freedom", in *International Journal of Research*, 1 (2): 37-56.

Chatterjee, P. (2014), "Caste adds another layer to the double rape, murder in Badaun", report in *The Indian Express*, June 6, 2014, Online [web], Accessed 15 Sept 2014, url : http://indianexpress.com/article/india/india-others/caste-adds-another-layer-to-the-double-rape-murder-in-badaun/

Dube, L. (1988), "On the Construction of Gender: Hindu Girls in Patrilineal India", in *Economic and Political Weekly*, 23 (18): WS11-WS19.

Impacts of Globalisation on the Rights of Women Workers.

Shevde, N (2008), "All's fair in love and cream: A cultural case study of Fair and Lovely in India", in *Advertising and Society Review*, 9 (2): 1-9.

Dogra, CS. (2013), "Jeans, mobiles and Khap Panchayats", The Hindu, 19 Oct 2013, Online[web], Accessed 26.9.2014, url: http://www.thehindu.com/news/national/jeans-mobiles-and-khap-panchayats/article5248924.ece

Bagri NT, (2013), "India scrambles to reassure tourists shaken by recent attacks on women", published in *The New York Times*, Accessed on 2 Sept 2014, Url: http://www.nytimes.com/2013/06/11/world/asia/rape-cases-are-making-tourists-wary-of-visiting-india.html?_r=02012 Delhi Gang rape, Accessed 10 Sept 2014, url: http://en.wikipedia.org/wiki/2012_Delhi_gang_rape

Report of the Committee on Ammendments to Criminal Law, Justice J.S.Verma (retd), Chairman, Justice Leila Seth (retd) (member), Justice Gopal Subramanium (member), January 23rd 2013, Accessed 8 Sept 2014, URL: *www.thehindu.com / multimedia / ... / Justice_Verma_Comm_1340438a.pdf*

9

Manual Scavenging and its Effects on Dalit Women in India

Sanghamitra Parida

"In India a man is not a scavenger because of his work. He is a scavenger because of his birth irrespective of the question whether he does scavenging or not."

(B. R. Ambedkar)

It a great shame on India, which is the largest democracy in the world promising equality, liberty/freedom, justice and fraternity through its living constitution, that a large number of its people particularly the so-called manual scavengers are being deprived of these very democratic principles that it is supposed to protect. It may not be out of place to say that even after more than sixty seven years of independence, manual scavenging in India continue to be more or less in the same state in which they were in the pre-independence days. Manual scavenging is a caste-based and hereditary occupation for Dalits in general and Dalit women in particular. Among manual scavengers, the majority happen to be the women who have no other option but to inherit the despicable job from their mothers or mother-in-laws. Needless to say that scavenging is the practice of manual cleaning of human excreta from dry latrines (without flush system) where the scavengers crawl into the dry latrines and collect the human excreta most of the times with their bare hands and carry it on their head in a container to dispose it off.

Hence, manual scavenging is a serious kind of social exclusion which, unfortunately, is the result of the structural features of our society. Moreover, in India, social exclusion revolves around some sections of the population, particularly, dalits, adivasis, women and minorities.

Manual scavenging and social exclusion

Social exclusion, simply speaking, refers to the process in which individuals or a particular section of society may become cut off from complete involvement in the wider society. It prevents individuals or groups from getting opportunities open to the majority of the population. Social exclusion is involuntary. That is to say, exclusion is practiced regardless of the wishes of those who are excluded. The term social exclusion broadly, indicates the relative deprivation of any person or group of persons on various predetermined criterion. Manual scavengers constitute one such socially, economically, psychologically and politically marginalised section of the society. They are the victims of social exclusion by caste, sex, and ethnicity and by religion. In the society, they are isolated, discriminated and deprived of equal access to social and economic opportunities. Thus, it is closely connected with poverty and illiteracy. Dalit women are the ignorant part of Indian society where they are excluded from the mainstream due to the caste and gender. They are facing the discrimination including isolation in village, caste- -based violence and gender-discrimination and so on. Thus, discrimination against dalit women cannot be seen as just a problem of Dalit women but it is affecting the rights and dignities of Dalit women. Therefore, in the Indian context, the core feature of social exclusion is the denial of equal opportunities by certain groups of the society which impose themselves upon others that leads the inability of an individual to participate in the basic political, economic and social functioning of society. Manual scavengers in India constitute one such socially excluded class.

Strictly speaking, manual scavengers are the untouchables (dalits of dalits) and they are considered to be so 'impure' that their mere touch severely pollutes members of all other caste. Although other low castes are also subjected to subordination and exploitation to some extent, they do not suffer the extreme forms of exclusion reserved for 'untouchables'. They are even prohibited from sharing drinking water or participating in collective religious worship, social ceremonies and festivals etc.

Manual scavenger means a person engaged or employed on regular or frequent basis by an individual or a local authority or a public or private agency, for manually cleaning, carrying, disposing of, or otherwise handling in any manner, human excreta in an insanitary latrine or in an open drain or pit into which human excreta from insanitary latrines is disposed of, or on a railway track, before the excreta fully decomposes. Many of us usually get confused between safai karmacharis and the people who do manual scavenging. The former normally include persons engaged as 'Sweepers' or 'sanitation/cleaning workers' in municipalities, government and private offices. They may be direct employees of these bodies (municipalities, government/ private sector organisations) or may be contract employees who happen to be working for these organisations. However, Safai Karamcharis, per se, are not manual scavengers. Manual scavenging is the removal of excreta (night soil) manually from "dry toilets", i.e., the toilets without modern flush system.

The system of building public toilets and employing people to remove excreta was introduced during British rule in India, when municipalities were constituted. That time, often containers were used in such toilets, which needed to be emptied daily. After the invention of flush type toilets, all other types of toilets disappeared from the western world. However, this inhumane practice continues in many developing countries including India. The scavenging castes which have known by different names in different States like Bhangi, Balmiki, Chuhra, Mehtar, Mazhabi, Lal Begi, Halalkhor etc. in northern India; Har, Hadi, Hela, Dom and Sanei etc. in eastern India; Mukhiyar, Thoti, Chachati, Pakay, Relli etc. in Southern India; and Mehtar, Bhangias, Halalkhor, Ghasi, Olgana, Zadmalli, Barvashia, Metariya, Jamphoda and Mela etc. in Western and Central India, also made an effort to get united and have a common name.

Manual scavenging and women

Discrimination both on grounds of gender and caste continue to trap successive generations of Dalit women in traditionally caste-based assigned occupations, as manual waste scavengers. Their job is to collect it with her broom onto a flat, tin plate, and pile it into her basket. When the basket is filled, they carry it on their head to a waiting tractor-trolley parked at a distance. But the most horrifying part is that their work is regarded so filthy that even when they are not at work and walking on the road most often people cover their noses when they walk past, as though they smell. They have to wait until someone turns on a municipal tap, or works a hand-pump, when they fill water, so that these are not polluted by their touch. In the tea-stalls, they are not allowed to sit with others on the benches. They are made to squat on the ground separately.

The houses of these scavengers are invariably situated outside the main residential area and they dwell in very poor and unhygienic conditions. It is needless to say that they are not allowed to dine and interact with the people of higher castes. It could be argued that this sort of ostracism is probably one of the major reasons that there is the prevalence of serious alcoholism and drug addiction among these communities, for example, alcoholism and drug addiction is very high among the Mehtar community.

As has already been pointed out that the occupation of manual scavenging consists in the removal of human excreta by hand in public streets, septic tanks or closed gutters and sewage. It, therefore, is characterised by the dramatically unhealthy and unsafe working conditions, which continue to exacerbate the practice of untouchability and marginalisation of the Dalits in general and the manual scavengers in particular. Adding to this is the unpalatable fact that more often than not the payment for a women scavengers' effort happens to be a single roti, a piece of Indian flatbread. Thus, the point that needs to be driven home is that discrimination on both grounds of sex and social origin continue to trap successive generations of Dalit women in traditionally caste-based assigned occupations like manual scavenging. Government estimates are testimony to the fact that manual scavenging is one of those occupations mostly held by women. For example, according to government estimates for 2005, 95 per cent of a total of 700,000 manual scavengers were women. Considering this huge number and also the role of women for the family, it is commonsensical that there should have been, at least, better provisions for the safety and decent working conditions for them. But, to no one's utter surprise, successive governments both at the Centre and the respective States have paid a callous disregard to the plight of these hapless Dalit women. Why is better protection needed for a scavenger is no rocket science? At all times, and especially during the rainy season, the contents of the basket will drip onto a scavenger's hair, clothes and body. A scavenger faces the dangers of daily contact of faeces exposing her to various kinds of faeces-borne illness. The use of hands by women manual scavengers, along with the certainty that they will have direct skin contact with human waste, in fact, is a very dangerous combination that is contributing to serious health conditions. Chronic skin diseases and lung diseases are very common among women manual scavengers.

In spite of its being "illegal" the practice and use of manual scavengers continues in many low-income urban and rural parts of India today. Men and women, often right from their teens, invariably the *Dalits of the Dalit* do this ignoble job. Mahatma Gandhi raised the issue of the horrible working and social conditions of *Bhangis* (manual scavengers) more than 100 years ago, in 1901, at the Congress meeting in Bengal. Yet it took about 90 years for the country to enact a uniform law abolishing manual scavenging. Struggling to find the means to a new livelihood in India often makes changes impossible and out of reach for women manual scavengers. According to law, children can receive scholarships for their education only as long as their family continues to work as scavengers. Indian government officials say these scholarships are meant only for the children of people engaged in "insanitary occupations". But once women manual scavengers quit their work it becomes clear that there are no more scholarships for their children. This is the reason that many women have returned to this work after quitting it once.

In this context it is pertinent to point out here that the very existence of dry latrines affects the society in three major ways. Firstly, it affects users of the dry latrines by exposing them to all types of health hazards, much worse than those caused by open field defecation, especially women and children who are in the house for most of the times in the midst of stinking environment and flies, exacerbated further by delay in cleanliness. Second, it violates the very constitutional principles of liberty, equality and justice guaranteed to all the citizens of the polity by making a particular community cling on to such an ignoble practice like manual scavenging. That is to say, this practice of manual scavenging helps continue the various forms of discrimination and oppression that our constitutional democracy would like to get rid of. Third, it affects the communities of manual scavenging directly including the future generation, for they get deprived of the fruits of India's overall development. Because, this profession of manual scavenging is by birth and this had been their ancestral profession. They consider it as their profession. They do not see any taboo or any social evil attached to this work. But the hard truth is that it is the only way they can earn their livelihood. Of course, there is a section of people who wanted to get rid of this work but due to lack of any other employment opportunity they were forced to take this work. There are also instances that some people wanted to get rid of this socially backward work but the people in their villages who are having the dry latrines restricted them to adopt any other work. Similarly, there are many manual scavengers who are not ready to leave their age old profession, for they are skeptical of the promises made by the government in general and that it takes much time to get some things done from the government.

Considering the gravity of the situation of the so-called manual scavengers one wonders as to what needs to be done to bring these people out of this humiliating practice. One gets tempted to offer the following two solutions. The first solution is that the Government of India should press all states to implement the Employment of Manual Scavengers and Construction of Dry Latrines (Prohibition) Act, 1993, and prosecute officials responsible for the perpetuation of the practice. The second solution is that the Government of India should ensure that all manual scavengers are rehabilitated according to the law in all states throughout the country. These are in fact well within the ability of the democratic polity called India. It's indeed a shame that even after more than six decades of independence, despite many reports, meetings and humanitarian outcries on the continuing use of manual scavengers in India that the Government of India has still failed to eradicate this inhuman practice. It is not to say that the government has not tried to do anything at all. But, it is the non-seriousness in their implementation which has kept this practice going and also India seeing a plethora of acts and committees to mitigate the problem of the manual scavengers.

Government Initiatives

The government has periodically formed various committees to look into the plight of the scavenging community.

The Protection of Civil Rights Act, 1955: Initially the Untouchability (Offences) Act, 1955, had been enacted to abolish the practice of untouchability and social disabilities arising out of it against members of the Scheduled Castes. It was amended in 1977 and is now known as the Protection of Civil Rights Act, 1955. Under the revised Act, the practice of untouchability was made both cognisable and non-compoundable offence and stricter punishment was provided for the offenders.

The Scheduled Castes and Scheduled Tribes (Prevention of Atrocities) Act, 1989: The main objective of the Act is to prevent the commission of offences of atrocities against the members of the Scheduled Castes and the Scheduled Tribes, to provide for Special Courts for the trial of such offences and for the relief and rehabilitation of the victims of such offences and for matters connected therewith or incidental thereto.

Employment of Manual Scavengers and Construction of Dry Latrines (Prohibition) Act, 1993: The government enacted the employment of Manual Scavengers and Construction of Dry Latrines (Prohibition) Act, 1993 which provides for the prohibition of employment of manual scavengers as well as construction or continuance of dry latrines and for the regulation of construction and maintenance of water sealed latrines and matters connected therewith.

However, this act has done very little to eradicate manual scavenging. Inefficiency of the act are that did not address the more insidious forms of manual scavenging, such as cleaning open gutters, manholes and septic tanks. Second, Parliament did not create an individual right to file a complaints under the Act rather, only specifically appointed authorities can file complaints, and only within a limited time frame. Finally, Parliament relied too heavily on the States to enforce the ban on manual scavenging.

The Prohibition of Employment as Manual Scavengers and their Rehabilitation Act 2013: The 2012 Bill definition is fitting more elaborate and inclusive, and includes "a person engaged or employed... for manually cleaning, carrying, disposing of, or otherwise handling in any manner, human excreta in an unsanitary latrine or in an open drain or pit into which the human excreta from the insanitary latrine is disposed of, or on a railway track...". The 2012 Bill explicitly prohibits construction of dry latrines, and employment of manual scavengers, as also the hazardous cleaning of a sewer or a septic tank. But cleaning railway tracks has not been included, and "hazardous cleaning" is defined not by employers requiring workers to manually clean sewers or septic tanks, but requiring them to do so without protective gear. Under the new law, each occupier of an insanitary latrine is responsible for converting or demolishing it at his own cost. If he fails to do so, the local authority will convert the latrine and recover the cost from him.

Barve Committee

The erstwhile Government of Bombay, appointed a committee known as the Scavengers' Living Conditions Enquiry Committee in 1949 and submitted its report with late Shri V.N. Barve as Chairman to study and enquire into the living conditions of the scavengers in the State of Bombay and to suggest ways and means to improve their conditions of work and to fix their minimum wages.

Kaka Kalelkar Commission

The first Backward Classes Commission which was appointed in 1953 under the Chairmanship of Kaka Kalelkar submitted its report in 1955. The Commission described the condition of sweepers and scavengers as sub-human.

Malkani Committee

The Board in its meeting held on the 12th October, 1957 constituted a committee, known as Scavenging Conditions Inquiry Committee consisting of Professor N.R. Malkani as Chairman to prepare a scheme to put an end to the degrading practice of scavenging having to carry night soil in buckets or baskets. The Committee which submitted its report in

December 1960 recommended not merely for eliminating the practice of carrying night soil as head loads, but also for removing filth and indignity from all stages of scavenging and for improving the working, living conditions and social status.

Pandya Committee

The National Commission on Labour constituted by the Union Ministry of Labour appointed a sub-committee (1968-69) under the chairmanship of Shri Bhanu Prasad Pandya to look into the working and service conditions of sweepers and scanvengers. One of the important recommendations of the committee was that "the Central Government should undertake a comprehensive legislation for regulating their working, service and living conditions which should also provide for adequate inspectorate and enforcement machinery."

Conclusion

The evil practice of manual scavenging is, undoubtedly, a complete violation of human rights and dignity. The successive governments both at the Center and the states have failed to abolish this abominable practice even after more than six decades of the working of the Constitution of India guaranteeing liberty, equality and human dignity to all. The society in general and the civil society in particular are also responsible for this failure. Hence, there is an urgent need of the time that the government(s), various civil society organisations, and the society as a whole work in tandem to get rid of this inhuman practice. Moreover, this caste-based occupation stands on the way of the very democratic process of the country by preventing the so-called manual scavengers to communicate with others freely and take part in the economic, political and social life of the community. Abolition of manual scavenging can be possible through provision of alternative livelihoods, abolishment of dry latrines and imparting free education to both to them and to their children. For, their condition can be improved only through education which can be provided by vocational training mainly by open-minded teachers. Education is essential to train them for alternative ways of living and it also will also create awareness among them regarding their rights and violation of their rights. Furthermore, as a starting point to rehabilitate them, it is possible, particularly for women, to provide jobs in different sectors like agriculture, selling of fruits and vegetables, tailoring of clothes, and handicrafts. Above all, the most important and urgent step to eradicate the practice of manual-scavenging has to do with the abolishment of dry latrines and establishment of flush latrines or eco-friendly latrines. Of course, all these would be possible only when there is a systematic implementation of government policies and programmes and also stringent punishment for those who violate the laws pertaining to the abolition of the shameful practice of manual scavenging.

Notes

Singh R. K. (2009), "Manual Scavenging as Social Exclusion: A Case study", *Economic and Political Weekly*, 44(26/27): pp. 521-523.

"Manual Scavengers: Welfare and Rehabilitation", *Lok Sabha Secretariat Parliament Library and Reference, Research, Documentation and Information Service (LARRDIS)*, No. 18/RN/REF/AUG 2013.

Ministry of Social Justice and Empowerment, Instructions Manual, February, 2013, pp. 19-20.

Ibid.

LAARDIS. No. 18/RN/REF/AUG 2013.

Ibid.

Harsh Mander, "Bare Foot: Burning Baskets of Shame", *The Hindu*, [18/12/2012].

Srivastava, B. N. (1997), *Manual scavenging in India: a disgrace to the country,* Concept Publishing Company: New Delhi.

Ibid.

Ibid.

References

"Beginning of the End: Manual scavenging persists, but community and political mobilisation of workers has initiated change" (November 20, 2010), *Economic & Political Weekly*, xlv(47).

Baruah, A. (2014), "The Prohibition of Employment as Manual Scavengers and their Rehabilitation Act, 2013: A Review", *Space and Culture and India*, 1(3).

Dhar, Aarti, (2012), "Hiring people for inhuman work will attract jail", *The Hindu*, New Delhi, [27/08/2012].

Ghose, Sagarika (Spring 2003), "The Dalit in India", *Social Research*, 70(1): 83-109.

Guru,Gopal (Summer 2000),"Dalits from margin to margin",*India International Centre Quarterly*, 27(2): 111-116.

"Human Rights and Manual Scavenging" (2011), National Human Rights Commission Faridkot House, Copernicus Marg: New Delhi.

J. Venkatesan, (2012), "Cabinet has cleared bill on manual scavenging, court told", *The Hindu*, New Delhi, [27/08/2012].

"Manual Scavengers: Welfare and Rehabilitation", *Lok Sabha Secretariat Parliament Library and Reference, Research, Documentation and Information Service,* No. 18 /RN/Ref./August /2013.

Mander, Harsh (2010), "Barefoot: burning baskets of shame", *The Hindu*, [8/05/2010].

Permutt, Samuel (2011), "The Manual Scavenging Problem: A Case for the Supreme Court of India", 20:277.

S. Vishwanath (2011), "This is the right method", *The Hindu*, [19/112011].

Staff Reporte (2013), "Yatra against manual scavenging reaches Mumbai", *The Hindu*, Mumbai, [7/1/2013].

Nevile, A. (Apr., 2007), "Amartya K. Sen and Social Exclusion", *Development in Practice*, 17(2): 249-255.

Singh, Rajeev and Ziyauddin (June, 2009), "Manual scavenging as social exclusion: A Case study", *Economic and Political Weekly*, xliv (26 & 27).

Singh, Rajeev and Ziyauddin (July 2009), "Manual Scavenging", *Radical Humanist*, 73(4).

Singh, Rajeev (Jun. 27- Jul. 10, 2009), "Manual Scavenging as Social Exclusion: A Case Study", *Economic and Political Weekly*, 44 (26/27): 521-523.

Ravichandran, B. (March 26, 2011), "Scavenging Profession: Between Class and Caste?", *Economic and Political Weekly*, xlvl (13).

Menon, Meena (2012), "The lives of others", *The Hindu*, [5/06/2012].

Dhar, Aarti, "Blotch on the social scape", *The Hindu*, [31/08/2012].

"India's continuing shame", *The Hindu* [18/05/2013].

Seelan, Samuel (December, 2013) "Neglect of Sewage Workers Concerns about the New Act", *Economic and Political Weekly*, xlviii (49).

"Manual Scavenging: stigma, discrimination and justice" (August 2012), Safai Karmcahari Andolan, New Delhi.

Mander, Harsh (2012), "India's great shame", *The Hindu*, [17/11/2012].

Palshikar, Sanjay (Dec. 17-23, 2005), "Understanding Humiliation" *Economic and Political Weekly*, 40(51): 5428-5432.

10

Women and Human Rights Violations in India A Comparative Study of Manipur and Odisha

Dr Padmalaya Mohapatra

Introduction

November 25 is celebrated as International Day for the Elimination of Violence against Women. Yet it is a shocking statistics that "worldwide, more than 700 million women alive today were married as children, 250 million of whom were married before the age of 15 years. Girls who marry before the age of 18 years. are less likely to complete their education and more likely to experience domestic violence and complications in childbirth". To Quote Nicole Kidman, 'Violence against women is an appalling human rights violation. But it is not inevitable. We can put a stop to this'. Additionally, according to an article in the Health and Human Rights Journal, regardless of many years of advocacy and involvement of many feminist activist organisations, the issue of violence against women still "remains one of the most pervasive forms of human rights violations worldwide." Essentially, violence against women in India is one of the major issues. In fact, it is rooted in societal norms and economic dependence, discriminatory practices, lack of proper policing and delayed justice delivery. Eventually women victims lack proper protection. It is a fact that the issue of violence against women in India was glaring after the atrocious and shocking gang-rape of 23 years old Nirvaya in Delhi on 16 December 2012. The December incident highlighted the challenges Indian women are facing today. And particularly the epidemic is more attitudinal and behavioural than systemic deficiencies. It is a fact that the sex ratio between men and women indicates 940 women to a 1000 men (2011 census data). It is yet the lowest sex ratios in the world. Another fact is approximately 35 million women in India are "missing". The highest number of missing women at birth is in the north-western states of Punjab, Rajasthan and Haryana.

The French Historian Michel Foucault highlights sexuality as a construct and presents its genealogical history. For him, sexuality is made by which one understands the exercise of power and how a certain kind of 'sexual' subjectivity encourages the disciplinary mode of power. By crafting a certain kind of imagery for the female body and its sexual desires the woman is absorbed into the normative structure of society that is defined by patriarchy. Patriarchy is an endemic historical and cultural practice that exacts an all encompassing hegemony.

Moreover, Sylvia Walby defines Patriarchy "as a system of social structures and practices in which men dominate, oppress and exploit women." When Walby uses the term social structures she is implying that this system of control, domination and oppression is not biologically determined. Contextually 'Patriarchy' is based on a system of power relations which are hierarchical and unequal where men control women's production, reproduction and sexuality. Acceptance of traditional masculine gender roles in a patriarchal society is closely connected with escalating violence towards women. Virtually all masculinity norms (anti-feminity, toughness, self-reliance, aggression and sexual contest) reinforce this fact. When men are granted permission to subordinate women in patriarchal societies sexual terrorism is a common result. Sexual terrorism includes sexual intimidation, threat of violence and overt violence.

Throughout the life cycle woman absorbs different kinds of pain. As a matter of fact WHO has given the following data.

Charlotte Watts and Cathy Zimmerman also had given a diagram of typology of violence against women over time.

Phase	*Types of Violence*
Pre-birth	Sex-selective abortion, effects of battering during pregnancy on birth outcomes.
Infancy	Female infanticide, female genital mutilation, physical, sexual and psychological abuse.
Girlhood	Child marriage, physical, sexual and psychological abuse, incest, child prostitution and pornography.
Adolescence and Adulthood	Dating and courtship violence (e.g. acid throwing and date rape economically coerced sex) (e.g. school girls having sex with "Sugar daddies" in return for school feeds), incest, sexual abuse in the workplace, rape, sexual harassment, forced prostitution and pornography, trafficking in women, partner violence, marital rape, dowry abuse and murders, partner homicide, psychological abuse, abuse of women with disabilities, forced pregnancy.
Elderly	Forced "suicide" or homicide of widows for economic reasons, sexual, physical and psychological abuse.

Figure 1: WHO: Violence against Women throughout the Life Cycle.

To combat violence against women Government of India and other world organisations are implementing a variety of programmes. In global arena the major accomplishment of the women's rights movements against violence on women are the "Declaration on the Elimination of Violence Against Women", "the Convention on Elimination of all forms of Discrimination Against Women (CEDAW)." and the declaration of 25 November as International Day for the Elimination of Violence against Women by UN General Assembly. Again in 1993, for the first time the Vienna World Conference on Human Rights, violence against women was addressed under the framework of International Human Rights.

It is necessary to note that not all victims of Gender Based Violence (GBV) are female. Men are victims of GBV as well. For example, gay men who are harassed, beaten and killed because they do not conform to socially acceptable norms of being a man.

1. Violence against Women: What it Includes?

To be clear VAW includes the followings:

- **Psychological Violence**

Psychological violence encompasses various tactics to undermine a woman's self-confidence such as yelling, insults, mockery, threats, abusive language, humiliation, harassment, contempt and deliberate deprivation of emotional care or isolation.

- **Physical Violence**

Physical violence is the most obvious ranges from pushing and shoving to hitting, beating, and physical abuse with a weapon, mutilation and murder.

- **Sexual Violence**

Any form of non-consensual sexual activity i.e. forced on a person- ranging from harassment, unwanted sexual touching to rape. This form of violence also includes incest.

- **Financial Violence**

It encompasses various tactics for total or partial control of a couple's finances, inheritance or employment income. It could also include preventing a partner from taking employment outside the home or engaging in other activities that would lead to financial independence.

- Spiritual abuse

  Words to destroy an individual's cultural or religious beliefs through ridicule or punishment, forbidding practice of a personal religion or forcing women or children to adhere to religious practices that are not their own etc.

2. The Concept: Violence against Women

The United Nations Declaration on the Elimination of Violence against Women (DEVAW) defines VAW as:

"Any act of gender-based violence that results in, or is likely to result in, physical, sexual or psychological harm or suffering to women, including threats of such acts, coercion or arbitrary deprivation of liberty, whether occurring in public or in private life." (DEVAW, Article 1) To this end the "Reasons" that sustain and escalate Gender Based Violence are:

- Cultural Gender –specific socialisation
- Culturally demarcated roles for men and women
- Expectations of performing fixed roles in familial relationships
- Women's economic dependence on men
- Limited rights over land and property
- Limited employment opportunities and adverse employment conditions
- Legal discriminatory laws on marriage, divorce, property and violence
- Low levels of legal literacy
- Insensitive treatment of women and girls by the police and judiciary
- Political Under-Representation of women in positions of power in politics
- VAW not considered as a serious political issue
- Notions of the family being private, beyond State intervention."

3. Underlying Causes

The UN has indentified six underlying causes of VAW. As a matter of fact it is interesting to highlight the causes of violence against women.

- **Historically Unequal Power Relations**

  The political, economic and social processes that have evolved over many centuries have kept men in a position of power over women.

- **Control of Women's Sexuality**

Many societies use violence as a way to control a woman's sexuality, and likewise in many societies violence is used to punish women who exhibit sexual behaviour, preferences and attitudes that violate cultural norms.

- **Cultural Ideology**

Culture defines gender roles and some customs, traditions and religions are used to justify VAW when women transgress these culturally assigned roles.

- **Doctrines of Privacy**

The persistent belief in many societies that VAW is a private issue seriously impedes attempts to eradicate this violence.

- **Patterns of Conflict Resolution**

Links have been identified between VAW in the home and community in areas that are in conflict or that are militarised. Often heightened insecurity means that tensions within the home are more pronounced and can contribute to the perpetuation of VAW in the family. Equally, because eyes tend to be on the conflict, women's suffering is often overshadowed. VAW is also frequently used as a formal military tactics.

- **Government Inaction**

Government negligence in preventing and ending VAW establishes a tolerance of VAW throughout the community.

4. Globalisation, the State and Violence against Women

Capitalist globalisation with its tools of development and progress, including some aspects of modern science and technology, free market, rational knowledge system and the militarised State seems to be intensifying existing violence and creating grotesque new forms against the already vulnerable-particularly women. The growing number of dowry murders, that are a direct outcome of increasing consumerism and devaluation of women, female foeticide that is fostered by new forms of reproductive technology, the total destruction of women's livelihood in the process of industrialisation and the absolute exploitation of women's skills and labour in sweatshops of the corporate free market, are just some cases of the growing myriad forms of violence against women. Violence in its various forms is getting accentuated under the New Economic Policy being pursued by the Sate. Thus, the State far from being the protector and custodian of the rights to its people has become its greatest violator- both through commission of violence and through omission to stop or end violence. While on the one hand it is granting more rights to women, on the other it is also creating conditions where women are being rendered more vulnerable and increasingly violated. "For example, while on the one hand globalisation has allowed a larger number of women to join the workforce, at the same time the State has not made enough effort to create enabling and safe working conditions for women at work."

5. Types of Violence: Rising Victims Worldwide

The Figure 3 below exhibits the common forms of violence against women at global sphere. This has also an important bearing on India which has been examined later.

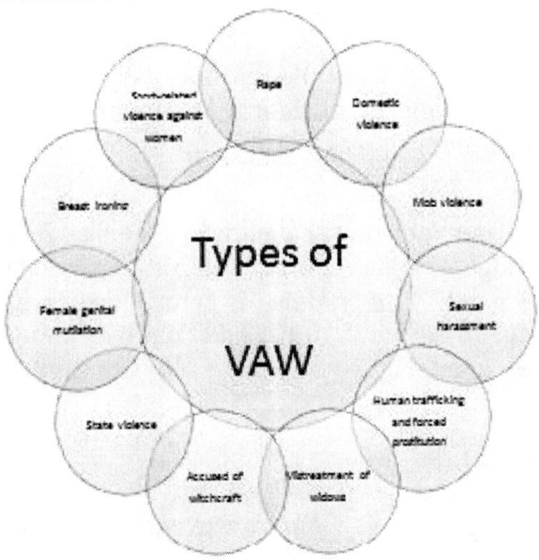

Figure 2 : Typology of VAW - Global Scene.

- **Rape- Rape is a type of sexual assault**

- **Domestic violence**

It is a fact that women are generally victimised by some related persons. This is called "intimate partner violence" or (IPV). Women are more frequently murdered by an intimate partner. WHO reported that "globally, as many as 38 per cent of murders of women are committed by an intimate partner." "A UN report compiled from a number of different studies conducted in at least 71 countries found domestic violence against women to be most prevalent in Ethiopia."

- **Honour killings**

Honour killings are a common form of violence against women. These are rampant in Afghanistan, Egypt, Iraq, Jordan, Lebanon, Libya, Morocco, Pakistan, Saudi Arabia, Syria, Turkey, and Yemen. In India these are sporadic incidents.

- **Dowry violence**

Dowry is generally found in South Asia. Particularly it is unbridled in India. In turn it gives rise to Bride burning, Dowry death, suicide etc. To put it in clear terms Dowry violence is frequent in India, Pakistan, Bangladesh and Nepal. As per the National Crime Records Bureau 8,618 dowry deaths were reported in India during 2011.

- **Acid throwing**

Acid throwing is also called acid attack, the purpose of acid throwing is injuring or disfiguring women out of jealousy or revenge or unilateral love affairs.

- **Forced marriage**

Another form of violence against women is forced marriage. It is a marriage in which one or both of the parties are married against their will. This malaise is reigns particularly in South Asia, the Middle East and Africa. Additionally the custom of bride kidnapping exists in Kyrgyzstan, Kazakhstan, Uzbekistan, Caucasus and Ethiopia.

- **Mob violence**

As per Amnesty International Report in 2010 mob attacks against single women were taking place in Hassi Messaoud, Algeria.

- **Sexual harassment**

Sexual harassment is abusive, in the work place. This may include intimidation, bullying or coercion of a sexual nature.

- **Human trafficking**

Human trafficking is a common form of violence against women. A 2006 study in Europe on women trafficking found that "the women were subjected to serious forms of abuse, such as physical or sexual violence, which affected their physical and mental health."

- **Forced prostitution**

  Forced prostitution is prostitution by women under force.

- **Mistreatment of widows**

  Maltreatments to widows are common in India. Widow Inheritance is also a problem area in India. Practice of *Sati* is prevalent. Example of this type is sati of Roop Kanwar (1987), as well as several incidents in rural areas in 2002 and 2006. (Arrests in Indian ritual burning. BBC News. 7 August 2002)

- **Witch Hunting**

  Witch hunting were common in Europe and in the European colonies in North America. Currently, these are found in Sub-Saharan Africa, rural North India, and Papua New Guinea. In most cases women are accused of being witches and are subjected to serious violence.

- **State violence**

  War rape and sexual slavery during military conflict are very common.

- **Forced sterilisation and forced abortion**

  To add to it, Forced sterilisation and forced abortion are other forms of violence against women. These procedures are generally practiced in Uzbekistan and China.

- **Violence by the police**

  Generally police officers misuse their power as agents of the state to physically and sexually harass and assault women victims.

- **Female genital mutilation**

  World Health Organisation (WHO) defined Female genital mutilation (FGM) as "all procedures that involve partial or total removal of the external female genitalia, or other injury to the female genital organs for non-medical reasons". UNICEF report in 2013 stated that, "125 million women and girls in Africa and the Middle East have experienced FGM". And it is to be noted that owing to globalisation and immigration, FGM is spreading from Africa and Middle East, to Australia, Belgium, Canada, and France, New Zealand, US, and UK.

- **Breast ironing**

Painful Breast ironing is commonly carried out by the girl's mother. The object is to keep the girl away from sexually attractive to men and boys. In consequence her virginity is protected. This inhuman activity is practiced in Cameroon. Also few cases are also reported in West and Central Africa.

- **Sport-related violence against women**

Sport-related violence against women athletes are also reported in some countries. Such events as the 2010 World Cup, the Olympic and Commonwealth Games have highlighted the connections between sports spectatorship and intimate partner violence.

6. India and Violence against Women: Typology

At present violence against women has become a prominent topic of discussion in India. A great focus is placed on the issue due to continuously escalating trends during 2008-2012. (Crimes against Women. National Crime Records Bureau, 2013).

No doubt violence against women is rising day by day. The record is placed below:

Violence to Women - Rising Trend

Year	*Reported violence*
2008	195,856
2009	203,804
2010	213,585
2011	213,585
2012	244,270

Source: Wikipedia

The National Crime Records Bureau of India reported the incidents of crime against women are increased to 6.4 per cent during 2012. Further a crime against a woman is committed every three minutes. As stated above, a total of 244,270 incidents of crime against women were reported in 2012. The figures for 2011 were 228,650 incidents. In January 2011, the International Men and Gender Equality Survey (IMAGES) reported that 24 per cent of Indian men had committed sexual violence at some point during their lives.

Rape in India

Year	*Reported rapes*
2008	21,467
2009	21,397
2010	22,172
2011	24,206
2012	24,923

Source: Wikipedia

To this it is to be noted that total reported number of rape crimes in 2012 were highest in Madhya Pradesh. The shocking status is followed by Uttar Pradesh and West Bengal. Further among major cities, Delhi reported the highest number of rapes in 2012. This is followed by Mumbai. According to another record the rape rate per 100,000 people was highest in Mizoram (10.4), followed by, Meghalaya, Sikkim and Assam. According to sources among foremost cities, Delhi's rape rate of 4.1 per 100,000 people was highest in India. The rape rate per 100,000 people was lowest in Gujarat (0.98).

In this context another aspect is that the highest number of victims, and majority of victims, was in the 18-30 year age group. Moreover, rape of minor (below age group 19) is nearly one in three rape victims in India. To put in other terms of all rapes, 12.5 per cent of total (or 3,125 rapes) victims in India were minors. Another glaring fact is unreported rape cases. Two estimates are given here; Madiha Kark estimates 54 per cent of rape crimes are unreported in India. Contrary to it Mihir Srivastava estimates 90 per cent of rapes go unreported in India. The Government of Odisha assess that 60 per cent of sexual assaults go unreported.

Domestic violence

In India, 70 per cent of women are victims of domestic violence. Again 38 per cent of Indian men admit they have physically abused their partners. To minimise it the Indian government passed legislation–Protection of Women from Domestic Violence Act, 2005.

According to different reported sources in websites fact is in every nine minutes, a case of cruelty is committed by either of husbands or a relative of the husband. Further during 2011 to 2012, there was a 7.5 per cent increase in cruelty by husbands and relatives. For example, in West Bengal, there were 19,865 cases (accounting for 18.7 per cent of the national total), and in Andhra Pradesh, there were 13,389 cases (accounting for 12.6 per cent of the national total).

Acid Throwing

Moreover it is to be noted that 72 per cent of reported acid attacks in India are on women. In 2010, there was a high of 27 reported cases of chemical assaults.

Dowry Deaths

Dowry death is a major form of violence against women in India. However, the incidents of dowry deaths have decreased 4.5 per cent from 2011 to 2012.

To be specific the reported cases of dowry deaths were 2,244 in Uttar Pradesh, (accounting for 27.3 per cent of the dowry deaths nationwide) and 1,275 in Bihar (accounting for 15.5 per cent of cases nationwide).

Honour killings

Honour killings are practiced in a big way in north India. Especially they are prevalent in Punjab, Haryana, Bihar, Uttar Pradesh, Rajasthan, Jharkhand, Himachal Pradesh, and Madhya Pradesh. These dreadful incidences had impact on Supreme Court of India to issue notice to six States to take preventive measures in 2010. Honour killings can be very violent. For example, in June 2012, a father chopped off his 20 years old daughter's head with a sword in anger. In September 2013, a young newlywed couple who was brutally murdered because of having love affairs.

Insult to modesty

Another form of violence against women is insult to modesty. The staggering cases are placed below:

Year	*Assaults with intent to outrage modesty*	*Insults to the modesty of women*
2008	40,413	12,214
2009	38,711	11,009
2010	40,613	9,961
2011	42,968	8,570
2012	45,351	9,173

(*Source*: Wikipedia)

The above data shows from 2011 to 2012, there was a 5.5 per cent increase in reported assaults on women with intent to outrage her modesty. Mainly, Madhya Pradesh had 6,655 cases, (accounting for 14.7 per cent of the national incidents). Again it is to be marked from 2011 to 2012, there was a 7.0 per cent increase in reported insults to the modesty of women. Andhra Pradesh had 3,714 cases, (amounting to 40.5 per cent of the national cases) and Maharashtra had 3,714 cases, (amounting to 14.1 per cent of the national cases).

Sexual Harassment at the Workplace

Sexual harassment in the workplace is considered as a common form of violation of human rights, and an affront to the dignity of the person harassed. It is viewed as a manifestation of violence against women that results in creating an atmosphere of discrimination against her. It is seen as unacceptable conditions of work which have detrimental effects for both female employees and the employer.

Sexual harassment can take the form of harmless banter or unwelcome physical conduct. Sometimes, a boss may use sexually tinged language with a female colleague, demand that she meet him after office hours for a relaxed and quiet dinner for two or even threaten her career options using sexual harassment to silence her. Sexual harassment at the workplace violated one's freedom and personal dignity, goes against the right to work in a healthy environment free of discrimination, and is unequal and discriminatory behaviour.

A survey conducted for the National Commission for Women (NCW) in July 1998, covering over 1,200 women in both the organised and unorganised sectors, found that nearly 50 per cent had experienced gender discrimination or physical and mental harassment at work. Yet, 85 per cent of them had never heard of the existence of any law against sexual harassment. Only 11 per cent of them were aware that they could seek legal redressed in cases of sexual harassment, and that sexual harassment was an offence punishable by law.

The NCW survey found women in the unorganised sector more vulnerable to sexual harassment than women in the organised sector. Apart from sexual harassment, 32 per cent of the women covered in the survey also reported discrimination in salaries, leave, promotions, work distribution and working hours.

Vishakha Case

The horrific story behind the inception of the Supreme Court's Vishakha Guidelines against sexual harassment at the workplace, etches into celluloid in the 2000 film "Bawandar". Bhanwari Devi, a 50-years-old social worker in Rajasthan, fought as a Saathin against the insidious practice of child marriage. As part of her job in the villages, she tried to stop the wedding of a minor girl, less than a year old. Outraged by the audacity of this low caste woman, who was challenging tradition, five men from the upper-caste family of the minor girl gang-raped Bhanwari Devi in the presence of her husband.

In the immediate aftermath of the rape, Bhanwari Devi's unthinkable trauma only festered as the village authorities, the police and doctors all dismissed her situation. A trial court acquitted the accused. Appalled at the blatant injustice and inspired by Bhanwari Devi's unrelenting spirit, saathins and women's groups from all over the country launched a concerted campaign to bring her justice. They filed a petition in the Supreme Court of India, under the collective platform of Vishakha, asking the court to take action against sexual harassment faced by women in the workplace. Bhanwari Devi had attracted the wrath of the men solely on the basis of her work. The result was the Supreme Court judgement of 1997, popularly known as the Vishakha Guidelines. Justice Burma Commission Report is an improvement of Visakha Guideline. On the basis of this Criminal Law Amendment Act, 2013 was passed.

Female foeticide

Killing of female foetus after amniocentesis test is a heinous crime perpetrated against a female child in the mother's womb. "1,600 female foetuses were aborted everyday in the country following sex selection tests."

Join and mark the 16 Days of Activism against Gender Violence Campaign

The 16 days of Activism against Gender Violence is an international campaign. Participants chose the dates-November 25: International Day against Violence against Women, and December 10: International Human Rights Day- in order to symbolically link violence against women and human rights and to emphasise that such violence is violation of human rights.

Work with Men

By and large, men tend to disclaim responsibility for their violent behaviour, often justifying it or simply refusing to admit it. According to Kathy Grogan, project manager with STOP (Start Treating Others Positively), based in Leeds (UK): "For men to stop being violent it is important for them to identify and take responsibility for feelings that are masked by rage. The connection between the probation against showing vulnerable feelings and the tacit societal permission to vent this rage on a woman is a crucial one to be made in programmes with male perpetrators.

Crime Clock

Crime Clock of National Crime Records Bureau is put here in brief.

- one crime committed against women every three minutes.
- one molestation case every 15 minutes.
- one sexual harassment case every 53 minutes.
- one kidnapping and abduction case every 23 minutes.

- one rape case every 29 minutes.
- And these are only the reported and recorded statistics.
- WHO has reported that up to 70 per cent of female murder victims are killed by their male partners.

7. Demographic, Economic and Social Profile of Manipur: Road to Violence against Women?

(a) The north-eastern region of India consisting of the seven sister states faces not just political, economic and cultural marginalisation but even emotional alienation from the so-called mainland India. Every passing day witnesses scenes of violence enacted on its soil, undermining the already fragile textures of national consolidation in the region. The turn of the century has seen turbulence of increasing intensity adversely affecting socio-economic development and political normalisation.

(b) The state of Manipur is one of the smallest north-eastern states in India having a total area of 22,372 sq. km. With a population of 41,947,358 crores sex ratio in Manipur are 987 females per 1000 males as against 940 per 1000 males in the rest of India. The female literacy rate is 73.17 per cent as against 86.49 per cent male literacy rate.

The more egalitarian tribal culture of the north-east region, coupled with the absence of some rigid practices prevalent in other parts of India, like seclusion (purdah) and dowry amongst the non-tribal populace of the region, certainly gives the women of the region an edge over other women, in terms of visibility and mobility. The concept of solidarity amongst women's groups is fairly strong. This is often seen in traditional cooperative systems, women's markets and other forms of cooperative village action, which seem to sustain and perpetuate an order of social cohesiveness. Women's collective work pattern has well been embedded through traditional and conventional value systems, which is often reflected in the functioning of groups and village organisations.

Women's contribution in the economic sphere is great and unlike in other parts of the country women of some of the communities not just contribute towards the economy but also enjoy considerable economic autonomy. Many of the main market areas of these communities are handled by women. The Ima Keithal or Mother's market also referred to as Keithal Nupi or Women's Market of Manipur is especially famous. It is one of the largest markets of the country managed exclusively by women.

In fact, the Keithal has been the facilitating space for women's activism in the state of Manipur. The women's movement in Manipur is famous for two agitations called Nupi-lan that the women staged against the British in 1904 and 1939. The first was a revolt against punitive labour levies or civil rights violation and the second was a protest against British interference in the rice trade. The British attempted to strengthen their colonial economic position by destroying the self-sufficiency ofthe village economy. As they tried to take over the economy traditionally controlled by women, the colonial rulers had to face an extremely tough and at times violent opposition from the women. The focus of the movement gradually shifted from the export policy of the colonial government to the freedom movement.

This great spirit of the women is evident today in the Meira Paibis or Torch Bearers' Movement. Started in the 1970s, initially, as a women's movement against alcohol abuse related public disorder, the Meira Paibis focus is the community as a whole. Its genesis has been the impact of crises on women and as such the outreach has gone far beyond the management of alcohol related trauma and abuse. Traditionally, the Meitei women also had women's courts known as Paja, where offences against women including domestic violence were heard by women, and justice dispensed.

None of the traditional institutions of governance accept women. Even where women have come in, the roles assigned to them are either peripheral of figurative. A major hurdle to the participation of women in decision-making is the much revered customary laws and practices.

In Manipur too, discriminatory customary laws and practices are strictly adhered to in many areas. In some communities these laws sanction polygamy and child marriage, in others; land, property rights and custody of children are given only to the males. In addition, women are debarred from taking part in decision-making. Besides, the inherent gender biases of the traditional systems, greater contact and exposure to other cultures have also resulted in acculturation and dilution of some of the positive and women-friendly aspects of the indigenous cultures.

In North East India, among tribal communities, there exists collective ownership of land. This is recognised by the Government of India under its Sixth Schedule. According to Anna Pinto, an activist and senior member of CORE (Centre for Organisation, Research and Education), a Manipur-based organisation, displacement in the course of armed conflict means that the community cannot be rebuilt again on the same traditional lines. The host community on whose lands re-settlement takes place are justifiably unwilling to surrender traditional controls over their land.

Most women in North-Eastern States like their counterparts in the other parts of the country do not enjoy inheritance rights. Even in the few communities in the area where woman are given such rights, resettlement due to armed conflict results in the loss of all such property.

But in the North East India mostly women enjoy greater mobility and visibility than women of other communities in the country. Practices such as dowry and bride-burning are not prevalent in the region. This is often cited to portray a picture of equity between men and women in the region and has given rise to the presumption that violence against women is not a major concern in the area. But data collected by the North East Network (NEN) however, suggests that violence against women particularly domestic violence is on the rise in the North-East.

The ongoing armed conflict situation prevalent in the North East India has intensified the violence faced by women which takes the form of sexual, mental or physical abuse, killings and clashes. The region under the shadow of conflict has witnessed a resurgence of patriarchal values and norms which have brought with them new restrictions on the movement of women, the way they dress and more overtly physical violence such as rape which is systematically used as a tactics against a particular community. All this is compounded by the long social, economic and psychological trauma of armed conflict.

The gender development indices of Assam and Manipur reflect the unequal treatment meted out to women in the areas of health, education and income. Due to the patriarchal structure of society many forms of domestic violence have received public sanction. Dr R.K. Lenin, Assistant Professor, Psychiatry Department, regional Institute of Medical Sciences, Imphal had revealed that

10 per cent of the total women population suffers from mental illness out of which one per cent are very severe. He has observed that women came for treatment only in extreme cases when pathological problems manifest themselves in the form severe headache, backaches, depression or general ill health.

8. Women in armed conflict

India's north-east region has been witness to ongoing low-intensity conflicts for almost three to five decades now. While the entire populace of the region continues to suffer, women living in such conditions are most vulnerable due to the restrictions on their mobility, the limited access to health services and most importantly, the lack of opportunities for education, employment and even leisure. In fact, it has been found that in this region, women regard leisure as synonymous with church gatherings or women's meetings.

Earlier studies conducted by NEN on women in situations of conflict have highlighted that the most critical element of disadvantage suffered by women in such conditions is violence. This violence is different from the violence experienced by them in 'normal' times for here even the state, which is supposed to be a guardian of their lives and rights, poses a threat to them. In ethnic clashes, women and children are easy victims and often the first ones to be killed. Even when they manage to survive direct physical violence, they have to bear heavy economic responsibility. It has been found that the conflict in the north-east region has resulted in an increase in female-headed households. Women have had to cope with these situations without any support from either the state or the society.

9. Few Cases: State of Manipur

The psychological trauma associated with sexual violence and with the loss or disappearance of family members lasts long after peace returns. A case in point is that of Gracie. She has been living in fear since the day two soldiers held her hostage in her very own house and coaxed her to divulge the whereabouts of her husband, whom they suspected to be a militant. During an interview, Gracie told the NEN team, "I could not comprehend what they were looking for because they spoke so fast. When I tried to ask them what they wanted they would interrupt and rudely point the nozzle near my jaw. How can I ever face such an encounter again when I travel alone in the bus or in the fields? For instance, in most tribes, including the Kukis if a woman does not have a son, inheritance is near impossible. In such cases, after the death ofher husband, custody of the children as well as property rights is automatically with her in-laws".

Among the Meitei community in Manipur, polygamy is still practiced. It is a widely held belief that polygamy was adopted by necessity rather than by design when the loss of men in the Manipuri – Burmese war was significantly high. The unequivocal need for social security gave way to elders sanctioning polygamy as a means of security and protection to women. This has however become an accepted practice now not just among the Meiteis but among the other tribal communities in the region as well.

The following case highlights the discrimination that women have to face in such situations:

Binalakshmi had been married to Arun for two years and lived in Imphal, Manipur. Right from the day of her marriage she was taunted by her in-laws and her husband, about her looks. She said, "I thought that things would change after I gave birth to a son. However, they did not. Within a couple of months he got married to another woman. Whenever he would get into a fit of anger, he would beat me and lock me out of the house. Unable to bear this any longer, I finally got the courage to leave him and start living on my own".

Binalakshmi has been living away from her husband for a couple of years now. She has been struggling to earn a livelihood and has recently remarried. She has been at the receiving end of a lot of criticism from family members and members of the community about being a 'bad' wife, a 'bad' mother and a 'bad' woman. Thus, women are often denied the right of residence at their marital homes if they are driven away from their husband's home.

Sexual violence has increasingly been used as a tool of war in the north-east region. There are two major kinds of conflict taking place in this region: intra-ethnic conflicts and conflicts that see the ethnic groups pitted against the state. Non-State armed groups in the region have thus very stringent codes of conduct. Hence, for a long time, most cases of sexual violence resulting from the armed conflict involved state armed forces.

The past couple of years have however seen an increase in the inter-ethnic violence. Rape and sexual assault have been used as a tactics by one ethic group to attack the honour of another group and to force people to flee their homes and communities in fear.

The following case studies illustrate the use of sexual violence in armed conflict scenarios:

- "Krishna Devi, a 30 years old woman, lived with her husband and three children in Lignsiphai, Churachandpur. She looked after cows and did the agricultural work. One morning while she was tending to cows in the jungle, two men from the Indian Reserve Battalion, who were undergoing training in the nearby BSF camp caught her, beat her up severely and then raped her till she fainted. She was admitted to the hospital in an unconscious state and was only released after a month of treatment. Women's organisations in Manipur took up the case and put pressure on the police to arrest the culprits. When nothing was done, they themselves caught the perpetrators and handed them over to the police. The rapists are now in jail. There has been increased pressure to let the perpetuators go free. Non-governmental organisations in Manipur, have however, stood by Krishna and her family and have managed to counter all such moves. Many women's groups in Manipur express their helplessness in dealing with cases of violence against women, especially when it involves the state armed forces.
- Security officials say that Thangjam Manorama Devi was a dangerous member of the separatist People's Liberation Army in Manipur. According to the army, she was responsible for a number of bomb blasts, including one that killed some soldiers. Her family insists she was a peaceful activist and was not involved in any criminal activities. Most human rights activists and journalists agree privately that she was a member of an underground group, but differ on the details, including what role she played.

The truth may never be fully known because no police complaint was ever filed against Manorama. She was never given an opportunity to be tried in court and found guilty or innocent. Instead, on July 11, 2004, the 32-years-old was arrested from her home by soldiers of the paramilitary Assam Rifles and killed while in their custody. Her bullet –ridden corpse was left in a field not far from her home where it was discovered by villagers. The Assam Rifles claimed she had been shot dead while trying to escape. It has been alleged that she was raped before being shot through her vagina.

10. Demographic, Economic and Social Profile of Odisha

Odisha lies in the Eastern Coast of India. It attained statehood on 1st April 1936 on the basis of language. But the princely states were merged in it after 1948 to form 13 districts. Later for administrative convenience in 1990 these districts were bifurcated in to form 30 districts. Odisha has the highest percentage of ST population after North-Eastern states. Total ST population: consists of 4,066,783 males and 4,078,298 females. Sex ratio among tribals is 953 females' per1000 males. Around 62 tribes are residing in the state with their specific culture and living style which is unique in the country. There are 12 major tribes such as Kondha, Gondh, Koya, Santhal, Saura, Kolha, Munda, Paraja, Bhuyians, Kisan, Oraon and Gadaba. The tribal's constitute one-fifth of the population of the state. As per 2011 census Odisha has a population of 41,947,358 crores. Sex ratio is 978 per 1000. Total literacy is 73.45 per cent out of which male literacy is 82.40 per cent and female literacy rate is 64.36 per cent. In Odisha the sex ratio till the age of six vis-à-vis boys has declined from 952 in 2001 to 934 in 2011.

Social status of women

The patriarchal social framework in Odisha and a value system based on preference for a son have resulted in discrimination and neglect of the girl-child. Further, proliferation and abuse of advanced technologies coupled with social factors such as dowry, concerns with family name and looking up to the son as a bread earner has led to an alarming rise in the practice of female foeticide.

The status of women in Odishan society is a major cause of concern that influences biases against women. The state has accorded high priority in ensuring gender equity in education, political participation as well as economic and employment opportunities.

Female work participation rate is usually considered an important indicator to assess women's participation and involvement in various economic activities and their access to income. A study of all the districts of Odisha reflects that tribal districts with more population of SC and STs have a higher FWPR. The developed and coastal districts such as Cuttack, Khurda, Puri, Kendrapara etc. have a participation rate less than 15 within the total women workers more in household industries followed by agriculture as labouers. Gender disparity in wages is a matter of concern. Equal pay for equal work is never a reality for at least casual workers. This has been found by WSS (55th Round) survey.

The political representation of women in the parliament and Assembly is very low. In 2009, the data reveals that Odisha has no woman in Lok Sabha and three women MPs in Rajya Sabha (30 per cent). The Assembly of 2004 had only nine women MLAs out of which two had received ministerial position. The assembly of 2009 has only seven women (4.8 per cent).

Cases of Violence against women in Odisha

As per the Annual Report of Commissionerate police released in 2014-15 the twin city recorded 440 cases of crimes against women in 2014. In 2013, the number of crimes against women were 320. In the Pipili Gangrape case the 19 year old Dalit girl was allegedly targeted as she was the prime witness of the gang rape case that took place in her village in 2008. The Pipili Police initially had not registered the case but later registered it on Jan. 9, 2011 following a direction from the State Human Rights Commission.

However, in order to curb atrocities on women, the State Government had initiated several measures. The Chief Minister of Odisha announced a special wing which had been functioning in the Odisha Police. It is styled as Human Rights Protection Cell under the charge of an Additional DG of Police. It exclusively deals with crime against women, particularly dowry-related offences like case of dowry homicide, suicide, torture and non-dowry torture and all cases registered under the SC and ST (PA) Act.

The National Crime Records Bureau reported 6,249 cases of violence against women, including 799 rape cases, 547 abduction cases, 334 dowry deaths, and 1,671 cases of cruelty by husband and relative, among others in Odisha.

The Dalits, who constituted 16.53 per cent of the State's total population, were neglected sections. About 52.30 per cent of the Dalits lived Below Poverty Line. The National Crime Records Bureau reported 1,439 cases of crimes against the Dalits in Odisha. Their houses were burnt and they were denied access to public places and services such as community tube well and temples.

Trafficking was rampant in Odisha. A study conducted by the Bhubaneswar-based Institute of Socio-Economic Development in collaboration with United Nations Development Fund for Women (UNIFEM) revealed that the holy place of Puri remained the main destination of victims of trafficking with 43.83 per cent, followed by capital city of Bhubaneswar with 30 per cent. The study covered 13 out of the State's 30 districts and identified 559 cases of trafficking from 275 villages in 83 blocks under 21 districts.

11. A Final Word

The North-Eastern region of India does not have a common platform where problems of women, especially those of domestic violence as well as ethnic violence are addressed. It is a fact that interventions from external social organisations in terms of training and confidence building are frequently offered. It is felt that building a constituent base is an important step in generating public support for addressing gender based violence. This responsibility lies with civil society on the one hand and State Agencies on the other in the context of both Manipur and Odisha.

A healthy partnership between Women's Groups and the State Apparatus can tackle this problem in an innovative way. Women's groups must protect their independence on certain issues. They have to believe criminal justice system, and fight to protect the rights of women victims. National Literacy Mission and other organisations engaged in Sarva Shiksha Abhiyan should also be assigned responsibility of educating the rural men and women regarding the significance of human rights and empowerment of women.

On the other hand, both print as well as electronic media can play a vital role in restructuring the rural society both in Manipur and Odisha. Further social media's role in this coveted direction is also praiseworthy. It can act as an agent of political socialisation for inculcating the values of gender equality and gender justice. Section 19 of the Human Rights Act must be suitably amended to make the verdict of Human Rights Commissions more binding. Restricting on the commission's jurisdiction over armed forces must be removed. Cultural appropriateness and value additions are essential for effectiveness in reducing violence against women. It depends upon balancing traditional beliefs about family and community relationships with new consciousness about human rights, gender equality and non-violence.

Above all optimistic vision that a multipronged approach to violence against women in both societies of Manipur and Odisha will result in far-reaching changes, transforming attitudes and practices so that women and men can live a life of equality and dignity.

Moreover, "We must unite. Violence against women cannot be tolerated, in any form, in any context, in any circumstance, by any political leader or by any government" said Secretary-General Ban Ki-moon. And in honour to dignity and security of women today time is ripe to think about it. Above all, attitudinal change is necessary to check the malaise." Furthermore moral policing, community awareness, women empowerment, popularisation of community police system are the guider to check Violence Against Women in coming days. To this Barack Obama's idea is worth noting 'Young men need to show women the respect they deserve and recognise sexual assault and to do their part to stop it'. Let us promise to take all possible steps including a Woman Security law for protection of Rights of women in particular and women in general.

Notes

- Agnes Flavia (1990): "Journey to Justice", (Mumbai, Majlis).
- Coomaraswamy, Radhika (2005): "Human Security and Gender Violence", *Economic and Political Weekly*, pp. 4729-4736.
- "Domestic Violence: A Short Legal Primer by Breakthrough": (www.breakthrough.tv)
- Fact Sheet: National Family Health Survey NFHS-III 2005-06. (Ministry of Health and Family Welfare, Govt. of India.)

- Fernades, Walter, Melville Pereina, Khataso, Vizalenu: "Customary Laws in North-East India: Impact on Women", (Report of National Commission for Women, New Delhi).
- Gonsalves, Lina (2001): "Women and Human Rights", New Delhi, APH Publishing Corporation.
- Hmar, Isaac L, "Violence Against Women" (www.atimes.com)
- India: Report of the Malimath Committee on Reforms of the Criminal Justice System: Some Observations (September 19, 2003): (www.amnesty.org)
- Lawyers Collective (1992): "Domestic Violence, New Delhi, Kali for Women.
- Pannu, Gurpreet, "Gender Violence Vis-à-vis Human Rights of Women: International and National Perspective" published in Singh, Awadhesh Kumar, Choudhury, Jayanta (Ed.) (2012): "Violence against women and children: Issues and Concerns", New Delhi, Serials Publications.
- Sehgal, Rashme (2006); "Delays do not bode well for Domestic Violence Bill", (www.infochangeindia.org.)
- Sen, Srijoni and Ambast, Sanhita (2005): "The Domestic Violence Act, 2005: A New Direction", (www.indlaw.com).
- Saikia, Nandita (2007): "Vision 2020 and Domestic Violence in India" published in Satpathy, Sachidananda (ed.) Youth Vision 2020: Towards Building An India of our Choice, New Delhi, Serials.
- "Violence against women on the rise in Odisha", Odisha diary, com viewed on Tuesday, February 28, 2012.
- WHO Multi Country Study on Women's Health and Domestic Violence Against Women, (2007): Geneva: World Health Organisation.
- WHO, Domestic violence: A priority public health issue in Western Pacific Region. (2001) : Western Pacific Regional Office.

References

Walby, Sylvia (1997), Theorising Patriarchy, Oxford, Basil Blackwell.

"Local action/ Global Change: Learning about the Human Rights of women and Girls" (1999) Julie Mertus with Mallika Dutta and Nancy Flowers, (Centre for Women's Global Leadership and the United Nations Development Fund for Women -UNIFEM).

Changing the stream: Backgrounder on the Women's movement in India by Shubha Chacko (Mumbai) (Centre for Education and Documentation).

www.dnaindia.com

These fellow must be eliminated": Relentless violence and impunity in Manipur (Human Rights Watch Report).

11

Violence Against Women: From Silence to Empowerment An Empirical Study

Dr Ms. S.D. Sasi Kiran

"Would thou the earth and heaven itself in one sole name combine?

I name thee, O Sakuntala! and all at once is said. (Tr. E. B. Eastwick)

Abstract

This study investigates the role of distinctive societal, and specific or systematic representation of factors represented in Indian Writings – Regional and English Languages - which influence opportunities for female advancement. This study is an analysis of the barriers or opportunities that are more or less favourable to women's advancement reflected in Indian fiction in English and Regional Literature, here Telugu. The study combines and contrasts results drawn from selected novels of Indian Literature in English.

Type of study

Empirical

Description of data and sample

Selected novels of Jumpa Lahiri (The Namesake); Anitha Desai (Fire on the Mountain); Sudha Murthy (Mahaswetha & Gently Falling Bakula); Chalam (Mydanam).

Introduction

Violence can include, but is not limited to:

- Physical violence (slapping, kicking, hitting, or use of weapons).
- Emotional violence (systematic humiliation, controlling behaviour, degrading treatment, threats).
- Sexual violence (coerced sex, forced into sexual activities considered degrading or humiliating).
- Economic violence (restricting access to financial or other resources with the purpose of controlling a person) (the World Bank's Gender and Development Group).

Literature Review

Violence as physically injurious assault by highlighting the interrelated range of abusive, coercive, controlling behaviours causing psychological, sexual or physical harm, which often accompany or precede the use or threat of physical force. However, researchers have given considerably less attention to sexual, psychological and other forms of abuse (Bergen 1999, O'Leary 1999, Dekeseredy 2000, Saunders 2002). Some issues of terminology remain actively contested, such as whether domestic violence should be a gender-specific or neutral referent and/or encompass all forms and incidence of abuse in all types of intimate relationships (Muehlenhard and Kimes 1999, Mullender,1996).

There is no single or universal definition of gender-based or sexual violence. Understandings differ according to country, community and legal context. For instance, prevalent definitions of sexual violence exclude children. The lack of a clear and commonly accepted language inhibits the development of an effective reporting system and/or databases, and thus restrains prevention, monitoring and advocacy efforts (Baker, 2007).

The term *sexual and gender based violence*, in its widest sense, refers to the physical, emotional or sexual abuse of a survivor. This review focuses exclusively on the sexual elements of abuse, and discusses the management of physical and emotional abuse only where it relates to accompanying sexual abuse. The term *gender-based violence* is widely used as a synonym for *violence against women*, in order to highlight the gender inequality in which much violence is rooted (IGWG of USAID, 2006). Violence against women and children, of both sexes, has gained international recognition as a serious social and human rights concern affecting all societies. Social, economic, and gender issues are increasingly recognised as significant factors in India.

Research indicates a link between maternal experience of violence and evidence ofincreased mortality and under nutrition among children of abused mothers (Jejeebhoy, 1998; Ganatra *et al.*, 1998; Asling-Monemi *et. al.*, 2003, in Kishor and Johnson, 2004). Hence, Gender violence is a subject matter to be discussed at larger frames to achieve Global wellbeing.

This paper sketches out promising standpoints headed for '*violence' showcasing that* the influential formation and significance of *violence* in both life and *literature*.

'*Autopsy*' of Selected Novels: *See for yourself*

When violence is loomed, it is fell out one dimensional as physical clash among fictional characters in literature. Violence in text, resembling violence in human world, is multifaceted that works at different intensity and is effected by diverse motivations, and is practiced in a variety of ways. Critics of modern literature have by and large attributed the new trend to: (a) the breathtaking pray of violent actions and (b) its embryonic to dumbfound readers by shuddering their viewpoints.

Creative writers, especially novelists expressed the anxieties of human world and in which human aggression threatened. Images of violence in all literary forms have so generalised that the destructive human potential appear unlikely at best. Thus, violence has become a subject that most modern writers who wish to pass on the historical, psychological, and artistic landscape of the modern world would brazen out with.

'Violent means key factors in the existential perception of human bonds broken under the modern philosophy of power were adopted to cleanse and reorder the world through fascism, collectivism, and imperialism.' (*On Violence,* Hannah Arendt)

Literature is the best tool for highlighting any issue or reiterating any position. Indian women writers have eloquently voiced women's side of life – the experiences of man's other. They are able to sensitively portray a world that has in it women rich in substance. Their women are real flesh-and-blood protagonists who make you look at them with awe with their relationships to their surroundings, their society, their men, their children, their families; their mental make-ups and themselves. In *The Namesake*, it becomes a process that can be seen in Ashima by contrasting her character in different stages of her life in the United States. However, here I would like to add Lahiri into that category of writers, since not only has she demonstrated the importance of in-between space, but also has, by deconstructing the narrow national and cultural identity for the immigrants, attempted to locate them into the mainstream white society. She suggests that identity based on national culture is a "potent site of control and domination within modern society" (Ashcroft, Griffiths, and Tiffin, *Key Concepts* 150). In other words, as long as immigrants are resistant to adopting a multiplicity of identities, they risk being the victims of discrimination. *The Namesake* is a cross-cultural, multigenerational story of a Hindu Bengali family's journey to self-acceptance in Boston. Jhumpa masterfully explores the themes of the complexities of the immigrant experience and foreignness, the clash of lifestyles, cultural disorientation, the conflicts of assimilation and the tangled ties between generations and paints a portrait of an Indian family torn between the pull of respecting family traditions, and the American way of life. It's a tale of love, solitude and emotional upheavals with an amazing eye for detail and ironic observation.

Anitha Desai's Ila Das in *Fire on the Mountain* comes to typify the sticky situation of ill fated women whose lives are worn out under the unbearable weight of tragic eventualities. The character of Ila Das has been portrayed to carry generous nuances. She lived her life on the margins of isolation and solitude with courage to counter the formidable dominant forces with her ability. However, tragic her untimely death might have been, she had succeeded to make her existence felt, against which her loss of chastity seemed to be a small price. Ila Das had to pay in the all consuming struggle with brute forces. She redeems the sanctity of her life by her indomitable spirits. When Ila Das is raped and killed, that violent action happens "offstage" at the end of the novel, the reader is prepared for the horrific ending by carefully embedding violence in her imagery and in her symbolism. "I, too, overflow; my desires have invented new desires, my body knows unheard-of songs. ... And I, too, said nothing, showed nothing; I didn't open my mouth, I didn't repaint my half of the world. I was ashamed. I was afraid, and I swallowed my shame and my fear. I said to myself: You are mad! What's the meaning of these waves, these floods, these outbursts? Where is the ebullient infinite woman who...hasn't been ashamed of her strength? (Helene Cixous)

Sample was also drawn from Sudha Murthy, an Indian industrialist, social worker and author of two selected novels - *Mahaswetha*, the female protagonist Anupama; who has met her match a handsome Dr Anand, just like the story of Cinderella and gets a life dream come true. This all is shattered when she discovers that she has leukoderma which is still treated in India as a curse.

Post-modern linguistic theory, which theorises the collapse of distinctions between self and other, and copy and original, fits right into gender theorists who would like to denaturalise compulsory heterosexuality, gender roles and the masculine-feminine binary.(Judith Butler) The other novel *Gently Falling Bakula* is about a bright young man and a girl, who knows each other from their school-days fall in love and gets married in spite of a family feud. Shrikant graduates from IIT-Bombay, joins a software firm and is on his way to become its director. Shrimati though more intelligent than him, gives up her further studies and manages his house. After almost half a decade of marriage, she realises that her husband has become too focused on his career and has no place for family matters or to think about her. Eventually, she takes a decision that leaves their family life shattered. The turning point of the otherwise settled life and easy going is when Shrimati realises, how easily she has made her husband's ambition as her ambition and in the process has lost not only her identity but herself respect too. An attempt has been made to test a hybrid notion that both gender norms and societal norms may partially account for the behaviour of female at middle and elite levels.

Many are incredible with Joseph Campbell's theory of the hero's journey, the idea that every man from Moses to Hercules grows to adulthood while battling his alter-ego. This paper explores the heroine's voyage in Telugu Literature *Maidanam* as Rajeswari, the female - protagonist searches through romancehood. Foucault plans to explore the self-awareness of the individual as the subject of sexuality. (*The History of Sexuality: An Introduction*. New York: Vintage Books, 1990). Abundant stories from cultures as varied as Hindu and Muslim divulge her who battle for love, thereby upsetting popular notions of the passive, gentle heroine. Only after she has reintegrated, can the heroine become the bestower of wisdom, the protecting queen and arch-crone. "We must kill the false woman who is preventing the live one from breathing." (Helene Cixous) In *Maidanam*, Chalam's most popular Telugu novel, Rajeswari, the heroine, deserts her husband who is a worldly person lacking an aesthetic sense and elopes with Amir. Rajeswari lives with him in poverty and in a barren land devoid of any conventional beauty. The third and the toughest phase comes with the entrance of an adolescent Meera to whom she gives herself as a token of gratitude, motherhood and a love beyond all earthly reasoning. Thus, her character accomplishes the three phases of evolution –physical, psychological and spiritual. The real self of the *Stree* was deliberately marred by the male chauvinism. She was totally chained from all corners in the conventional society. She was chased by the quality of chastity. Chalam roared against the marital violence. He tried to shock the conventional minds by criticising vehemently differentiating love and sex. Lust could not be considered as love. The illegal relationship between man and woman that was not accepted by conventional society had pervaded much of the Chalam's writings. *Maidanam* tells a tale of love of a real, flesh-and-blood woman who runs away to the open plain where Rajeswari liberates herself from the bondages imposed upon her. The open plain is especially important to Rajeswari because this is where Rajeswari comes to realise that she has the strength and ability to go beyond her limitations as a woman.

Chalam's *Maidanam* is widely perceived and highly appreciated by modern readers as a feminist text, which advocates the notions that women are entitled to true love, happiness and independence. They also highly value Chalam's *Maidanam* for it shows the conflicts and struggles a woman goes through while challenging the social norms. In the novel, Rajeswari at first behaves and considers herself a reserved and inhibited person not accustomed to intimacy. After she develops a relationship with Amir, it is her passion for him and the sensual stimulation by him bring her sensual joy and awaken her. While her rebellion against the social conventions is regarded as a very strong characteristic of feminism that highlights Rajeswari's intense emotional capacity, it may be that she is a solitary and a conflicted woman, and it is her desperate loneliness that leads to her tragedy. Chalam took solitude as the central theme of the novel. Interestingly, the word, alone, occurs many a times throughout the novel. It is safe to say that Chalam portrays Rajeswari as a solitary woman who struggles to make up for her loneliness. In the interpretation of her awakening, she is seen as a woman who awakens to her sensuality that brings her physical joy. Later on, she awakens once again to realise that she is all alone in the world and can never overcome this state of being. To dispel this intolerable sense of solitude, she chooses to welcome Meera into her life. She does not possess the strength to live her life alone and is therefore driven to seek the security of Meera's company. Her final act of destruction has a quality of uncompromising sensuous fulfillment. It is her answer to the inadequacies of life, a literal denial and reversal of the birth trauma she has just witnessed, a stripping away of adulthood, of limitation, of consciousness itself. In short, she first awakens from sensual pleasure followed by the realisation of an unbeatable sense of solitude.

Significant findings

Women are ever ready to rise to the situation in India too from time immemorial. The modern women are ready to face the challenges to attain aggressive gender-conscious promotion. Creative writers show that the mission of literature is to advance equity for women and girls through advocacy, education, training and philanthropy. We find female protagonists like Ashima, Ila Das, Anupama, Srimathi and Rajeswari grow through shaded experiences showcasing the feminine vibrating energy.

References

- Anita Desai: *Fire on the Mountain*. Penguin, London,1977.
- Jhumpa Lahiri, *The Namesake*, 2004.
- Sudha Murty, *Mahashweta*, Penguin Books, India, 2007
- Sudha Murty, *Gently Falling Bakula*, Penguin Books, India, 2008
- G.V. *Chalam, Maidanam*, Vijayawada: Aruna Publishing House, 1927.

- G.V. *Chalam*, Stree, Vijayawada: *Premchand Publications*, 1930.
- Franzak, J., and Noll, E. (2006). Monstrous acts: Problematising violence in young adult literature, *49*(8), 662-672.

Bio – profile: Dr Ms. S.D. Sasi Kiran MA, M.Sc IT, PGDTE, M.Phil PhD, Associate professor of English, S & H Department, Vignan's University, Vadlamudi in Andhra Pradesh hails from Kakinada and a senior academician interested in the field of Translation. Her thesis at doctorate level 'Translating the Regional Invisibility: A Discourse Analysis of Telugu Translated Works' belongs to the area of Translation Studies. Her areas of interest are: Translation, Translation Studies, Language and Literature of English and Indian Writing in English. Her contribution in publication, both research and creative, has been rich and commendable. She is a co-editor/ Reviewer of Online – Journals – 'Cyber Literature', 'Journal of Medical and Science and Technology', 'SISAL', 'AWEJ' and 'International Journal of Sociology and Anthropology' and actively involved in the activities of the journals and also a member of various teaching associations like TSAP, ELT@I, Teaching professionals and SIG. Her article "A Brief Survey of Translated Telugu Literature in English" has been included as study document to Lecture Notes on Indian literature with University of Sussex, UK. Her translated stories from English into Telugu and some other articles are published in Telugu daily paper 'Saakshi' and her poems are published online. She released three books. Her short story 'Madhura Meenakshi' in translation is published in Sahitya Academy's Indian Literature Journal. She is dynamically engaging engineering - students in mini projects. She is currently translating a biography and R. Vasundhara Devi's short stories.

12

Women as Victims of Violence in India

Dr Beulah Shekhar

Abstract

This theoretical research paper attempts to draw the need of women victims of crime in India. It discusses the plight of women victims of crime vis-à-vis, India's commitment to international instruments. The salient features of the UN documents pertaining to victims the Justice Verma Committee Report are highlighted. Attention is drawn to the absence of victim friendly legislations and the alternate state initiatives that come to the rescue of the women victims of crime in India. The role of public interest litigations, alternate dispute resolution and the proactive role of NGOs and frontline professionals are elucidated. The road ahead for redressal for women victims of crime are argued.

***Key words**:* United Nations adopted the Declaration of Basic Principle of Justice for Victims of Crime and Abuse of Power. Handbook on justice for victims, the Guide for policy-makers, Justice Verma Committee Report, CEDAW report, Public Interest Litigation, Alternate Dispute resolution, Role of NGOs.

'Justice isn't served until crime victims are'......John Scarr

Much water has below the bridge since activists spoke about the womb to tomb victimisation of women in India. Now, the time is ripe to approach this concern with a rights based approach for women victims of crime in India. To begin on a positive note with regard to redressal for women victims of crime, the United Nation's Convention on the Elimination of All Forms of Discrimination against Women (CEDAW) in the report of the Committee on the Elimination of Discrimination against Women, (CEDWA Report, 2014) commended the progress achieved since 2007 the adoption of: The Criminal Law Amendment Act, 2013; The Sexual Harassment of Women in the Workplace (Prevention, Prohibition and Redress) Act, 2013; The Protection of Children from Sexual Offences Act, 2012. Having said this, on the flip side however remains the hiccups in the implementation of these women friendly legislations here in India. While embarking on the task of this research paper, attention should be drawn to Andre Gide quote 'Everything that needs to be said, has already been said, but since no one was listening, everything needs to be said again' this is stated with reference to the Law Commission's 84th Report in 1980, the 172nd Report of 2000, the Supreme Court's judgment of 2006 in Prakash Singh's case, the Justice Malimath Commission report, the 2nd Administrative Reforms Commission report the National Police Commission Reports and last but not the least the Justice Verma Report. All these documents repeatedly recommend autonomy and improving in the quality of the police force, which is the principal machinery for the maintenance of law and order. The Justice Verma Committee report reiterates stricter implementation of existing laws, police reforms, gender sensitisation of the security agencies gender sensitisation of the judiciary, changes in the IPC to deal with the crimes against women particularly rape cases. It is interesting to note that the late Justice Verma in his opening remarks has expressed the fervent HOPE that the government will take the recommendations seriously, and ensure implementation of these in letter and spirit.

However, the data in National Crime Records Bureau (NCRB, 2012), reveals the large numbers of acquittal in cases registered for crimes against women, reveals that the challenges of making the Justice system in India victim friendly are multifold. Traced back as far as the Blackstone's formulation (also known as Blackstone's ratio or the Blackstone ratio) is the principle: "better that ten guilty persons escape than that one innocent suffer". Also, going back even further a Roman doctrine that states "it was better to let the crime of a guilty person go unpunished than to condemn the innocent." Both theses maxims it should be observed, when rephrased read as 'Better to deny ten victim justice than deny one perpetrator justice'. In simple terms it means that it is worse to convict innocent people than to acquit guilty people. Justice Malimath says 'Criminal justice system favours the accused' (The Hindu, April 22nd, 2003) Criminal Justice System focuses on the Perpetrator. From the very nomenclature itself it is evident that this is a Criminal Justice System. The center of attention is justice to the criminals. So, should the present Criminal Justice System be done away with, and replaced with a Victim Justice System or should there be a parallel Victim Justice System for victim justice? Moreover, in the present scenario, due to the docket explosion, the victim of crime in India is more often than not, found chasing justice, which like a mirage, moves further and further away, eluding him for decades. After all it is not for the victim for whom this Justice system exists. So the victim holds the key and he is the person the system should revolve around, as he is the one who sets the Justice system in motion when he initiates action in the form of an FIR. The recent Victimisation Surveys have captured the huge chasm between the reported crime and the unreported crime. The reasons for not reporting range from the attitude of the law enforcement to the judges. These dark figures are increasing steadily since the justice system is not victim friendly. Consequently, the victim seeks justice elsewhere giving rise to vigilantism or street justice. Then the present justice system in all its glory will become redundant. Having said this, while targeting the need for national legislations for victims to ensure Social Justice, it is dare said that denying Victim rights is absence of Social Justice because social justice is 'a fair and proper administration of laws conforming to the natural law that all persons, irrespective of ethnic origin, gender, race, religion, etc., are to be treated equally and without prejudice' (this list sadly omits, but should include the parties to a crime namely, the victim and the perpetrator.)– and the national laws in this country, sans Victim Laws, favour the perpetrator, thus making the Criminal JUSTICE system a sheer CRIMINAL Justice System (Reiman, 2006). Any well thought of or well conceptualised legislation is characterised by three points - First, that the legislation in question addresses a felt need, secondly, that it is broadly acceptable and finally it is an enforceable piece of legislation. (Shekhar and Wemmers, 2012) The latest amendment to the Criminal Procedure Code, which finally received the President's assent in 2010, after a year in abeyance, was encouraging. This legislation addresses some important aspects of victims' justice such as requiring the completion of investigations of rape and child abuse within three months; the right of rape victims to engage a lawyer of their choice to assist the prosecution; the ability of the trial court to award compensation in cases of acquittal to the victim under Section 357 of the Criminal Procedure Code; and the right of the victim to rehabilitation (Venkatesan, 2010). New legislation will allow judges' orders to reach victims and their families, assisting them in accessing justice and securing their rights. However, the Indian government has failed to implement both the letter and spirit of this new legislation law. Thus, the Indian legal regime has failed to protect victims' rights in two fundamental ways. First, by failing to enact suitable laws and secondly, when legislation is in place, by failing to monitor its implementation. (Sarkar, 2010)

Therefore, the journey through the criminal justice system, of a woman who is a victim of crime, is not smooth, to say least. This plight of the victim continues through the various phases like the reporting of the crime, police investigation, charge sheeting and pre-trial enquiry, trial or even after the trial. The Indian legal system's inexplicable persistence with its colonial past is reflected in its reluctance to break away from the pattern of institutionalisation of mechanism of adjudication and enforcement.(Muralidhar, 2003). This is doubly true for women victims of crime in their pursuit of justice through the criminal justice system in India. While the vulnerable victims from the disadvantaged sections, do not in the sense access the legal system to seek redress, they are nevertheless engage with it negatively and are drawn into the system as encroachers and defendants. These situations accentuate their denial of access to justice, to basic legal services, resulting in grave violations of their liberty. While the response of the governments to these endemic problems has been one of indifference, the judiciary and the civil society have attempted alternatives that require to be acknowledged and understood. In recent times, among the many reforms canvassed for improving the criminal justice system is the one that advocates a victim-orientation to criminal justice administration. Victim-orientation includes greater respect and consideration towards victims and their rights in the investigative and prosecution process, provisions for greater choices to victims in trial and disposition of the accused, and a scheme of reparation/ compensation particularly for victims of violent crimes. (Menon, 2004). Until 1970s the victims of crime were a forgotten entity in the criminal justice system. The attitude began to change as the discipline of victimology came into its own. (Srinivasan and Mathew, 2007) Having said this, across the globe, victims of crime are protected, assisted, restituted and compensated by appropriate laws and acts. But in India the victims of crime play only an insignificant role in the criminal justice process. The role of the victim in the Indian criminal Justice System which follows the common law colonial tradition, is restricted to that of a witness (Muralidharan, 2004). It has been over twenty-five years since the United Nations adopted the Declaration of Basic Principle of Justice for Victims of Crime and Abuse of Power. The Declaration played a key role in stimulating Member States of the UN to introduce victims' rights domestically and inspired the inclusion of victims' rights in the Rome Statute, which established the International Criminal Court. Today, many developing nations, such as India are just beginning to address victims' rights.(Shekhar and Wemmers, 2012)

STATE INITIATIVES FOR VICTIM JUSTICE: It is pertinent to note that in India in spite of Professor Upender Baxi's (while calling attention to the fact that there is no dearth of laws in India), statement at the Criminology conference where he coined the term 'Gross Legislative Product (GLP)', India has not a single victim legislation. Therefore, in the absence of victim legislation the State initiatives and the role of the judiciary in furthering the victim justice in India are a way forward for women victims of crime in India. Though India till date does not have comprehensive victim legislations, to further the aims of the UN declaration that it has ratified, it has taken initiatives in the form of Alternate dispute resolutions, Public Interest Litigations, Lok Adalats, and Tribunals Commissions. Unlike the case of the USA or Canada, the legal aid/ public interest movement in

India has been almost entirely initiated and led by the judiciary. (Bhagavathi, 1985).

Public Interest Litigation : The PIL though not uniquely a creature of Indian public law, has achieved an identity of its own in the jurisprudence of the sub-continent. The emergence of the concept and, even more strikingly, its unrepentant dimensions in the current practice of Indian courts, clearly in conflict with traditional norms of judicial detachment and objectivity, represent a bold but controversial response to the perceived implications of social inequality and economic deprivation (Peiris, 1991). The PIL has been used as justice to both victims of crime and victim s of abuse of power since 1979. Through an expansive reading of the fundamental rights, informed by commitment to the (non-enforceable) social welfare objectives of the directive principles, the courts have sought to read substance into otherwise formal guarantees. (Article 37) Since 1981 when the apex court open the issue of locus standi in public interest litigation in favour of the citizen and public interest litigation on his behalf this has allowed a stranger to a cause, be he a journalist, social worker, advocate or an association of such persons initiate action before this court in matters alleged to be involving public interest (Noorani, 1982). As a result of this many public spirited citizen of the country, had a locus to present the plead on behalf of the victim in numerous matters involving life and liberty of a citizen, and the courts in India have given justice to victims by their proactive judgments. Public interest litigation (PIL) in India can serve as a vehicle for creating and enforcing rights and is critical to the sustenance of democracy. PIL in India can address the needs of its citizens when legislative inertia afflicts it PIL can serve as a model for other developing nations struggling with legislative inertia and can provide recourse to marginalised and disadvantaged communities. Furthermore, while PIL obscures the traditional boundaries of power in a liberal democratic polity, democracy is in fact strengthened by the expansion of standing to include any citizen who has suffered a rights abuse.(Holladay, 2012). It is refreshing to note that despite the fact that no separate laws for Victims of crime have been enacted in India, Victim justice has been rendered through the proactive action of the apex court and ensuing judgments (Shekhar and Wemmers, 2012). In the Vishaka judgment, the petition was presented as a class action by certain social activists and NGOs with the aim of focusing attention towards the 'societal aberration' and also to a system finding suitable methods for realisation of the true concept of gender equality. There was also a prayer that sexual harassment of women in all workplaces must be injuncted through judicial orders until the vacuum in the existing legislation was replaced. (JVCR, 2013) This movement has been discussed by judges in the popular press and academic literature, and it is clearly informed by strong socio-political views and commitments and have the following distinctive characteristics liberalisation of rules of access and standing, creative and activist representation of legal and fundamental rights remedial flexibility and ongoing judicial participation and supervision (Cassels, 1985). Past interest in the phenomena of Public Interest Litigation has concentrated on a legal justification of PIL based on arguments of "access to justice" for the underprivileged masses (Baxi, 1987; Desai and Muralidhar, 2000). In the context of developing countries going to court may not even be a matter of choice to a large number of affected people who are unacquainted with their legal rights and, in the face of damages, simply do not have the means to file a case in the court (Desai and Muralidhar, 2000). In spite of so many ills which plague the judicial system, the overflowing docket explosion is evidence of the faith in the judiciary, but state of affairs is that the number of Judges is highly disproportionate to the population. Recently it has gone upto 13 Judges per million as against an estimated requirement of 50 judges per million of the population, though the apex court has expressed the need for at least 50 per million. (Kumar, 2012) Past interest in the phenomena of public interest litigation has concentrated on a legal justification of PIL and on arguments based on "access to Justice" for the poor. PIL can be justified as an economically efficient choice of redress if certain conditions are fulfilled. (Raja and Rajarathinam, 2005)

Free legal Aid: To address the access to justice for victims through the state has responded with the Article 39A which emphasises that free legal service is an inalienable element of 'reasonable, fair and just' procedure, for without it a person suffering from economic or other disabilities would be deprived of the opportunity for securing justice. The Legal Services Authorities Act, 1987 made the much needed modifications in the arena of legal services by providing free and competent legal services to the weaker sections of the society to ensure that opportunities for securing justice are not denied to any citizen by reason of their economic status and to organise Lok Adalats to secure that the operation of the legal system promotes justice on a basis of equal opportunity.

Alternate Dispute resolutions : The state had statutorily provided for arbitration as an alternate ADR and recently overhauled the statutory framework but arbitration has become entrapped in the mould of the formal legal dispute resolution and is struggling to emerge from it. Another initiative by the state to increase the access to justice for victims is the setting up of tribunals for dispute related to family, labour and consumers have been lamented by the but efforts are being made to use these bodies to effectively respond to the victims and to the formal legal system. Establishment of the fast track courts and Special Courts is a more recent response of the state to address the issue of access to justice but they seem effective only in some states and not others. (Muralidhar, 2003)

However, in spite of the National Consultations on judicial reforms, comprehensive victim legislation has yet to see the light of day in India. While several National Commissions (e.g. National Commission on Human Rights) have been put in place to help victims of human rights violations, child victims, women victims and the victims of the scheduled caste or tribe, these commissions remain toothless tigers without enforceable victims' rights and, hence, contribute to the secondary victimisation of these hapless victims. (Shekar and Wemmers, 2012)

Amicus curiae Courts are obliged to do justice in individual cases and must deal with the inability of the accused to engage a lawyer when no lawyer is willing to appear for him/her. Thus, the resort by the court to a friend, amicus curiae, forms an important pillar of the justice delivery system in the Indian context. Article 39A of the Constitution of India obliges the state to ensure that the legal system promotes justice on the basis of equal opportunity to all citizens, and the state shall, in particular, provide free legal aid to ensure that opportunities for securing justice are not denied to any citizen because of economic or other disability. The right to legal representation has also been read into Article 21 of the Constitution. Thus, the right to legal representation in all cases exists not because the Constitution provides for it, but because it is a fundamental condition for the sustenance of the rule of law, which in turn is a constitutional goal. Even if a person has committed a crime, which may be heinous in nature, it is a requirement under the ideals protected by constitutionalism that there should be a trial where the person has full opportunity to satisfy the court of his or her innocence. Such a right is equally available in so-called "open and shut" cases. In fact, it is in "open and shut" cases that in addition to the accused being tried, democracy and the values of the Constitution are put to test. Reactions by bar associations making it difficult for the accused to get legal assistance after gruesome incidents such as the Parliament House attack, the 26/11 attack, or the Nirbhaya case, have all compelled the courts to crystallise a new jurisprudence.

Abuse of power: Way back in 1893 Justice Mohamed in a special bench the Allahabad High Court prior to the decision of Ridge vs Baldwin which enunciated the principles of natural justice and recorded his lone dissent, that was ignored by the remaining English judges, ahead of his time, when he held that the appeal of an accused against his conviction could not be decided without hearing being heard for his decision, in a case of deciding his jail appeal. 'sentinel on the qui vivi'

INTERNATIONAL INSTRUMENTS FOR VICTIMS: First, the United Nations Declaration on Basic Principles of Justice for Victims of Crime and Abuse of Power, 1985, which has been duly ratified by India as a member state, promulgates access to justice and fair treatment for Victims of Crime, restitution (compensation from the perpetrators), compensation (from the state) and last but not the least assistance to victims of crime. This Declaration is descendant to the UN Universal Declaration of Human Rights adopted in 1948. This Declaration gives victims a legitimate place in the universal agenda of Human Rights. The United Nations Declaration on The Basic Principles of Justice.

This declaration is rightly called the Magna Carta for Victims of Crime. It further propagates that victims of crime have ten rights namely,

1. The right to be treated with dignity and respect
2. The right to information
3. The right to present their views to the court

4. The right to free legal aid / advice
5. The right to protection of privacy and physical safety
6. The right to informal dispute resolution
7. The right to social and medical assistance
8. The right to restitution by the perpetrator
9. The right to compensation by the state
10. The right to capacity building and co-operation.

Rights bring with them an obligation to respect a person's right. One person's rights presuppose another person's duties; hence Hohfeld (1964) argues that there cannot be a right without a duty. So the Government has a duty to ensure these rights.

This declaration gives a very comprehensive definition, (has recently found a place in the Indian statues) the Articles 1 and 2 where it says that "Victims" means persons who, individually or collectively, have suffered harm, including physical or mental injury, emotional suffering, economic loss or substantial impairment of their fundamental rights, through acts or omissions that are in violation of criminal laws operative within Member States, including those laws proscribing criminal abuse of power. A person may be considered a victim, under this Declaration, regardless of whether the perpetrator is identified, apprehended, prosecuted or convicted and regardless of the familial relationship between the perpetrator and the victim. The term "victim" also includes, where appropriate, the immediate family or dependants of the direct victim and persons who have suffered harm in intervening to assist victims in distress or to prevent victimisation.

Next, the other document the Handbook on justice for victims serves as a tool for implementing victim service programmes and for developing victim-sensitive policies, procedures and protocols for criminal justice agencies and others who come into contact with victims. This elaborates on the following in the five sections, the impact of victimisation; victim assistance; the role and responsibility of frontline professionals to victims; advocacy, policy-making and law reform and working together at the international level. These may include police and other law enforcement personnel, prosecutors, legal and other victim advocates, judges, correctional personnel, health and mental health providers, social workers, ombudsmen, spiritual leaders, civil organisations, traditional leaders, human rights commissions, legislators and elected representatives. It applies similarly those to whom victims reach out in their immediate circle—to their family, friends and neighbours—and to various informal, spontaneous and indigenous support structures.

Finally, the Guide for policy-makers which is a 39 page companion to Handbook, defines tasks to achieve the goals of the Declaration. It encourages governments to develop and support programmes. It reminds policy-makers that victims deserve respect for their dignity, privacy and security. It stresses importance of establishing partnerships with all agencies. Many jurisdictions have noted that special categories of victims may require particular attention, owing to the problems they face in coping with the victimisation and/or their limited access to justice. Women, children, the elderly, persons with disabilities, sexual assault victims, domestic violence victims, survivors of homicide, victims of drunk or drugged driving crashes, victims of hate crimes, refugees as victims and victims of large-scale crimes. For all these categories special measures may be necessary to ensure adequate and/or equal treatment.

Now the UN declaration will be discussed in the light of the Justice Verma Committee Report with reference to access to justice, compensation, restitution, and assistance that the document envisage for women victims of crime. The voluminous, 630 page report begins introduction of the methodology talks about constitutionalism, republicanism, and gender equality in the first chapter goes on to talk about gender justice and India's obligations under international conventions in the next chapter. Then follows the chapter on rape and sexual assault, sexual harassment at the workplace other offences against women, trafficking of women and children, child sexual abuse, khap panchayats and honour killings, sentencing and punishment. The last few chapters talk about the provisions of adequate safety measures and amenities in respect of women, medico-legal examination of the victim, police reforms, electoral reforms, education and perception reforms. The committee proposed the bill of rights, criminal law amendment, amendments to the Representation of People Act, 1951, emergency response system and have suggested guidelines for medical examination of sexual assault survivor, protocol for psychological interventions in sexual assault/rape. Considering the length of the Justice Verma

Committee Report, only in a nutshell can it be scrutinised to observe how the principles of the three United Nations documents relating to victim rights have been imbibed in the report. As far as victim justice is concerned, it for the first time, by transgressing the frame of the terms of reference, while moving the spotlight away from the perpetrator to the victim and while ignoring the deafening clamour for punishments of death penalty and chemical castrating for the perpetrators, focused on the relief for women victims of crime besides the treatment of sexual assault victims by the Justice system. The Committee also did not recommend mandatory chemical castration of any type as punishment for sex offenders because in its view that would "contradict human rights standards". Moreover, the report rightly emphasises the urgency of implementing police reforms in order that our country may "attain a standard of policing, which is based upon a positive and cooperative relationship between the civil society and the police service". It would ensure that the victim rights are addressed.

Access to justice: The recommends that it should be a statutory right as a part of due process of access to justice so that the victim /complainant will be able to engage a lawyer of his or her choice – that is, the victim's advocate should have a right of audience in his/her own right, and not merely in a support capacity to the prosecutor. The Committee believes that this will add an additional level of oversight in the trial process. The manner in which the rights of women can be recognised can only be manifested when they have full access to justice and when the rule of law can be upheld in their favour. The proposed Criminal Law Amendment Act, 2012, should be modified as suggested, to secure public confidence, be promulgated forthwith. Since the possibility of sexual assault on men, as well as homosexual, transgender and transsexual rape, is a reality, the provisions have to be cognisant of the same. A special procedure for protecting persons with disabilities from rape, and requisite procedures for access to justice for such persons is also an urgent need. Amendments to the Code of Criminal Procedure, which are necessary, have been suggested. The Committee has recommended that the archaic form of medical examination of the sexual assault victim with the two finger test be done away with.

Compensation: In relation to crimes against women, the Central and State governments must contribute substantial corpus to frame a compensation fund. Subsequently, the Law Commission of India, in its report in 1996, stated that, 'The State should accept the principle of providing assistance to women victims of crime out of its own funds, in cases of acquittals; or where the perpetrator is not traceable, but the Victim is identified; and also in cases when the offence is proved'. It is interesting to note that in Canada one dollar of every fine collected for traffic violations goes in to the Victim fund. If this strategy was adopted the fund would have a huge corpus/ but this statement would come with a rider, provided the corruption of traffic police is checked. They has recommended that the Duties of the Police towards women, poor and general public should include, immediate medical aid to victims of road accidents or victims of other crimes, or police action and notification of their families about the accident or incident. The sets out the duty to advise the victims of road accidents about their rights and privileges and assist accident victims or their heirs or their dependents, the Bureau of Police Research and Development and the training manual for police sub-inspectors, with such information and documents as would facilitate compensation claims. The report sets out the duty to prevent harassment of women, children and weaker sections of society. The judiciary has the primary responsibility of enforcing fundamental rights, through constitutional remedies. The judiciary can take suo motu cognisance of such issues being deeply concerned with them both in the Supreme Court and the High Court. An all India strategy to deal with this issue would be advisable. The Chief Justice of India could be approached to commence appropriate proceedings on the judicial side. The Hon'ble Chief Justice may consider making appropriate orders relating to the issue of missing children to curb the illegal trade of their trafficking etc. Social activists involved in curbing this menace could assist the court in the performance of this task. The question of award of compensation and rehabilitation could also be considered in such cases by the court. Rape victims can claim compensation from the state as this is not only a sexual offence but also violates Articles 14, 19 and 21 of the constitution. Victims of sexual harassment case at work place – compensation is to be paid by the company. As recommended by the Women's Role in Planned Economy, domestic workers also must be compensated for household labour and chores from the family income. WRPE report dealt with equal pay for equal work and also raised the question of compensation for household labour by absolute claim on a portion of the household income.

The report has referred to the decision in Nilabati Behera vs State of Orissa and Others. This was an important pronouncement to ensure that an enforceable right of compensation was also a part of the enforcement of guaranteed rights. Thus, what can happen in respect of an offence like rape is that there could be not only an offence as defined in the IPC but simultaneously there would be a constitutional violation of Articles 14, 19 and 21 and which would also enable the victim to claim right to compensation. The report stipulates that a right to claim compensation will lie against the State in the event the State is unable to secure safe conditions / safe spaces for women. It is under these circumstances that the norms and guidelines were actually prescribed in Vishakha case by the Supreme Court. The report further suggests that suitable provisions should be added to the Bill to make payment of compensation to a woman who has suffered sexual harassment, which is to be paid by the company and be determined by a Tribunal. It is also proposed that domestic workers should also fall within the ambit of the proposed legislation. This would facilitate protection from situations where their wages are withheld arbitrarily as also to provide a basis for monetary compensation in the event of sexual harassment/assault besides steps taken under the general criminal law.

Restitution: The Justice Verma Committee Report recommends that acid attacks be specifically defined as an offence in the IPC, and that the victim be compensated by the perpetrator. With regard to the punishment for rape he recommends that the perpetrator also be liable to pay compensation to the victim, which shall be adequate to meet at least the medical expenses incurred by the victim. The gender specificity and discriminatory nature of this offence does not allow one to ignore this offence as yet another crime against women, and that acid attacks are specifically defined as an offence in the IPC, and that the victim to be compensated by the perpetrator. However, in relation to crimes against women, the Central and State governments must contribute substantial corpus to frame a compensation fund, after noting that the existing Criminal Law (Amendment) Bill, 2012, does include a definition of acid attack. It also talks about voluntarily causing grievous hurt through use of acid shall also be liable to pay compensation to the victim, adequately to meet at least the medical expenses incurred by the victim. The committee also recommends compensation for lately defined crimes like assault or use of criminal force to women with intent to disrobe her, trafficking, stalking and voyeurism.

In this context it would be pertinent to elucidate the roles and responsibilities of the frontline professionals who deal with women victims of crime. The judge should be balanced, humane and ensure protection of the dignity of the vulnerable victim. There should be no expression of gender bias in the proceedings. No humiliation of the witness should be permitted either in the examination in chief or the cross examination. The investigating officer recording the statement of the child victim shall ensure that the victim is made comfortable before proceeding to record the statement and that the statement carries accurate narration of the incident covering all relevant aspects of the case. In the event of the child victim being in the hospital, the magistrate concerned shall record the statement of the victim in the hospital. To create a child friendly environment, separate rooms be provided within the Court precincts where the statement of the child victim can be recorded. Orientation is to be given to the doctors, who prepare MLCs or conduct post mortems to ensure that the MLCs as well as post mortem reports are up to the mark and stand judicial scrutiny in courts. While conducting medical examination, child victim should be first made comfortable as it is difficult to make her understand as to why she is being subjected to medical examination.

Assistance: The recommendations related to assistance women victims are the assistance of a counsellor and a social worker with the doctor and the police. At the very outset the counsellor must inform the victim about the procedure to ensue and also make her aware of her rights. There should also be a readily available set of names and telephone numbers of lawyers at the Centre and a lawyer from the list will be contacted by the counsellor to render assistance during recording of her statement by the police. As per the order passed by the Delhi High Court in Delhi Commission for Women Vs. Delhi Police W.P of comprehensive guidelines to police, hospitals/doctors, committees, sessions courts, magistrate courts, prosecutors and other. The said guidelines have comprehensively laid down protocols and procedures to be followed for medical examination of the victim. In our opinion, these guidelines, which are extracted below ought to be the starting point for arriving at a standardised protocol for medical examination which adheres to international standards.

The Justice Verma Committee Report recommends that short, long and medium term ongoing counselling support be given to women victims of crime in reintegration, healing and recovery; emotional support during court appearances has to be provided. It mentions the Rape Trauma syndrome and the need for assessment of mental health by the counsellor. It also stipulates that the role of a counsellor in the acute stage or immediately after rape to fill gaps in services such as (a) Psychological Safety including support, ventilation, validation (b) Information about emergency contraception (c) Information about post-exposure HIV prophylaxis, STDs (d) Sensitive Discussion about medical and forensic examination. The Justice Verma Committee Report also gives emphasis to the impact of the victimisation and talks about psychological interventions in sexual assault; acute phase or initial phase as the time period immediately after the rape; the subsequent reactions which is the second phase as the weeks and months that follows the sexual assault

Advocacy, Policy Making and Law Reform. The right to be protected from sexual harassment and sexual assault is, therefore, guaranteed by the Constitution, and is one of the pillars on which the very construct of gender justice stands. This right is buttressed by the directive principles of State policy contained in Articles 38, 39 and 39A of the Constitution, which are to be construed harmoniously with the fundamental rights in Part III; and these fundamental principles bind the State in performance of its task of governance of the country. They thought it necessary that this imbalance is set right by express statutory provisions, which are outlined in the form of a draft

Bill of Rights appended to this Report. Empowerment of women means the advancement of women as contemplated under Articles 14 and 21 of the Constitution through integrated strategies, frameworks, programmes, plans, activities, budgets, which aim to eliminate structural inequalities, which enable women to gain power and control over decisions and resources that determine the quality of their lives in a sustainable manner.

Women victims of crime should receive the necessary material; medical, psychological and social assistance through governmental, voluntary, community-based and indigenous means.Victims should be informed of the availability of health and social services and other relevant assistance. Police, should receive training to sensitise them to the needs of women victims of crime, and guidelines to ensure proper and prompt aid. Victims with special needs treated without distinction of any kind, such as race, colour, sex, age, language, religion, nationality, political property, birth or family status, ethnic or social origin, and disability. There is a dire need for the Justice system to network with the NGO (non-governmental organisation) due to the dismal ratio of professionals like police and public or judges and public. Police-public ratio in India is far below the UN standard. As per information furnished by BPR&D, the sanctioned and actual total police per one hundred thousand population (police-population ratio) at all-India level is 145.25 and 117.09. Some sources give the ratio as 1:694 passing on the adverse police public ratio. The present judge's strength in India is 14 per million populations. Government has already increased the Judge strength in the High Courts by 152. The Law Commission in its 120th Report recommended that the strength of judges per million populations may be increased from 10.5 to 50 judges. The Tamil Nadu police registered 5,861 cases of violence against women, many of them for years, without filing a charge sheet. Of the 834 rape cases in the bunch registered in Chennai, 21 have been pending for more than four years. Various courts across the state have a tendency of 14,545 cases of crime against women, including 1,751 rape cases, 3,581 molestation cases and 2,320 sexual harassment cases. In 2012, police registered 584 cases of rape, 721 molestation cases, 1,379 kidnapping cases and 656 sexual harassment cases. For the same period, 667 rape cases are pending trial. (Times of India, 24th Jan 2013) Given this situation, it is obvious that by sheer number the protection of the victim- is a force to reckon with. God cannot be everywhere, so He created mothers, an old Yiddish proverb. In the Indian context one could rearticulate that Yiddish proverb and say 'Government cannot be and is not everywhere, hence the need for Non-Governmental Organisations in India'. NGOs over the days have become the watch dog of the Criminal Justice System or a Guardian of the System. Therefore, the NGOs play a significant role in India in trying to represent the Human Face of the Criminal Justice Systems and make the process more Victim Friendly. However, one should also be cautioned of the 'bad apples' in the basket of public spirited NGOs. The YWCA of India, for example, has ratified the SGMA – the standards of good management and accountability at the Nairobi convention in 2007 as World YWCA had brought the issue of maintaining standards and being accountable to the civil society that they representing. Other NGOs should also follow suit and wear the 'HAT' of Honesty, Accountability and Transparency, which will go a long way in gaining the confidence of the public who they represent. The NGO representatives serve as volunteers on the Mobile Police Unit, are involved in the training in the police training academy and in the working of the All Women Police Station. NGOs participate as protection officers and run protection homes in the filing of Domestic Incidence report under the Domestic Violence Act, Representation in Dowry harassment cells, All Women Police Stations, a pioneering initiative of the state of Tamil Nadu in India. Since it's commissioning in 1992 the number of AWPS in India has grown to 524 (National Crime Records Bureau, 2009). The AWPS is operated by one woman Inspector, one Sub-Inspector and ten women police constables. NGO representatives function as Psychologists, Counsellors, Social workers from Crisis Intervention centers, Medical aid, etc. This helps further the aims of All Women Police Stations, which are to provide immediate relief to women in distress, to rescue girls and missing children, assist policemen in the raids to curb immoral trafficking, to conduct Public order duties at large gatherings where women congregate. Investigate crime cases against women under Indian Penal Code, Dowry Prohibition Act, Tamil Nadu Prevention of Women Harassment Act, Domestic Violence Act, Child Marriage Act, Medical Termination of

Pregnancy Act, Child Labour Act, Juvenile Justice Act, Prevention of Immoral Traffic Act. The All Women Police Station also provides 24x7 women helpline. NGOs play a vital role of training the Judicial academy and the in-service Training centers. The Women's cell of the free legal Aid Unit is run by NGOs. There is the presence of a NGO representative with specified qualification on the following: The Lok Adalat or People's Court and the Parivarik Mahila Lok Adalats, the Juvenile Justice Board formed under the Juvenile Justice Act 2000, the Family Court or the Mahila Court, the National Commission for Women, Children, Scheduled Caste and Scheduled Tribe, Human rights. The role of NGOs in the Mahila/ Family Courts which deals exclusively with cases relating to offences against women headed by District and Sessions Judges for speedy trial and disposal of cases of offences committed against women and also cases under other social laws enacted by the Central and State Governments for the protection of women. To ensure that these places are manned by trained personnel who are sensitised to the needs of women as victims of crime. The Aims of Women's /Mahila/ Family Courts are to promote conciliation and secure speedy settlement of disputes relating to offences against women, family affairs and for matters connected to marital affairs. They ensure that persons who are appointed to these courts are committed to the need to protect women and ensure that the court is a safe space for women. They should promote the settlement of disputes by conciliation and counseling. They are to associate with institutions engaged in promoting welfare of families, especially women and children, or working in the field of social welfare to facilitate satisfactory resolution of disputes concerning the women through a forum that works expeditiously and in a just manner and with an approach ensuring maximum welfare of society and dignity of women.

At the UN Crime Congress at Salvador 2010, specifically, paragraph 7 of the declaration says, 'We recognise the importance of adopting appropriate legislation and policies to prevent victimisation, including re-victimisation, and to provide protection and assistance to all victims of crime'. This being the pulse of the international community, it is noted with anguish at the predicament of women victims of crime in India, who still languish in the charity mode when their counterparts, the world over have their rights established through national legislations that give them their rightful place in the justice system, both as stakeholders and as participants through their victim impact statements. When the UN declaration was ratified, India made a commitment, as a signatory, to maintain the basic principles. So, if these and other recommendations materialise and see the light of day first, the quality of life for many women victims of crime would be improved; second, the cause of justice for all would be strengthened; third, crime prevention would be enhanced it has been reiterated that victim assistance is crime prevention; fourth, survivor volunteer who work for other women victims of crime would be supported and finally the people would be empowered with the "will to change". The World Society of Victimology and the Indian Society of Victimology are working towards a legally binding convention.UN Convention on Justice and Support for Victims of Crime and Abuse of Power and have submitted a draft convention in 2006. The binding nature of the convention will ensure the enactment of victim legislation. Also since the CEDAW Committee has urged the government to implement the recommendations of the Justice Verma Commission regarding violence against women; promptly enact the draft Communal Violence (Prevention, Control and Rehabilitation of Victims) Bill, ensure that it provides for a comprehensive system of reparations for victims and for gender-sensitive victim-centred procedural and evidentiary rules; amend the Criminal Law (Amendment) Act, 2013 ensuring that marital rape is defined as a criminal offence, as requested by the Committee in its previous concluding observations and expanding the scope of protection of the Act to cover all prohibited grounds of discrimination, and defining gang rape as constituting an aggravating factor calling for a more severe punishment; enact specific legislation to introduce heavier sentences for perpetrators of acid attacks, to regulate the sale and distribution of acid substances, and to conduct large-scale campaigns to raise public awareness on the criminal nature of such attacks; strengthen the efficiency of the police, ensure that police officers fulfil their duty to protect women and girls against violence and are held accountable, adopt Standard Procedures for the police in each State on gender-sensitive investigations and treatment of victims and of witnesses, and to ensure that FIR (First Information

Reports) are duly filed; establish, without delay, one-stop crisis centres providing women and girls victims of violence and rape with free and immediate access to medical attention, psychological counselling, legal aid, shelters and other support services; provide systematic training on women's rights to all law enforcement personnel, to medical staff and judicial officials; put in place an effective system to monitor and evaluate the implementation, effectiveness and impact of legislation to combat sexual violence; take efforts towards eliminating any criminalisation of same sex relations by studying the possibility, as accepted by the State party at the Universal Periodic Review (A/HRC/21/10/Add.1), and take notes of the ruling of the Indian Supreme Court (Suresh Kumar Koushal v. Naz Foundation, 2013) in this regard; take urgent measure to adopt its National Plan of action for improving the girl child sex ratio; and allocate sufficient resources for the immediate enforcement of legislation on violence against women and for the establishment of special courts, complaints procedures and support services envisaged under that legislation in a time bound manner.

With the swords of Damocles, in the form of pressure to conform from international organisations and the NGOs India, hanging over the heads of politicians they have no choice but to enact legislations sooner than later and ensure protection of women victims of crime. As with most analysis of the position of victims this has not been able to assess the needs and position of all victims, many remain largely hidden. Whilst politically and in popular rhetoric the system in India includes victims needs and rights, often these are given moral priority rather than legal power, and a holistic inclusion of the rights of victims in the system is still at its infancy.

References

CEDAW committee report July 2014 available at http://www.wilpfinternational.org/wp-content/uploads/2014/07/CEDAW-Concluding-Observations-India.pdf

Guide for Policy Makers (1999), available at http://www.uncjin.org/Standards/policy.pdf accessed on 7th March 2013.

Handbook on Justice for Victims (1999) available at http://www.uncjin.org/Standards/9857854.pdf accessed on 7th March 2013.The CEDAW committee report July 2014 available at http:/

/www.wilpfinternational.org/wp-content/uploads/2014/07/CEDAW-Concluding-Observations-India.pdf

Hohfeld, W. N. 1964, Fundamental Legal Conceptions as Applied in Judicial Reasoning. Ed. Walter Wheeler Cook. New Haven: Yale University Press.

Justice Verma Committee report full text http://www.firstpost.com/india/full-text-recommendations-of-the-justice-js-verma-committee-report-599874.html

Menon, N.R. (2004), Victim Compensation Law and Criminal Justice: A Plea for a Victim-Orientation in Justice. In Vibhute, K.I. (ed.) Criminal Justice – A Human Rights Perspective of the Criminal Justice Process in India. Lucknow: Eastern Book Company, pp. 362-369.

Muralidhar S, (2003a), Access to justice http://www.ielrc.org/content/n0501.pdf

Muralidhar, S, (2003b), 'India: Public Interest Litigation - Survey 1997-98'. Found in Annual Survey of Indian Law 525.http://www.ielrc.org/content/n0501.pdf

Muralidharan, S., 2004, Rights of Victims in the Indian Criminal Justice System available at www.ielrc.org/content/a0402.pdf accessed on 4th April 2012

Muralidharan, S., 2004, Rights of Victims in the Indian Criminal Justice System available at www.ielrc.org/content/a0402.pdf accessed on 4th April 2012

NCRB report of Conviction Rate of IPC Crime Cases During 2012, http://ncrb.gov.in/CD-CII2012/CIIMaps2012-finalPDF/74 Conviction Rate of IPC Crimecases-PercentTotal-Map.pdf

Reiman, J and Leighton, P. 2006, The Rich Get Richer and The Poor Get Prison: Ideology, Class, and Criminal Justice 8th Edition ISBN-10: 0205461727.

Sarkar, S., 2010, The Quest for Victims' Justice in India available at ww.wcl.american.edu/hrbrief/17/2sarkar.pdf accessed on 15th April 2012

Shekhar and Wemmers, 2012, 'SMARTER' Rights for Victims, The Victimologist Volume 14, Issue 1.

Shekhar, B., 2005, Victim rights are also human rights, in the Human Rights Global Focus, August 2005, Volume 2, Nos. 3, pp. 40-46.

Shekhar, B., 2012, 'Justice isn't served till crime victims are' The Peoples reporter, Mumbai, March 24th, 2012.

Shekhar, B (2012), Ed. Dimensions of Violations and Victimisations, pp.1-16. Manonmaniam Sundaranar University, Tirunelveli, India.

Shekhar, B, 2012, Victims of the System - Crime as a Cause of Crime Ed Publication Division, Manonmaniam Sundaranar University, Dimensions of Violations and Victimization, pp. 1-16 ISBN No: 978-93-81402-27-6.

Srinivasan, M and Mathew E.J.(2007), Victims and the Criminal Justice System in India:Need for a Paradigm Shift in the Justice System TEMIDA Jun 2007, str 51-62ISSN: 1450-6637 DOI: 10.2298/TEM0702051S

The Hindu dated 22nd April 2003,

The Law Commission in its 120th Report available at http://lawcommissionofindia.nic.in/101-169/Report120.pdf accessed on 7th March 2013,

Times of India 24th Jan 2013 available at http://timesofindia.indiatimes.com/search.cms

UN draft Convention on Justice and Support for Victims of Crime and Abuse of Power available at http://www.justice.gov.za/vc/docs/international/2006_DraftUNConventionVictims.pdf

UN Declaration on Basic Principles of Justice for Victims of Crime and Abuse of Power 1985, available at http://untreaty.un.org/cod/avl/ha/dbpjvcap/dbpjvcap.html Venkatesan, J., 2010 Cr.P.C. amendments come into effect, The Hindu, Jan. 2, 2010, available at http://www.hindu.com/2010/01/02/stories/20100 1025310 1200.htm

13

Bourgeoning Crime Against Women in Odisha: Introspecting the Instrument of Governance Dealing with Gender Violence

Pramod Kumar Ray

Statement on the Problem

The position and condition of women of India in the twenty-first century, indeed has not only become terrible so also highly deplorable. Recent years have recorded an alarming increase in atrocities and crime against women in the country. Bourgeoning crime against women in form of ill-treatment, humiliation, exploitation, female feticide sexual slavery, forced pregnancy, rape including marital rape and domestic violence, trafficking etc. has exposed the insensitivity of our society towards our better halves. The record of Odisha in perpetuating crime against its women, is also no lagging behind rather has stood very high ranking eighth in percentage share. The paper, while analysing the psychosocial dynamics of the bourgeoning crime against women in the state also has made on introspection of the instrument of legal and institutional measures devised for its containment. The author urged for a composite psychosocial legal and political approach to deal with the terrible insensitivity against women in our society.

Keywords : Bourgeoning crime, Gender vulnerability, Insensitivity, heinous, progressive social Legislation, domestic violence, incremental discrimination, psychosocial dynamics differential treatment, Protective discriminations, Gender just humanism.

Introduction

Crime against women is not something new, the threat of violence that stalks their lives from cradle to grave, was prevailing since time immemorial. Violence against women in India found to be existing since dawn of civilisation. Indian mythology has both valorised and devolarised women. Indian mythology, while has depicted women as 'Shakti' –"the symbol of power" also at the sametime has justified women as commodity and subjected to torture. Sant Tulsidas justified the torture of women in his writings as he says "Dhol, Ganwar, Shudra, Pashu, Nari/Ye Sab Tadhan Ki Adhikari" (Drum, rogue, salve, animal and women, they deserve beating and condemnation). All through ages, crimes against women continue to exist and in recent years, there has been an alarming increase.

Women in India are ahead of women in other places so far as social legislation protecting their rights are concerned. But implementation lapses of these legal and institutional measures has worsened their condition and pushed them to further deplorable situation. In reality, while all men are not potential abuser or violator of women rights, but all women could be consider as potential victims of violence and crime. Violence or crime against women creates barrier for women to enjoy their basic human rights and fundamental freedoms. It is a major stumbling block on the way of achievement of the objective of the equality, development and peace in society.

Conceptualisation of violence against women: It's Prevalence in India

Violence against women is found to be all pervasive through ages. The scourage of crime against women continues to wreck havoc on a nation's innocent women, who are denied to live in dignity and right to life. It exists in every country, cutting across boundaries of culture, class, education, income, ethnicity and age. The term "Violence against women" means any act of gender-based violence that results in, or is likely to result in physical, sexual or psychological harm or suffering to women, including threats of such acts, coercion at arbitrary deprivation of liberty, whether occurring in public or private life. The Beijing declaration does not restrict the act of violence against women to this limit, it rather adopts a wider connotation to explain the term. According to the Beijing Declaration, violence against women includes;

(i) Physical, sexual and psychological violence occurring in the family, including battering, sexual abuse of female children in the household, dowry related violence, marital rape, female genital mutilation and another traditions practices harmful to women, non-spousal violence and violence related to exploitation;

(ii) Physical, sexual and psychological violence occurring within the general community, including rape, sexual abuse, sexual harassment and intimidation at work, in educational institutions and elsewhere, trafficking in women and forced prostitution;

(iii) Physical, sexual and psychological violence perpetrated or condoned by the state, wherever it occurs. The Beijing conference also pointed out other forms of violence against women such as violation of human right of women in situations of armed conflict, in particular, systematic rape, sexual slavery and forced pregnancy. It also pointed out that forced sterilisation and forced abortion, forced use of contraceptives, female infanticide and prenatal sex selection.

Thus, gender based inequality exists in all stages of women's life from infancy to old age and manifests in the form of several act of violence.

The worst manifestations of violence against women, is found in South Asia, which is known as the most gender insensitive region in the world. South Asia is witnessed for record of highest incidences of violence against women in the world. India has become increasing gender insensitive and the official statistics from the National Crimes Record Bureau (NCRB) reveals a trend of rising crimes against women. Other cultural practices in India such as dowry, child marriage, sati, the 'Devadasi' tradition and ill-treatment of widows enhance girls and women's vulnerability to the experience of violence, gender differential treatment in nutrition, healthcare, education, mobility and other life opportunities places girls and women at a highest risk of violations of all kinds.

In India crime against women has been classified into two broad categories;

(1) The Crimes under the Indian Penal Code (IPC) and (2) The Crimes under special laws (SLL)

The Crime under Indian Penal Code include–

(i) Rape (Section 376 IPC)
(ii) Kidnapping and abduction for different purposes (Sections 363-373 IPC)
(iii) Homicide for dowry, dowry deaths or their attempts (Sections 302/304-B IPC)
(iv) Torture both mental and physical (Section 498-A IPC)
(v) Molestation (Section 354 IPC)
(vi) Sexual Harassment (Section 509 IPC)
(vii) Importation of girls (up to 21 year of age) (Section 366-B IPC)

The Crime under the special laws include–

(i) Immoral Traffic (Prevention) Act, 1956
(ii) Dowry Prohibition Act, 1961
(iii) The Child Marriage Restraint (Amendment) Act, 1979
(iv) Indicent Representation of Women (Prohibition) Act, 1986
(v) Commission of Sati (Prevention) Act, 1987

Various study findings have revealed that crime against women in India proportionately very high in comparison to the rate of total crime. It was found that during 1992 to 2001, the growth of total crimes registered under IPC was 0.20 per cent per annum. While the annual growth rate of crime against women was proportionately very high, 2.18 per cent per annum. The nature of crime against women varies from simple harassment to even denying them the very right to exist. As per 'Crime in India report 2001', there are four molestation cases, one sexual harassment case, six cases of cruelty by husband and relatives, two rape cases and one dowry death case reported every hour in the country. However, a WHO report says 'nearly 42 women are raped everyday in India, one in every thirty five minutes. The scourge of rape continues to wreck havoc on the nations thousands of innocent women: Caste Hindus rape harijans; teacher rapes their students and colleagues, students rape their colleagues, doctor rape their patients and nurses in hospitals and Nursing homes, Prison staff rapes prisoners, old men and young men alike enjoy the pleasure of sex out of wedlock; and even women suffering from T.B. or other ailments undergoing treatment as indoor patients, pregnant, lunatic, deaf and dumb and blind women suffering from Leprosy are not spared.

In India, despite many positive developments in security of women's human rights, the reality of the situation on the ground for women continues to be extremely harsh. Strong patriarchal values govern formal as well as informal institutions within the country. A majority of women face nutritional discrimination within the family, eating last and least. Women are legally and socially discriminated against in land and property inheritance rights. Most women do not own any property in their names and do not get a share of parental property. These discriminatory practices make women socially, economically and emotionally dependent on men in the family- father, husband or son – and make them vulnerable to various kinds of threats and acts of violence. The National Crime Record Bureau (NCRB) indicates that in India the violence against women are very high. These include rape, kidnapping, dowry deaths, mental and physical torture, molestation, sexual harassment and trafficking.

Women and girls in India are vulnerable to several forms of violence throughout their life. It is observed that women and girls are more at risk of violence within the family than from strangers, which shatters the myth that the family is the safest place for women.

Crime against women: The Odisha Scenario

Crime against women in Odisha is also very high. As per National Crime Record Bureau (NCRB) data crime against women in Odisha constitute 4.91 per cent of the national crime against women and it ranked eighth in percentage share. According to one study crime against women in Odisha has increased from 2131 to 4897 during 1993 to 2001, recording 130 per cent in the crime. Crime against women which constituted 4.12 per cent of the total crimes in the state in 1993, constitutes 10.49 per cent of total crimes by 2001, indicating a more than proportional rise in crime against women in the state. If we compare the rate of crime against women in Odisha with that of national average, the crime against women in Odisha was below the national average in the year 1993-1994 and 1995 onward the state record a steady rise in crime against women in comparison to the national average. The rate of crime against women in Odisha which was much below the national average and was reported to be 9.8 per cent in 1995 has gone up above the national average and touched 14.6 per cent by 2001. Odisha occupied 14th rank among states in the crime rate against women and 11th rank in respect of percentage share of Odisha to the total crime against women in India.

Odisha is second in dowry related crime (16.45 per cent) as against Andhra Pradesh with 27.78 per cent. It accounted for 6.38 per cent of dowry deaths cases registered in India putting it fifth on the crime map. With regard to crime pertaining assult on women, Odisha ranked third accounting for 9.23 per cent of the total national average. In 2011, a total of 1139 girls and women were kidnapped and such cases were increased to 1364 in 2012. Odisha alone recorded 1458 cases of rape in 2012 ranking Seventh nationally.

The state white paper, 2012 also clearly indicates a steady rise in violence against women in the state. It categorically highlighted the rise in some of the specific crime such as incidences of rape increased from 1112 (2011) to 1458 (2012). Further, dowry related crimes such as dowry murder, dowry torture and suicide in Odisha has been reported very high in the latest state white paper. Odisha's crime record on domestic violence although is not very high but is higher than the national average. The NFHS 3 data reveals that quite a large proportion of women (42 per cent) experience emotional, physical and sexual violence in Odisha with wife beating a common phenomena.

Crime against women related to witchcraft is wide spread in the state. A large number of women in the state are killed, tortured and partially naked due to witch hunting that goes unreported. Such violence, if not reduced will remain one of the greatest challenge before women of the state. The state passed the prevention of witch hunting Bill 2013 but implementation is yet to start. The state in order to contain crime against women, along with legal measures also has devised some support services.

Instruments of Governance to deal with crime against Women in the State

Earlier we have discussed about the legal and constitutional measures in shape of Indian Penal Code (IPC), Criminal Procedure Code (CrPC) and crime under special laws (SLL) to protect women from violence and crime.

Under IPC section 376 deal with rape, section 363-373 deal with kidnapping and abduction, section 302/304 deal with homicide and dowry death, section 498 deal with mental and physical torture, section 354 deal with molestation, section 509 deal with sexual harassment, section 366-B deal with importance of girls upto 21 year of age.

Besides there are some special laws to prevent crime against women. They include;

(i) Immoral Traffic (Prevention) Act, 1961

(ii) Dowry Prohibition Act, 1961

(iii) The Child Marriage Restraint (Amendment Act, 1979)

(iv) Indicent Representation of Women (Prohibition Act, 1986)

(v) Commission of Sati (Prevention) Act, 1987

In addition to the legal measures there are some support services to help out the women victims of various crimes.

(i) State women commission; a quasi judicial body, established on November 1993 takes care of criminal cases against women related to marriage and dowry, rape, kidnapping, criminal abduction, eve-teasing, immoral trafficking of women and even cases of medical negligence relating to child bearing of child birth. It acts as civil court and on the basis of complain received, it looks into atrocities against women and recommends criminal Prosecution against persons accused of crime against Women.

(ii) Orissa State Social Welfare Advisory Board established in 1954 provide services to women victims of crimes through short stay homes and family counselling programmes. Through support of NGOs it provides preventive, curative and rehabilitative services, provides family counselling, create awareness among women on safety measures.

(iii) The Odisha Mahila Vikash Samabaya Nigam, established on 8th March 1991, work towards economic empowerment of women. It takes up income generation programme for women, conducts training programmes. The most important function of the organisation is conduct of gender sensitisation programmes for removal of gender discrimination and developing leadership qualities in women.

(iv) Dowry Prohibition Advisory Board. To address the Dowry related issues, the state government in line with the Dowry Prohibition Act, 1961, formulated the Odisha dowry Prohibition rules in 2000. Accordingly Dowry Prohibition Advisory Board was set up and the sub-divisional magistrate of each sub-division worked as dowry prohibition officer. The main function of the Board constitutes; creating anti-dowry awareness, settling of dowry dispute by counselling expedite police investigation, provides evidences to investing officers on dowry related crime, act as advisor to public prosecutor on dowry crime trial.

(v) Complaint committee on Sexual Harassment of women at work place . Such committees established at district level under the chairmanship of senior lady officer looks into cases of sexual harassment of women at work place. It receives complain from victims and takes action against the offender.

(vi) District level committees to counter atrocities against women. These committees play the role of facilitator by guiding, monitoring, directing cases of atrocities against women. It provides legal aid to the victim and spreads legal literacy among women.

(vii) Legal support services. To render free legal services to the women victims of atrocities, the state government by virtue of Odisha state legal services Authority Rule 1996 have constituted legal service authorities at state, district and taluka level. Such legal service authorities by organising Lok Adalat within their respective jurisdiction, delivers justice to the poor women victim without any expenses.

(viii) Human right Protection Cell (HRPC). The Government of Odisha, for smooth and speedy trial of cases of crime against women, has constituted HRPC in 32 police districts. The SP of the district directly controls the cell and remains responsible for its functioning. The cells directly monitor the progress of investigation, persecution and trial of cases of crime against women. It involves NGOs for awareness generation among communities. It organises multi stake holder sensitisation programmes, seminars, symposiums.

(ix) Short Stay Homes. Girls and women, who are exposed to moral dangers or are victims of family discord, are provided the facility of such institutional services. For the social rehabilitation of the victims, the SSHs provides counselling and guidance, medical and psychiatric treatment. For the economic rehabilitation, it provides vocational training to the victims.

(x) Family Counselling Centres. Through the family councelling centres preventive, curative and rehabilitative services are provided to the women victims of atrocities and exploitation. Some 13 FCCs in Odisha are running by NGOs with support from Central Social Welfare Board. These centres have become instrumental in settling family disputes and maladjustment.

(xi) Mahila Police Station. To make the police station approachable and less intimidating to women victims, Mahila police stations have been set up in Odisha, fully managed by women staffs only. The first such police station was started in 1994 in Cuttack and subsequently were set up at different parts of Odisha. These exclusive police stations function for an effective and impartial deal of crime against women such as rape, kidnapping, abduction, eve teasing and immoral trafficking.

(xii) Task Force on Women and Violence. To provide quick and effective services to the women victims of atrocities and violence, the Task force has been set up in Odisha in 1994. The main function of the task force is to monitor the gender violence cases by police and courts and it intervenes for prompt and swift action and fair play of justice in favour of the victim.

Introspection of the Efficacy of the Instrument of governance dealing with crime against women in the state:

Various study findings on Instrument of governance dealing with crime against women in the state closely observed that despite the plethora of laws and institutional support services devised by the state, the incredible apathy towards women who are victim of heinous crime, the enforcement deficit and the incredible support services with lack of commitment and concern has multiplied the plight of the women victim subjected to violence and atrocity. It is also observed that, a women victim seeking protection from the law enforcement agency and support service institutions, has invited more trouble to them. The situation has become like, the victim trying to run away from the devil offender of the crime has emerged in the deep sea like protector. Various research and study findings have revealed that, the law enforcement agency, the police, other institutional support service agencies, who are supposed to be trouble shooter have turned trouble makers. The victims are increasingly losing confidence on police and other support service agencies because of their callowness and lack of concern in taking action against the suspect/accused/offender. The redressal mechanisms have found to be non-commitant in follow-up action of the reported cases. The nexus between the political class and the police, politicisation of police forces has diluted the integrity of policing. The Odisha experience has more than once exposed the dominance of political class and extra constitutional authorities over the instrument of governance dealing with crime against women have vitiated and manipulated the investigation and fair trial of cases. Various incidents in the state have exposed the fraud, untruthfulness and the insincerity of every institution directly involved in dispension of justice to the victims of crime against women. The enforcement agency, the politician are found to be insensitive to the issues related to safty of women and crime against women. Most often lack of clarity in our laws on crime against women failed to protect the victims. Kiran Bedi, the then Joint Commissioner, Special Branch had observed that "The laws of rape are not just a few sentences. It is a whole book, which has clearly demarcated chapters and cannot be read selectively. We cannot read the preamble and suddenly reach the last chapter and claim to understand and applied it."

There are several cases where the integrity of judiciary has been in question while protecting sexual violence against women. One such classic example of the judicial pronouncements in rape cases "in the cases of Bhanwari Devi, where in a judge remarked that the victim could not have been raped since she was a Dalit, while the accused hailed from an upper caste, who would not stoop to sexual relations with a Dalit." In Odisha, it is reported that the failure to deliver justice is highest with police and state commission for women, both bodies need revitalisation.

This is high time we need to introspect our legal procedure and institutional support services for the women victims of crime and atrocities. It is equally important to introspect our political leadership, political culture and instruments of governance that claims elimination of all forms of violence against women.

Conclusion

Considering the increase in crime against women at geometrical progression rate and inadequate protection mechanism against them, the need of the hour is to change the existing legal procedure; IPC, CrPC, Indian Evidence Act. Crime against women in India despite being deterred by means of passing of various Acts still a bourgeoning social problem and has became an increasing concern widening gender disparity and imbalances. However, a comprehensive sustainable progressive policy measure for the women is the need of the hour. However, initiatives that have been taken till now should get unnoticed. Combating violence against women required challenging the way that gender roles and power relations are articulated in the society. Changing people's attitude and mentality towards women will take a long time. India should follow the Beijing declaration on elimination of all forms of violence by promoting an active and visible policy of mainstreaming a gender perspective in all policies and programmes related to violence against women. Government should initiate implementing measures on programmes aimed at increasing the knowledge and understanding the causes, consequences and mechanism of violence against women among those responsible for implementing these policies i.e. police personnel, law enforcement officers, judicial, medical and social workers. Above all the media should play a proactive role in informing and educating people about the causes and effects of crime against women and should initiate stimulating public debate in the topic.

Notes

Desai, Dhruv (2013), "Sexual Harassment and Rape Laws in India", in Udaya India, January 26, 2013, p. 35.

Fourth world Conference on women; Beijing Declaration and The Platform for Action (1995) New York, Department of Public Information, p. 73.

Ghosh, SK (1984), "Women in a Changing society", New Delhi: Ashis Publishing House.

References

Fourth world Conference on women; Beijing Declaration and The Platform for Action (1995) New York, Department of Public Information, p. 73.

Violence against Women in India – a review of trends, patterns and responses for UNFPA India, 2004, p. 4.

Mohanty, Bedabati (2005); "Violence against women: An analysis of contemporary Realities", New Delhi: Kanishka Publishers, Distributors.

'Crime in India Report 2001' quoted in Bedamati Mohanty, *Ibid.*

Vasudev, Shefalee and Methil Renuka (2002), "RAPE" in India Today, September 9, 2002, p. 50.

Ghos, SK (1984), "Women in a Changing society", New Delhi: Ashis Publishing House.

National Crime Report Bureau (NCRB), 2012.

Mohanty, Bedabati, *Ibid*, p. 33.

Ibid, p. 33.

National Crime Report Bureau (NCRB), 2012.

NFHS.www.nfhsindia.org/factsheet.html

Pati, Bibhuti (2014), "Despite Newlaws cases of witch hunting continue to surface in Odisha" Merrinews, 9 January 2014.

Desai, Dhruv (2013), "Sexual Harassment and Rape Laws in India", in Udaya India, January 26, 2013, p. 35.

Ibid, p. 35.

Mohanty, Bedabati, *Ibid*, p. 152.

14

Violence Against Women at Workplace - Current Challenges

Dr Dilshad Shaik

Abstract

Every woman has a constitutional right to participate in public employment, but this right to participate is denied in the process of sexual harassment which compels her to keep away from such employment. Workplace violence solely targeted against women is one of the most underreported crimes in our society. The prevailing forms of harassment at workplace include the sexual desire-dominance paradigm which conceptualises the hostile work environment harassment (Dugar and Deora, 2011). Sexual harassment at workplace is a violation of the right to life and personal liberty as mentioned in Article 21 that no person shall be deprived of his life or personal liberty. Right to livelihood is an integral facet of the right to life. Sexual harassment is the violation of the right to livelihood too. For meaningful enjoyment of life under Article 21 of the Constitution of India every woman is entitled to the elimination of obstacles and of discrimination based on gender (Radhakrishnan, 2009). Since the 'right to work' depends on the availability of a safe working environment and the right to life with dignity, the hazards posed by sexual harassment need to be removed for these rights to have a meaning. By any measure workplace violence is emerging as a prominent local, state and national issue. Clearly, the place of employment rather reflects the larger societal context. The Supreme Court commented Gender Equality includes protection from sexual harassment and right to work with dignity which is a universally recognised basic human right. Recently, Sexual Harassment of Women at Workplace (Prevention, Prohibition and Redressal) law was enacted. The new law stands substantially changed. The focus of this paper is to address the current challenges in the implementation of existing laws to curb sexual harassment at workplace and also takes stock of the ways in which the new amendments re-framed sexual offences in the law, their significance and the challenges that remain. While being far from comprehensive, these changes substantially transform the way legal redress for sexual offences have been framed in the law.

Key Words: Workplace Violence, Gender Equality, Sexual Harassment, Constitutional Provisions, Right to Work.

Introduction

Violence in the workplace is rampant in India. These days it has become a problem for employers too. One form of violence which is solely targeted against women is sexual harassment. The prevailing forms of harassment at workplace include the sexual desire-dominance paradigm which conceptualises the hostile work environment harassment (Dugar and Deora, 2011). The United Nations defines violence against as: 'any act of gender-based violence that results in, or is likely to result in, physical, sexual or mental harm or suffering to women, including threats of such acts, coercion or arbitrary deprivation of liberty, whether occurring in public or in private life' (WHO, 2011). Sexual harassment at the work place is rampant but no one talks about it- **17 per cent of working women in major cities have admitted** to it. However, most of these women said the harassment wasn't physical. The prevailing forms of violence at workplace include the sexual desire- dominanace paradigm which conceptualises the hostile work environment. It was very important for the courts to recognise that gender discrimination which can take the form of sexual overtures. Of all the forms that violence against women can assume, sexual harassment is the most ubiquitous and insidious; all the more so because it is deemed 'normal' behaviour and not an assault on the female entity. The data on workplace violence is scattered and inadequate to understand the extent of the problem. Many acts of non-fatal violence and threats in the workplace go unreported because there is no coordinated data-collection system to process the information. The rights of women were enshrined in the Constitution as fundamental rights with right to equality in Article 14, non-discrimination by the State in Article 15(1), equality of opportunity in Article 16, equal pay for equal work in Article 39(d), special provisions by the State in favour of women and children in Article 15(3), renounces practices derogatory to the dignity of women in Article 51(A) (e), and provisions to be made by the State for securing just and humane conditions of work and for maternity relief in Article 42 (Menon and Shivkumar, 2001). Despite these protective measures women are discriminated at work because of their gender variance. The women are subjected to harassment at their workplace due to their unequal status. Harassment at work is termed as a form of violence against women. It is one of the social mechanisms which forces women into subservient position and accords power quotient to the other gender. In spite of all these provisions the occurrence of sexual harassment at the workplace is widespread in India, now it has been recognised as an infringement of the fundamental rights of a woman under Article 19(1)(g) of the Constitution of India.

It is the duty of the state to provide for the wellbeing and respect of its citizens to prevent frustration, low self-esteem, insecurity and emotional disturbance, which, in turn, could affect business efficacy, leading to loss of production and loss of reputation for the organisation or the employer. In fact, the recognition of the right to protection against sexual harassment is an intrinsic component of the protection of women's human rights. It is also a step towards providing women independence, equality of opportunity and the right to work with dignity. Every woman has a constitutional right to participate in public employment, and this right to participate is denied in the process of sexual harassment which compels her to keep away from such employment. Though this right is only available against the state, it is a recognised right in all the major international conventions. Sexual harassment of women at workplace is also a violation of the right to life and personal liberty. Right to livelihood is an integral facet of the "Right to Life." The General Assembly Resolution 48/104 on the Declaration on the Elimination of Violence Against Women, The International Convention on the Elimination of all forms of Discrimination against Women (CEDAW) adopted in 1979 at Beijing, which has been ratified by India, also recognised the right of women to equality at the workplace and it states that women shall not be subjected to sexual harassment at the workplace as such harassment vitiates the working environment and the Charter of Fundamental Rights of the European Union are the international initiatives that lay down appropriate measures to eliminate discrimination against women in all fields including sexual harassment. Highlightings the issue of sexual harassment at workplace – an often subtle but disturbing form of aggression - Jane Hodges, ILO, director of the Bureau for Gender Equality, on March 6, 2013 said, "Sexual harassment and other forms of harassment and abuse – physical, verbal or psychological – bullying, mobbing, work-related stress and violence affect all professions and sectors and both women and men."

Sexual Harassment-Judicial Approach

There are various cases on sexual harassment at workplace had come before the courts in India. Sometimes precedents by the court also acts as legislations where guidelines were laid about the measures to be taken by the employer to ensure the safety of women employees. In Apparel Export Council Vs. A.K. Chopra: The Supreme Court declared that sexual harassment is gender discrimination against women and also said that any act or attempt of molestation by a superior will constitute 'sexual harassment'. In Mrs Rupan Deol Bajaj Vs. Kanwar Pal Singh Gill. This case has changed the meaning of the terms 'modesty' and 'privacy' in such a way that, any kind of harassment or inconvenience done to a women's private or public life will be considered as an offence. In Radhabai Vs. Ramachandran: The Supreme Court in 1995 passed the judgement in her favour,with back pay and perks from the date of dismissal. In Visakha and others Vs. State of Rajasthan: In this case, the Supreme Court while disposing of the writ petition with directions, held that, "The fundamental right to carry on any occupation, trade and profession depend on the availability of 'safe' working environment. The right to life means life with dignity. The primary responsibility for ensuring such safety and dignity through suitable legislation and the creation of a mechanism for its enforcement, belongs to the legislature and the executive."

When however, instances of sexual harassment resulting in violations of Articles 14,19 and 21 are brought under Art. 32, effective redressal requires that some guidelines for the protection of these rights should be laid down to fill the vaccum.' In light of these deliberations, the court outlined certain guidelines which are significant because for the first time sexual harassment is identified as a separate category of legally prohibited behaviour. These are subjected to all workplaces until any other legislation is passed by Parliament in this regard.

The guidelines are:

- It is the duty of every employer to deliver a sense of security to every women employees.
- Government should make strict law and regulations to prohibit sexual harassment.
- Any act of such nature should result in disciplinary actions. Further criminal proceedings should also be brought against the wrongdoer.
- The organisation should have a well set up complaint mechanism wherein the complaints made by the victim should be disposed off within a reasonable time.
- This complaint mechanism should be in the form of complaint committee which needs to be headed by a woman member and at least 50 per cent of the committee members should be women, so that the victims do not feel ashamed while communicating their problems this complaint committee should also have a third party involvement in the form of NGO or other body which is familiar in dealing with such type of issues. Issues relating to sexual harassment should not be a taboo in the workers meeting and should be discussed positively.
- It is the duty of the organisation to aware the female employees about this right.

- The employer or the person-in-charge is duty bound to take the necessary and reasonable steps to provide support to the victim, even if sexual harassment takes place due to the act or omission of the third party.
- These guidelines are not limited only to government employees and should also be followed by employees in private sectors.

Recently, Sexual Harassment of Women at Workplace (Prevention, Prohibition and Redressal) Law was enacted. The new law stands substantially changed. This law can lead to higher penalties and even cancellation of licence or registration to conduct business. The new law brings in its ambit even domestic workers and agriculture labour, employees in both organised and unorganised sectors. This Act seeks to protect the women from sexual harassment at their workplace.

Features:

- The Act defines sexual harassment at the workplace and creates a mechanism for redressal of complaint. It also provides safeguards against false or malicious charges.
- The definition of "aggrieved Women" who will get protection under the Act is extremely wide to cover all women, irrespective of her age or employment status, whether in the organised or unorganised sector, public or private and covers clients, customers and domestic workers as well.
- While the 'workplace' in the Vishaka guidelines is confined to the traditional office set-up where there is a clear employers-employee relationship, the Act goes much further to include organisations, department, office, branch, unit etc. in the public and private sector, organised and unorganised, hospitals, nursing homes, educational institutions, sports institutes, stadiums, sports complex and any place visited by the employee during the course of employment including the transportation.
- The committee is required to complete the enquiry within a time period of 90 days. On completion of the enquiry, the report is required to be sent to the employer or the district officer, as the case may be, further they are mandated to take action on the report within 60 days.
- Every employer is required to constitute an internal complaints committee at each office or branch with 10 or

more employees. The District Officer is required to constitute a Local Complaints Committee in each district, and if required at the block level.

- The Complaints Committee has the power of civil court in gathering evidence.
- The Complaints Committee is required to provide conciliation before initiating an enquiry, if requested by the complainant.
- The Act casts certain obligations upon the employers such as to provide a safe working environment, to display conspicuously at the workplace, the penal consequences of indulging in acts that may constitute sexual harassment and the composition of the internal complaints committee.
- The Act obligate the employer to organise workshops and awareness programmes at regular intervals for sensitising employees on the issues and implications of workplace sexual harassment and organising orientation programmes for members of the internal complaints committee; to treat sexual harassment as a misconduct under the service rules and initiate action for misconduct.
- Penalties have been prescribed for employers for non-compliance of the provisions of the Act. It is punishable with a fine of up to Rs 50,000. Repeated violation may lead to higher penalties and even cancellation of license or registration to conduct business.

Conclusion

Implementation of these provisions may become a challenge for employers – to constitute an ICC at "all administrative units or offices". It may also become necessary for the employer to spend more time and efforts in training members of the ICC who are to be replaced every three years. There is also a lack of clarity as to who shall be a chairperson of the ICC in absence of a senior level female employee. Also, in such cases, the composition of the committee members should ideally have been an odd number in order for the committee to arrive at a decision based on majority. The law allows the employer to initiate action against the complainant in case of a false or malicious complaint. This provision, although meant to protect the employer's interests, is likely to deter victims from reporting such incidents and filing complaints, which may in turn defeat the purpose for which the law was enacted. Government and employers should ensure that women should be treated equally and gender discrimination should not take place at the workplace. Effective implementation of the policies can reduce the manifestation and mutilation of the sexual harassment to the minimum. This will reduce or eliminate glitches caused by this harmful transgression. Establish a zero-tolerance policy towards all forms of violence at work, including verbal and/or physical abuse and prevent sexual harassment. Train security staff and managers to recognise signs of violence against women and understand laws and institution policies on human trafficking, labour and sexual exploitation. In consultation with employees, identify and address security issues, including the safety of women travelling to and from work and on co-related works.

Notes

1. Bhasin, Alok. (2008). Sexual Harassment at Work, New Delhi: Eastern Book Company Conduct Rules.
2. Chorine, Christine, Mihir Desai, Colin Gonsalves (1999). *Women and Law,* Vol. I and II, Socio-legal Information Centre, Mumbai.
3. *Combat Law* (2003), the human rights magazine, special number on violence against women, September-October.
4. Court meeting (2003). Amendments to Ordinances and Appendices to Ordinances, No. 19, XV D Sexual Harassment, University of Delhi.
5. Dalal, Sucheta (2003). 'Bias in the Boardroom', *The Sunday Express*, May 18.
6. Desai, Dhruv. (2008). Sexual Harassment and Rape Laws in India, Retrieved from http://www.legalserviceindia.com/articles/rape_laws
7. Dugar, Jayashree and Deora,Yashwant. (2011). Sexual harassment at workplace in India. Retrieved from http://www.mightylaws.in/487/sexual-harassment-workplace-india
8. FAOW (1991). 'Moving...But Not Quite There — Evaluation Report of One Decade 1980-1990', Forum Against Oppression of Women, Mumbai.
9. Gupte, Manisha and Renu Khanna (2002). Process Documentation of Gender Training of Dilaasa, Mumbai.
10. IHRO (2009). International Human Rights Organisation: Violence against women, Retrieved from http://www.ihro.org.in/women_violence.html

11. Mathew, Mini (2002). Sexual Harassment at Workplace, India Centre for Human Rights and Law, Mumbai.
12. Menon, Kalyani, and Shivkumar, A. K. (2001). "Women in India: How free? How equal?", United Nations.
13. Mishra, R. C. (2006). Towards gender equality. Authors press
14. Nair, Meera (2003). 'The Seamier Side of Office Life — This Women's Day Let's Do Away With the Groping, Lecherous Advances Made by Male Colleagues at the Workplace, *The Indian Express*, March 6-12.
15. Patel, Vibhuti (2002). *Women's Challenges of the New Millennium*, Gyan Publications, New Delhi.
16. Patel, Vibhuti (2004). 'Crusade of University of Mumbai Against Sexual Harassment at Place of Work', presented at a seminar 'An Interdisciplinary Approach to the Unexplored Areas Related to Women', sponsored by University Grants Commission and organised by Maniben Nanavati College for Women, Mumbai, on July 30-31, 2004.
17. Report (1999). Workshop on Prevention of Sexual Harassment of Women at Workplaces, Department of Adult and Continuing Education and Extension, University of Mumbai.
18. Radhakrishnan (2009). Development of human rights in an Indian context. *International Journal of Legal Information*, Vol. 2.
19. Schultz, (1998). Reconceptualizing sexual harassment. *Yale Law Journal*, Retrieved from cyber.law.harvard.edu/vaw00/shultz.html
20. Sadani, Harish (2003). 'Man Against Violence and Abuse — MAVA', *Urdhva Mula,* Vol. 2, No. 2.
21. Sadashivan (1999), Policy for Prevention of Sexual Harassment in Educational Institutions and for Dealing with Cases of Sexual Harassment', Bombay University College Teachers' Union, Mumbai
22. Samhita (2001). *The Politics of Silence*, Kolkata Sophia Centre for Women's Studies and Development and India Centre for Human Rights and Law (2003), 'Sexual Harassment of Women at the Workplace', Department of Sociology, Sophia College, Mumbai.
23. The Times News Network (2003), 'Disclosures — What is Sexual Harassment?', *The Times of India,* June 15, 2003.
24. WHO (2011). World Health Organisation: Violence against women Factsheet, http://www.who.int/mediacentre/factsheets/fs239/

References

*Principal; Sri R.K.M.Law College Chittoor-517127; cell:09849000331; e-mail:dshaik786@gmail.com

Vishaka v. State of Rajasthan.

President Pranab Mukherjee on April 25, 2013 gave his assent to Sexual Harassment of Women at Workplace (Prevention, Prohibition and Redressal) law.

Workplace Violence Statistics, 2010.

These findings are part of the survey, 'Sexual Harassment at Workplaces in India 2011-2012', done by Oxfam India during a workshop at the India Islamic Cultural Centre. The report was released on 27th November 2012. It revealed high incidence of sexual harassment in both organised and unorganised sectors. The research was jointly conducted by Oxfam India and the Social and Rural Research Institute, a wing of IMRB International in Delhi, Mumbai, Bangalore, Chennai, Kolkata, Ahmedabad, Lucknow and Durgapur and covered 400 working women. http://www.womenstudies.in/elib/others/ot_sexual_harassment.pdf,

The constitution of India ensures and guarantees every individual right to practice any profession or to carry out any occupation, trade or business.

Sally Engle Merry, "Constructing a Global Law-Violence against Women and the Human Rights System", https://www.utexas.edu/law/centers/humanrights/events/adjudicating/papers/LawSocialInquiryArticle.pdf.

AIR.1999. SC 625.

AIR 1995(6) SC 309.

AIR 1995 SC 1476.

AIR 1997 SC 3011.

President Pranab Mukherjee on April 25, 2013 gave his assent to Sexual Harassment of Women at Workplace (Prevention, Prohibition and Redressal) law.

15

Delhi Rape Case: The Idea of Gender Justice, Social Mobilisation and Media Activism

Ishfaq Ahmad Shah *and* ***Monisa Qadri***

Abstract

Though violence against women is a universal phenomenon, the recent incidents of rape, molestation, domestic violence and other related crimes against women in India have witnessed a spurt. In wake of infamous New Delhi Rape of 16 December 2012 in Munirka and similar attempts on many foreigners, the media was forced to take a firm stand in shaping up a new order determining the safety of women in India. It was the continuous media trail of the Delhi gang rape that the government was compelled to enact stringent laws against the perpetrators of such heinous crimes. In this context, the study will attempt to study the role of leading National Newspapers in highlighting the case by analysing their content. This chapter is based on an empirical study of the interpretative reportage adopted by the sample newspapers *Times of India* and *Indian Express* which has led to some interesting findings regarding media activism and media advocacy for the cause of victim and for bringing the rapists to the book.

Key Words: Women; Violence; Gender justice; Media organisations; government.

Introduction

Women have always been at the receiving end of the numerous acts of violence perpetrated across the globe. Violence against women is a universal phenomenon. A spurt of incidents of rape, molestation, domestic violence and other related crimes against women has seen an upward graph during past few decades. Like other places, women in India too have suffered a lot as worst crimes against them are being perpetrated.

One of the heinous crimes committed against the women in India is rape. As per statistics, India stands at the third place in the world, where most number of rapes cases are reported every year. In such a scenario, it becomes very important that every stake holder plays a role in improving the status of women in the Indian society and a system of governance and judiciary be provided which delivers justice to the victims of this "heinous" crime.

Shift to intro: According to a report published in the India Tribune, India stands at number three after South Africa and USA in the list of most reported rape cases per year. The report claims that the police records show more than 21000 cases of rape are reported every year across India. (*India Tribune*, 2012). The intensity in the number of rape cases reported in India has reached such a level that it forced the United Nations Human Rights Chief to term it as India's National problem (The Economist, 2013).

The 2012 statistics reveal, New Delhi has the highest number of rape-reports among Indian cities, while Jabalpur has the per capita incidence of reported rapes. Sources show that rape cases in India have doubled between 1990 and 2008 (Arab News, 2013). According to the National Crime Records Bureau, 24,206 rape cases were registered in India in 2011 only, although experts agree that the number of unreported cases is much higher.

Delhi Rape Case: The infamous New Delhi Rape of 16 December 2012 that happened in and around Munirka area of the Indian capital in which a 23 years old female was gang raped and murdered has set an example of media and public activism. This event has been etched in the minds of people across the globe as a horrific event that once again brought to the public debate the issues of women safety and growing sexual assaults on them (Batra, 2013). It led to a pioneering role by Indian media and the common masses towards shaping up a new order for not only determining the safety of women in India but also ensuring justice to the victims of rape. There has been an ongoing call for stricter laws related to women's abuse in India. It was the continuous media trail of the Delhi gang rape that the government was compelled to enact stringent laws against the perpetrators of such heinous crimes. The media coverage has been instrumental in not just setting an agenda in media itself but also give space and airtime to the public agenda from different sections of the society. The study aims to analyse the role of leading National Newspapers (The Times of India and Indian Express) in highlighting the case by giving ample space and using Media as a tool for interpretation and activism.

Literature Review

Studies have shown news coverage about the crimes like rape indicate or frame a dominant preconception about the incident, the victim as well as towards the criminals. Marian Mayers (1954) argues that the predominant problem with media while reporting crimes against the women, under the societal influence, deny that male violence against women is serious and a systematic problem. In such a scenario it becomes imperative for the media to report the actual happenings in a clear and unbiased manner to bring the culprits to the book.

The methods adopted to highlight cases like rapes to influence the state as well as public opinion need an approach of advocacy and activism so that justice is delivered in a free and fair manner. The need for media activism becomes more relevant in such a scenario. Sützl and Hug (2012) explained how activists use communication and information technologies to effect social change by empowering sex workers with poetry and phone technologies, intervening social practices through performance and community programmes, stopping factory farms from polluting the environment and challenging the biotechnology industry.

Studies suggest that in India use of media for the various causes and issues. Sharma (2013) highlights that media activism is not a new concept in India as pre-independence era witnessed several attempts of using media as a tool of protest and social reforms.

It is a kind of activism which utilises media for social and political movements. A number of cases in Indian context may be mentioned like Jessica Lal, Priyadarshni Matto, Nitish Katara, Aarushi Murder etc. where media forced the judiciary and the law and order agencies to undertake a fair trial and punish the guilty.

The salience of Delhi gang rape case can be established by the fact that not only did the Indian media actively highlight this issue but it was given much space globally. While analysing media coverage given to this episode, Roychowdhury (2013) records that around 1,515 articles appeared in the United States alone within the two-month period following the incident. In cases like these, media has played an important role as an activist in terms of highlighting the incident and generating public opinion about the issue. Niazi and Townson (2013) argue that the response to a recent horrific gang-rape and murder case has highlighted the power of media to stimulate debate and change attitudes.

I believe through this case, media played an important role to pressurise the government to take some measures for protection of women. I hope because of media the family will also get justice for the girl.

Saeed Ansari, anchor of Hindi news channel Aaj Tak (as cited in Niazi and Townson, 2013).

An important part in raising this debate was played by the media, both national and foreign. As the news of the rape broke, the media went into frenzy, not just in tracking the case but in leading people to introspect. A responsible section of the media asked people to be part of radical reforms the country required while it continued to give expression to the public grief, the mourning and reconciliation as people watched in horror the victim's final moments. However, the media was also accused of activism and leading a trial of its own while covering the case. As the movement to bring the gang rape victim to justice went viral, the nation saw widespread protest that spilled on streets across the country. The media covered the demonstrations day and night, following the protesters to every street and corner, giving a voice to their demands for justice and bringing them to the centre of political debate. Moreover, it exposed the growing crime statistics, especially in the national capital, against women. Basically, the media led bare the growing frustrations of an entire emerging aspirational urban class and generation (Batra, 2013). Notwithstanding the role played by media actively, a recent editorial in the Journal for Public Health calls on the media to do a better job of reporting on sexual violence against women. It says, too often, the media focus on sensational crimes and fail to reveal the full scope of the problem (DeCapua, 2013).

Research Objectives

The present study has the following specific research objectives:

1. To study the role of two national newspapers in highlighting the Delhi gang rape case.
2. To analyse the content and the interpretative reportage adopted by these media organisations about the gang rape case and to influence the public opinion.
3. To study the outcome of consistent pressure from general public and media organisations on Government of India regarding the Delhi gang rape case.

Research Methodology

The methodology followed in the study is conducted as per the principles of content analysis.

The content analysis is one of the most authentic way to quantify and investigate the content of the print media, hence it is widely in use for carrying image related analysis. Content analysis is essentially an organised and systematic procedure and according to Walizer and Wiener (1978), it is systematic procedure designed to examine the content of recorded information. The chapter has studied content of the selected newspapers using this technique of analysis and the data has been analysed both quantitatively and qualitatively.

Unit of Study

The units studied include news reports, pictorial content, editorials and vox pop which reflect the editorial policies of these newspapers and also the resulting public opinion which the newspapers tried to highlight.

Sample

The Sample undertaken by the researchers includes print editions for one week from two leading Indian English Newspapers– *The Times of India* and *The Indian Express*. During the process, the researcher began by selecting the Newspaper issues dated 18-December-2012 to 24-December-2012 (Although the rape and murder took place at around 9:30 p.m on 16-December-2013, the information about the same was collected on 17-December-2012 and subsequently reported on 18-December-2013).

The time frame selected for collection of the sample seems enough as the information disseminated by both the newspapers was enough to generate public outcry and pressurise the government to take necessary measures.

As per Registrar for Newspapers in India report (2011-2012), The Times of India is the largest circulated multi-edition English daily with a circulation of 4575895 copies per year while as the Indian Express is believed to be one of the bold newspapers famous for fearless investigative reporting about scams.

Data Analysis

After thorough analysis of the data collected it was found that the issue was given widespread coverage by both the newspapers. It was found by the researcher that during afore-mentioned period, Times of India (TOI) published 94 stories about the issue on Front page as well as inner pages. Out of the total 94 stories published, 25 stories were on the Front page while as 69 stories were distributed on many inner pages. It was also seen that as many as 49 pictures and illustrations deliberating in detail about the issue and the subsequent protests were used with stories. The Indian Express (IE) came out with 50 stories related to the issue among which seven stories were on the front page while as 43 stories came on the inner pages of the newspaper.

Table 1: Number of Stories

Type	*The Times of India*	*The Indian Express*	*Total (TOI+IE)*
Front Page	25 (26.6 per cent)	7 (14 per cent)	32 (22.22 per cent)
On others pages	69 (73.4 per cent)	43 (86 per cent)	112 (77.78 per cent)
Total	**94**	**50**	**144**

Type? *Newspaper?*	*Front Page*	*Inner pages*	*Total*
The Times of India	25 (26.6 per cent)	69 (73.4 per cent)	94
The Indian Express	7 (14 per cent)	43 (86 per cent)	50
Total (TOI+IE)	32 (22.22 per cent)	112 (77.78 per cent)	144

Table 1 gives a detailed information about the number of stories published and the percentage with which the issue was raised in both the newspapers.

The placement of the stories on a particular page describes the newsworthiness or enhances the news value of the issue. While a story with a Banner Headline (headline spreading across all the columns of a page) is considered an information of utmost value, equally the lead story (often placed on the upper left hand side of the page) is also considered very important. After analysing the content, the researcher found out that TOI published six stories with banner headline on the front as well as inner pages. Fifteen stories were published on different pages as the lead stories by the TOI. The IE also published five stories with a banner headline and as many as 11 as lead stories.

The Editorial of a Newspaper is considered as the voice of the newspaper and tells the audience about the policy of a newspaper organisation. Evaluation of the data showed that no Editorial was published by the TOI while as the IE wrote twice on the issue in the Editorial.

Table 2 gives detailed information about the placement of the news in both the newspapers.

Table 2: Placement of News

Type	*Times of India*	*Indian Express*	*Total (TOI+IE)*
Banner Stories	6 (6.32)	5 (10 per cent)	11 (7.63)
Lead	15 (15.9)	11 (22 per cent)	26 (18.05)
Editorial	Nil	2 (28 per cent)	2 (14.28 per cent)

Similarly, the usage of photographs alongside the text adds more to the impact of a news story. Keeping the importance of the photographs in consideration both newspapers published a fair amount of pictures alongside the text. During the said time period, the TOI published 49 pictures related to the issue while as 32 pictures were published by IE on both the front as well as inner pages. Moreover, to generate public interest and to form a public opinion, the voice of people commonly known as *Vox Populi* in journalistic language was also included only by the TOI. On seven occasion, the Times of India asked the people including celebrities to comment of the issue. No Vox Pop was published in the Indian express. Table 3 gives detailed information :

Table 3: Pictures and Voice of People

Type	*The Times of India*	*The Indian Express*	*Total*
Pictures and illustrations	49	32	81
Voxpopuli	7	Nil	7

Date Interpretation

The language and tone in which a newspaper presents the content often determines the actual aim of the media organisation. If reporting is confined to mere highlighting the facts, the essence of the published report remains confined to informing people. However, the interpretation of certain information sometimes gives an idea to the audience to follow a path that may be helpful for them to determine their future.

Analysing the data regarding the gruesome rape and murder of this 23 years old female, the researcher found that while the Indian Express followed the simple path of reporting the spots and the actual happening during the reference period, the TOI took a different line to persuade, motivate and ask people to act against the crimes against the women.

The headline *"Enough talk, Let's make women safe, here is how it can be done"* which appeared on the front page of TOI dated 19-12-2013 gives a clear indication about the fact the newspaper was suggesting a clear path to its huge audience to follow and to persuade the authorities towards taking a firm stand against the perpetrators.

The ethics of journalism may not allow a journalist to editorialise and opinionate the news content but the text like "*Every time there is a rape in the city, we cringe at the reports in shame, wring our hands in frustration, and often cower in fear because our daughters, sisters and wives go out for work taking the very same routes stalked by depraved men who think nothing of violating, maiming and torturing women*" (The Times of India dated 19-12-2012) highlights the urge of the media organisation to compel people towards acting against crimes like rape and other forms of violence against the women.

The researcher also found that the TOI rather than writing an editorial on the issue came up with an innovative and novel concept of opinionated content and termed it as "The Times View" in which comments like "*Here's how rapes can be prevented*", "*Channel this anger to secure real changes*" and quotes from the victim like '*I won't vanish without a fight, they will have to pay*' were highlighted in such a way that it was clear the newspaper was pushing people to such an extent that they eventually came on roads to force government for enacting stringent laws against criminals perpetrating violence against the women.

Moreover, the selection of pictures depicting messages like "*Book culprits with death*" by both the newspapers indicated in sending a strong message.

Interestingly, both the newspapers came up with numerous measures suggesting women to take certain protective measures while in danger. Advertisements about certain applications for the android mobile phone users were also published in these newspapers believed to be helpful in sending speedy messages.

A dig at the politicians with selective use of words was also taken which is quite evident in an intro of one of the stories "*Law-makers who have been shedding tears over the Delhi gang-rape do not match their words with action.*"

Even though the Munirka rape case was not the first rape and murder case in New Delhi, however, this issue received widespread media attention which is clear by the amount of space, placement of news, the selective and interpretative approach of writing and the photographs that were published during one week.

Conclusion

The immense media coverage followed by huge amount of protests and criticism by the people forced the then Indian government to enact its law on prevention of sexual harassment act. The Sexual Harassment of Women at Workplace (Prevention, Prohibition and Redressal) Act, 2013 ("Sexual Harassment Act") was made effective from April 23, 2013. Moreover, the continuous media coverage about the court trail of the culprits and an incessant public resentment resulted in a historical decision of sentencing all four convicts to death by Delhi court on 14-09-2013.

The data analysed clearly indicated that media organisations under discussion haven't confined itself to mere normal happenings and the reporting of the event and the subsequent protests but advocated a cause to force the government to change its policy. Furthermore, an interpretative approach to reportage was adopted which subsequently prompted both masses as well as the government to make some drastic changes into their policies while dealing with crimes like rape.

The extensive focus of TOI and IE on this case through their news reports, editorials, photographs and other content reflects the salience accorded to the case and how it has helped in shaping the public agenda as argued by Dearing and Rogers (1996) that social issues that are widely recognised on the media agenda often demand attention on the public agenda, and in turn move quickly up the policy agenda, creating policy changes, which was visible through enactment of various laws relating to the case by the government and hastening of the legal process which are otherwise seen as much delayed and time consuming. This has giving a sense of confidence to women in general and rape victims in particular that gender justice has a place in this society.

Notes

1. Arab News (2012). Indian student gang-raped, thrown off bus in New Delhi http://www.arabnews.com/indian-student-gang-raped-thrown-bus-new-delhi.
Retrieved on 11-09-2013.
2. Dearing, James W., Rogers, Everett (1996). Agenda-Setting (Communication Concepts). SAGE Publications.
3. Human Rights Watch (2012). India: Rape Victim's Death Demands Action http://www.hrw.org/news/2012/12/29/india-

rape-victim-s-death-demands-action.Retrieveed on 15-09-2013.

4. India Tribune (2013). Rape statistics around the worldwww.indiatribune.com/index.php?option=com_content& view=article&id=10195:rape-statistics-around-the-world-&catid=107:coverpage&Itemid=471. Retrieved on 11-09-2013
5. Mayers, Marian (1954). *News Coverage of Violence Against Women: Engendering Blame*. California: SAGE Publications, Inc.
6. Pande, Mrinal (2009). "Indian Press: The Vernacular and the Mainstream Babel", in Ather Farouqui (ed.): Muslims and Media Images. New Delhi: Oxford University Press.
7. Ramagundam, Rahul (2005). "The 'State' Revealed in Newspaper Headlines" in **Economic and Political Weekly**, January 8.
8. Sützl,W. and Hug. (eds.) (2012). Activist Media and Biopolitics: Critical Media Interventions in the Age of Biopower Austria: Innsbruck University Press.
9. Sharma, Bindu (2013). Media Activism and Public Participation: A Case Study of Delhi Gang Rape with focus on Indian Print Media. http://amic.org.sg/conference/AMIC2013/Full%20Papers/F4/Bindu%20Sharma.pdf.Retrieved on 11-09-2013.
10. The Economist (2013). Rape and murder in Delhi http://www.economist.com/news/leaders/21569031-horrible-attack-could-prove-turning-point-indias-women-rape-and-murder-delhi. Retrieved on 11-09-2013
11. Walizer, M.H. and P.L.Wiener (1978). "Research Methods and Analysis." New York: Harper and Row.
12. Wimmer, Roger D. and Joseph R. Dominick (1983). "Mass Media Research: An Introduction." California: Wadsworth Publishing Company Belmont.

References

http://www.exchange4media.com/52025_vivid-media-activism-in-delhi-gang-rape-case.html

http://www.dc4mf.org/en/content/indian-media-pushing-change-after-gang-rape-case
http://www.voanews.com/content/rape-media-30apr13/1651676.html

Index

H

I

N